Sc and ...wise

Please remember that this is a library book,
and that it belongs only temporarily to each
person who uses it. Be considerate. Do
not write in this, or any, library book.

WITHDRAWN

PERSPECTIVES ON GENDER

Series Editor:
Myra Marx Ferree, University of Connecticut

*Pleasure, Power, and Technology: Some Tales of Gender,
Engineering, and the Cooperative Workplace*
Sally Hacker

*Black Feminist Thought: Knowledge, Consciousness,
and the Politics of Empowerment*
Patricia Hill Collins

*Understanding Sexual Violence: A Study of
Convicted Rapists*
Diana Scully

Maid in the U.S.A.
Mary Romero

*Feminisms and the Women's Movement: Dynamics of
Change in Social Movement Ideology and Activism*
Barbara Ryan

*Black Women and White Women in the Professions:
Analysis of Job Segregation by Race and Gender,
1960–1980*
Natalie J. Sokoloff

Gender Consciousness and Politics
Sue Tolleson Rinehart

Mothering: Ideology, Experience, and Agency
Evelyn Nakano Glenn, Grace Chang, and
Linda Rennie Forcey (editors)

For Richer, For Poorer: Mothers Confront Divorce
Demie Kurz

Rock-a-by Baby
Verta Taylor

Schoolsmart and Motherwise

Wendy Luttrell

Working-Class Women's Identity and Schooling

Routledge
New York and London

Published in 1997 by
Routledge
29 West 35th Street
New York, NY 10001

Published in Great Britain by
Routledge
11 New Fetter Lane
London EC4P 4EE

Printed in the United States of America on acid-free paper.

"'Becoming Somebody in and against School': Toward a Psychocultural Theory of
Gender and Self Making," by Wendy Luttrell, in *The Cultural Production of the Educated
Person*, edited by Bradley Levinson, Douglas Foley and Dorothy Holland permission of
the State University of New York Press. © 1996.
"The Teachers, They All Had Their Pets: Concepts of Gender, Knowledge, and Power,"
by Wendy Luttrell, in *Signs: Journal of Women in Culture and Society*. © 1993 by the
University of Chicago. All rights reserved.
"Becoming Somebody": Aspirations, Opportunities, and Womanhood," by Wendy
Luttrell, in *Color, Class and Country: Experiences of Gender*, edited by Gay Young and
Bette Dickerson © 1994. ZED Books.

Library of Congress Cataloging-in-Publication Data

Luttrell, Wendy.
Schoolsmart and motherwise: working-class women's identity and schooling/Wendy Luttrell.
p.   cm.
Includes bibliographical references (p.) and index.
ISBN (invalid) 0-415-91011-1 (alk. paper). —ISBN 0-415-91012-9 (pbk.: alk. paper)
1. Adult education of women—Social aspects—United States.
2. Group identity—United States. 3. Feminism and education—United States.
4. Working class women—United States—Biography. I. Title.
LC1663.L88 1997
371.822'071'5—dc21   96-39655
                                                                            CIP

[Contents]

for Robert, Mikaela, Liam, and Emma

[Acknowledgments]

My biggest debt is to the women who shared their stories and trusted me to make final decisions—for better or worse—about representing their lives. This book does not adequately convey, but has greatly benefited from, many impromptu conversations, gifts, moments of reflection and reconsideration, the willingness to be interviewed yet one more time—for all these extensions of good will, I am grateful.

I was fortunate to have my research financially supported by two separate awards. First, an award from the Rockefeller Foundation allowed me, as a Humanist in Residence at the Duke/University of North Carolina Center for Research on Women, to immerse myself in data analysis. Second, an award from the American Council of Learned Societies gave me respite from teaching summer school to finish the manuscript.

I have also had the benefit of working in a setting that provided invaluable intellectual and personal resources. I would like to acknowledge Jean O'Barr, Director of Women's Studies, Duke University, for creating and sustaining a space for feminist teaching and learning. I am especially indebted to Naomi Quinn, whose leadership of the Cultural Anthropology department enriched my life in inestimable ways. Through her mentoring and institutional advocacy on my behalf I have learned to better recognize my own voice and value. I cannot thank her enough.

Numerous Duke University students brought fresh insight and energy to this project; indeed, one of the most invisible (and hence devalued) kinds of scholarship arises from classroom discussions when students ask clarifying questions about one's research. This book has profited enormously from such classroom exchanges and I wish there was a way to personally acknowledge each student. I could not have completed the book without the help of two graduate student research assistants, Ingrid Byerly and Katherine Murawski, whose endless trips to the library freed me up to write. I am especially grateful to Katherine for her shepherding this book through numerous revisions and edits. She was unruffled by my hectic schedule, always efficient, and ever willing to xerox one more copy of the manuscript.

Many people contributed to the ideas presented in this book, offering encouragement and crucial advice along the way. I want to first acknowledge the members of my dissertation committee—Pam Roby, Carole Joffe, and Hardy Frye—who mentored me through the first stage of this research and whose support was paramount in my development. I am deeply indebted to those who read and provided critical comments on the entire manuscript: Katherine Borman, Arlene McLaren, Myra Marx Ferree, Naomi Quinn, Mary Rogers, Robert Shreefter, Jean Stockard, and John Wilson. I am also grateful to those who read parts of the manuscript: Jessica Benjamin, Nancy Chodorow, Deborah Dwork, and Dorothy Holland, and to those whose comments on papers or responses to presentations made me think about my research in new ways: Kathryn Anderson-Levitt, Ann Bookman, Francesca Cancian, Susan Chase, Bette Dickerson, Doug Foley, Mary Hawkesworth, Nancy Hewitt, Miriam Johnson, Bradley Levinson, Sandra Morgen, Rachel Rosenfeld, Carol Stack, Claudia Strauss, Edward Tiryakian, Lois Weis, Julia Wrigley, and Gay Young.

Special thanks are due to Myra Marx Ferree, editor of the Perspectives on Gender Series at Routledge. It was an exhilarating moment when she approached me after I had presented a paper and said, "Is someone already publishing your book?" ("I am writing a book?" I thought to myself.) Her belief in my work has sustained me during the hardest of times. She has nurtured so many women sociologists and I feel honored to be one of them. Jayne Fargnoli was the editor at Routledge who enthusiastically took on this project and I regret that she was unable to see her initial investment of energy come to fruition. I appreciate the excellent help of Routledge Press personnel: Anne Sanow, Alex Mummery, and Karen Deaver, who all contributed to the final product.

Several people were instrumental in making my prose more reader-friendly and whose "allergy to jargon" (Sherryl Kleinman's phrase) inspired me to keep rewriting. I thank members of my writing group: Jane Brown, Marcy Lansman, Fabienne Worth, Sarah Shields, and Sherryl Kleinman for listening with kind but critical ears to the worst of it. Their feedback spurred and sustained me during the book's final stages. Mary Rogers was more than generous with her time and green pen. She helped me in more ways than she will ever know. Lori Patel copy edited the book; she was the person who gave me the courage to give it up in the last hours with her reassuring suggestions.

There are people in my life whose support is so vital that this book could not have been written without them. Maureen Cawley and Ellen Tichenor were remarkable role models and are responsible for innovative educational opportunities afforded the Philadelphia women in this study. I thank Naomi Quinn for believing in my work more than I did at times and for making me and my family a part of hers. She stands out among those I know who combine schoolsmarts with motherwit. I thank

Deborah Dwork for our Wellfleet "mothers' swims" which strengthened my muscles and fortified my soul. Had I been able to take all her advice to heart, this would have been a better book.

I am grateful to my parents and siblings for their continued influence and interest in my work. My mother's willingness to travel a long way to help with my children made their lives happier and my life easier. My brother and sister-in-law, Scott and Laura Luttrell, gave me financial assistance in the face of economic difficulties and provided me a retreat in their Pinehurst home so I could work uninterrupted on several occasions. Cousins Naomi Kleid and David Heath generously allowed me to stay in their beach house to do the same.

Unbounded thanks go to Louise Allen, the most wonderful child care provider. I hope she will recognize her part in these pages and know the extent of my gratitude.

I cannot imagine writing this book without the presence of my children, Mikaela, Liam, and Emma. They were wholehearted participants in the research effort, accompanying me on interviews, making creative use of the reams of discarded paper I produced throughout the writing process, and demanding of my attention in unanticipated and joyful ways.

One special person influenced every phase of this project—my husband, Robert Shreefter. His vision and hard work as an activist, educator, and artist inspired and comforted me from the inception of this book to its completion. He listened to me clumsily articulate my observations and offered his own perspective as a teacher in the very programs I describe. He took over my literacy classes in North Carolina and enhanced this workplace education program in immeasurable ways. I am most grateful, however, for the way he treated my desires for intellectual and creative expression as something I was entitled to enjoy. His love, wit, and wisdom lit the way for this book.

[Preface]

I greet my class of sixteen students. Some have been out of school for more than twenty years. Others have more recent memories of school before marriage and babies. Joyce explains she is taking this class to "become somebody," and everyone nods knowingly. A mother and daughter arrive late and ask if they may take the course together. Doris, the mother, says she wants a high school diploma so she can wave it in her husband's face and say, "I know what I'm talking about." Two students are accompanied by their preschool children. They feel unsure about the child-care setting downstairs and would prefer to keep their children with them, if that is okay with me. Penny introduces herself, saying both her mother and her husband disapprove of her return to school, but ever since her son graduated high school last year, she feels the need to do the same.

I wrote this journal entry in 1976 and am struck by how Joyce's words distill my project. I later returned to the Lutheran Settlement House Women's Program, Philadelphia, from 1980 to 1984, to study (through participant observation and in-depth interviews) why these white, working-class women were in adult basic education classes and what it meant to "become somebody." Then in 1984–1988 I asked the same questions of working-class women of color (they called themselves black) who were enrolled in a work-place literacy program in North Carolina. The intertwining of family life, schooling, and work, how working-class women view themselves and are viewed by others in these contexts, have been my major preoccupation for many years.

This book is based on the life stories of working-class women in each program. I analyze these life stories for the insight they give into the twisted relations of selfhood, class, race, and gender identity, and schooling. By twisted I mean simultaneously entangled and at odds, interwoven and warped. Through the women's stories, we see how they viewed themselves and others—whom they thought was womanly, smart, credible, and worthy of respect, and why. The aim of my analysis is to reveal and disrupt images of what education can and should be. And the conclusion I draw is that schools should provide the space and resources for students to renew and reinvent themselves.

This book is about the women and the stories they told, but it is especially about the controlling images and ambivalent feelings that were evoked as the women recounted their lives. These images and feelings were bound up together in institutional, cultural, and psychological ways that the women were often unaware of. Above all, it is a book about how life stories may help us see ourselves better; how they may function for our protection, renewal, or transformation. One of my graduate school mentors once said that the measure of a good sociologist was her ability to tell a "good" story, one that has value, is believable and authentic.[1] At the time, I wasn't sure I believed him; the notion of "story" seemed too trivial for the task I envisioned. In retrospect, I understand the wisdom of his remarks.

I write across and in relation to many stories—the women's, my own, official stories about women's education, and several feminist versions of women's ways of knowing and identity formation. I write straddling two tendencies within feminism—what Ruth Behar (1993: 301) has called "opposite tendencies to see women as not at all different from one another or as all too different." She has warned that "to go too far in either direction is to end up indifferent"—and, I would add, unconnected—"to the lives of other women." I also straddle two narrative stances: that of "ventriloquist" and "activist."[2] As ventriloquist, I have at times mistakenly assumed myself to be an anonymous transmitter of the women's voices, as if I had no hand in the telling or no voice of my own. As activist, I have sought ways to translate what the women told me into accurate and useful stories about the issues and challenges women encounter in their lives, especially in school. I have tried to write in ways that challenge taken-for-granted assumptions, particularly assumptions about power and domination that structured the women's stories. I have striven to bring the women, as well as myself, into the narrative as real people who are invested in a variety of contradictory privileges, personal conflicts, and social struggles.[3]

A colleague recently told me that the fieldwork rule of thumb is that you double the number of years spent in the field to determine how long it takes to write about what one has learned.[4] She may be correct; it takes time to analyze fieldnotes, conduct and interpret in-depth interviews, and translate the results into prose. But there are other, more mundane issues that influenced the timing of this book—issues that I share with the women I interviewed and I suspect with many others. The demands of family and work life, coupled with unexpected emotional and financial hardships, have often meant putting my manuscript back up on the shelf as I dealt with other important and immediate matters.

But apart from these reasons, the women's stories have stayed with me for so long, in part because I find them so personally meaningful. [5] This insight serves as a theoretical anchor of the book as I draw upon feminist object relations theory and symbolic interactionism to discuss certain defensive strategies people use to tell their stories so that they will not be found lacking. This is a common feature of the women's identities and schooling, as their stories will illustrate.

In writing about women's identities I have worked to avoid a distanced "I-they" or a false "we" to convey what was learned. I actively solicited and received feedback from many of the women about my description and analysis and made appropriate revisions based on their remarks. The final version, however, is mine more than theirs. I have attempted to convey their stories in ways they will recognize, but also in ways that reveal underlying assumptions, as well as psychological and structural relations that they may not recognize or agree with.[6]

I have tried to write this book in a way that is accessible, annotating scholarly passages, references, personal anecdotes, and biographical information that have shaped my thinking. Notes are distracting; as one of the women I interviewed said, "There is nothing that ruins a good story more than those little numbers getting in the way." I hope readers will overcome this distraction and some will find the additional information useful.

Mostly I hope readers will find parallels between their life stories and those of the women I interviewed. Like these women, people tell about the past to help make sense of their present lives. People tell stories that use images about others as a way to shore themselves up or hold themselves together so that they may feel as if they are a "somebody." Personal narratives are often hard won. But most important, like the women in this book, people tell stories in ways that explain and justify social inequalities related to privilege, power, or respect as we, each in our own way, search for personal recognition and esteem in a society where some people count more than others.

Becoming Somebody

Doreen left school at age sixteen when she became pregnant. Ten years later she enrolled in a community-based women's adult education program in Philadelphia. "I don't think the world ends if you didn't finish high school," she announced to her classmates. "I didn't finish and I'm not a bum. But I always wanted to finish, just so I could feel like I was somebody." Beatrice, who was enrolled in a work-place literacy program in North Carolina, echoed Doreen's sentiments. "If you know how to read, write, do your figures— if you have that diploma, then you feel like you're somebody, you know."

Despite very different backgrounds, these two women agreed that receiving a high school diploma is self-defining—it allows you to "feel like you're somebody." Their views about bettering themselves through adult education, as well as their memories of school, shed new light on how social inequalities—understood in terms of who does and does not count as a somebody—get created, maintained, and institutionalized.

Doreen was born and raised in Fishtown, an Irish and Polish working-class, urban-industrial neighborhood in Philadelphia.[1] She was a student in my first adult education class and became an eager participant in my study. Describing her early school experiences as "uncomfortable," she explained that as an adolescent she could not wait to quit school so she could go to work in the local box factory. Having just sent her youngest child off to kindergarten, Doreen said she hoped to set a good example by returning to school.

Doreen's husband did not have a high school diploma; in her words, "he was never suited for school." But, she added, he was "no bum" either, for he earned adequate, though sometimes erratic, wages as an electrical apprentice. On the first day of class she told her classmates and me that, despite her husband's lack of enthusiasm about her return to school, she was determined to show him the benefits. Still, she cautioned, being "schoolwise" was not the only or the most important form of knowledge; having common sense, being "streetwise and mother-wise" had got her by in life. She continued to say that she was not as smart as her husband, who could "fix anything"; his "real intelligence" surpassed that of most professional and college-educated people she knew. Her comments elicited nods from several other women, who expressed pride and confidence in what they called their "common-sense" abilities to raise children and make ends meet in spite of financial and social difficulties. They too admired fathers, husbands, and brothers for their commonsense abilities to make things work.

Beatrice was born and raised on a South Carolina tenant farm. She attended a work-place literacy program at a North Carolina state university; like Doreen, she too was determined to show her children the importance of school by getting her diploma. She remembered her child-hood school days with fondness; she described going to the one-room schoolhouse as a "luxury"—reserved for those rainy days when she and the other black children in sharecropping families were not needed as laborers. Beatrice, a thirty-eight-year-old mother of four, worked as a housekeeper cleaning student dorms. Now she was "finally getting around to finishing something I started many years ago and should never have given up on so easily." She talked about being a "graduate of the school of hard knocks" and, as a result, saw herself as a wellspring of commonsense knowledge. Her claims to common sense elicited the same chorus of nods as did Doreen's, but Beatrice was more willing to identify her commonsense knowledge as valuable, as "real intelligence." Meanwhile, calling herself a "late bloomer," she reminded the class and me that "you don't need an education to be smart, but that diploma can really make you feel like a somebody." This sounded familiar, but the class discussion that followed put a new twist on who is considered smart and what education can and cannot do for you. According to these North Carolina women, a high school diploma had questionable value; they knew "plenty of black people with educations that have jobs that are no better than the ones we got here."

For both groups of women, commonsense knowledge is clearly split off from and at odds with book learning and school knowledge. Similarly, the "commonsense types" are different from, if not in conflict with, those who are "schoolsmart" or college-educated professionals, just as the "bums" are set against the "somebodies." Given these conflicts, what does it mean to return to school? What does becoming a "somebody" or feeling like one is a somebody have to do with being educated? The answers to these questions are complicated, especially when we consider the overlapping yet distinct educational experiences and views of northern, urban, white, working-class women and southern, rural-raised, working-class women of color.[2]

In this book I analyze the life stories of women such as Doreen and Beatrice to show the different ways that school impeded the women's sense of social value and self-worth. My goal is to explain how each group of women arrived at split and conflicted self-images, self-understandings, and social identities. I closely examine the historical, institutional, cultural, and psychological ways in which the women learned about themselves and their place in American society, and reveal the personal costs of these lessons. Throughout, I reveal that school is a crucial site where this learning takes place.

THE STUDY

I collected the women's life stories while I taught classes, developed curriculum materials, and performed certain administrative functions at each adult education program. First I established my participant role; then, feeling somewhat settled, I officially embarked on my research. I conducted thirty-minute, semistructured interviews with close to 200 women about why they were returning to school and any problems they were encountering as a result. I then selected fifteen women from each program to interview in depth about their family, school, and work lives.[3]

I mean to distinguish the women's life stories from a more comprehensive report of their life histories—that is, those stories that are told in discontinuous bits and pieces and revised over the course of a person's lifetime.[4] Life stories include "all of the stories and associated discourse units, such as explanations and chronicles," that a person tells to make a point about herself, not just about the way the world is (Linde 1993: 12). In this case, the women told many stories that were associated with their education, such as explanations about their school success or failure; stories about their common sense and varied forms of "intelligence"; cautionary tales about their childhood ambitions; stories about teachers, mothers; and so forth.

I gathered the women's life stories over the course of a year at each site, meeting with each woman for two to three hours at least three different times in her home. As these relationships evolved, I met family members and friends and often talked with them as well. I observed the women in their classroom settings, taking note of their informal conversations before class, their demeanor with different teachers, how they responded to class assignments, homework, and exams. These observations helped me better interpret their school stories and self definitions, because I could compare what they said about themselves as learners with how they acted and what they said in specific classroom situations.

Many factors influenced how the women narrated their life stories and the specific versions they told me.[5] Both their tales and my interpretations were undoubtedly shaped by my request for childhood memories of school and my assumption that there must be a story explaining why women who had seen themselves as school failures nonetheless decided to return to school as adults.[6] The way each woman made sense of her past in light of the present, and what she wanted me to know or not know about her life, also gave shape to the stories that were told.

There are many reasons people tell stories and the stories they tell can serve multiple purposes. For analytical purposes I treat the women's stories as "accounts." The account notion borrows from the mathematical—things must "add up" as people interpret daily events and interact with others. People's accounts commonly explain in advance what others might perceive as unexpected or inappropriate behavior. "Indeed, the giving and taking of accounts in everyday life represents one of the most fundamental characteristics of the social order" (Weinstein 1980: 591). From this perspective, the women's stories serve dual purposes. In one sense, they serve to defeat in advance any negative judgments that I, as a white, middle-class, college-educated person might have of them (Hewitt and Stokes 1978). In another sense, the women's accounts could be said to provide them a means to reconcile their past experiences, feelings, and self-understandings in school with their current lives. It is understood that these accounts are partial, yet they provide important insights into the conditions shaping the women's lives.[7]

Personal stories are also the means by which people fashion their identities. Hence, I analyze the women's stories for what they tell us about their membership in certain groups—for example, as women, as African Americans, as members of the working class, and so forth (Linde 1993, Plummer 1995);[8] and for how they established a positive moral image—in this case, that of a good student, daughter, worker, mother, and wife. To understand the "formative—and sometimes deformative— power of life stories" I take what has been called a critical theory of personal narratives (Rosenwald and Ochberg 1992: 1).[9] From this perspective, what the women emphasized and what they omitted in their stories provide insight into their multiple positions, sometimes as victims of, sometimes as rebels against, and sometimes unaware of oppressive cultural conditions.

The telling of personal stories, especially the recollection of childhood memories, can be emotionally arduous work for both the interviewee and interviewer. I was not always prepared for the intense feelings that the women's "memory work" (as one woman called it) would release.[10] Sometimes the women would tell stories and then later request that their names be withheld because they didn't want to hurt anyone's feelings. This happened most often when they spoke about their mothers. Their predominant openness and occasional desire for anonymity were crucial dimensions of the research process. Especially important was how the women viewed me as a college-educated, white, middle-class woman who had been their teacher and how they imagined I viewed them. Meanwhile, I had my own projections about and identifications with the women in each group (these will be considered in more detail in chapter 2).

SCHOOLS

School is by no means the only site where people define themselves and their social worth but, as these women's stories will attest, it is a formative one.[11] Their stories feature childhood experiences of exclusion, difference, and illegitimacy in school and explain how they learned to think about these in gender-, race-, and class-based terms. In their explanations, the women spoke of embattled and ambivalent relationships with other students, teachers, and (most surprising to me) their mothers. The women framed their problems according to each school context and mission (one rural-community and the other urban-bureaucratic). But in each institutional setting, they came to see themselves as less than equal —if not unworthy—students.

Taken together, the women's stories confirm the findings but illuminate the limitations of current school ethnographies and theoretical discussions that explain how this loss of self worth happens.[12] In one sense, the women's stories support a view of schools as trading posts where students bring different sorts of "cultural capital," i.e., different kinds of knowledge, dispositions, linguistic codes, problem-solving skills, attitudes, and tastes, only some of which get rewarded or valued by school authorities.[13] Those with the "right" (i.e., legitimated) cultural capital fare the best in school. For example, the streetwise or commonsense knowledge that these women brought to school was, in their view, at best disregarded and at worst ridiculed by the teachers. Students like themselves, who had "country ways" or "problems with authority," could not be expected to achieve. In contrast, students of higher social standing were automatically viewed by the teachers as smart. Similarly, those students with obedient or submissive behavioral styles and attitudes were the "teachers' pets" and were understood to be "going places." They were treated better and got more attention, which undoubtedly contributed to their school success. Such experiences confirm the importance of cultural capital, but the women's stories show that there are personal, cultural, and institutional conflicts that frame students' understandings of their lack of cultural capital which must be taken into account.[14]

NARRATIVE URGENCY

Whether talking about their childhood ambitions, early family life, school and work experiences, difficulties raising children, or frustrations with the men in their lives, the women expressed a narrative urgency to "tell it like it was" for them. As one woman put it, "You want to know about my childhood? I could write a book about my life, about what I've been through, about what I've learned." As if explanations of poverty, violence, or discrimination were not enough, the women seemed compelled to tell about their personal struggles to gain respect and legitimacy. Often they told of feeling falsely ridiculed or accused, not for having *done* something wrong, but for *being* wrong. Their stories also emphasized, however, a hard-won sense of uniqueness, a view of inner life "that is experienced as a struggle: a struggle against being like everyone else, a struggle to hold together or hold up, or a struggle simply to feel that one has a self."[15]

Similarly, the women narrated their school struggles with particular passion, however horrific these experiences were. Charlotte Linde (1993) attributes this school storytelling to a prohibition within American culture against talking about class as a legitimate explanation for why people end up in the social position that they do. She says there is an unspoken assumption that important life decisions are made in schools, decisions that contribute to or justify one's social standing. Put bluntly, talking about school is a code for talking about class. In a similar spirit, Richard Sennett and Jonathan Cobb (1972) note a "defensive" stance towards education on the part of the white, working-class men they interviewed, which they attribute to the hidden injury of class. Lillian Rubin (1976) also found conflicts and ambivalence toward education among the white, working-class husbands and wives she interviewed.

My research confirms these observations. But there is much more to say about how the women's school stories account for their social standing. Class was not the only or the primary unspoken or unrecognized reason why these women ended up in the social positions they did.

THEORIZING GENDER, RACE, AND CLASS

There are a host of theories explaining how people understand and negotiate their place in American society according to race, class, and gender hierarchies.[16] An individual's position in a web of intersecting privileges and constraints can often be experienced as paralyzing.[17] There is a tendency to identify one of the three—class, race, or gender—as "the" problem.[18] Indeed, the notion that it is either one or the other, or that there *is* a single problem, keeps people uninformed about the politics of these categories of "difference"—unaware, for example, that notions of race, gender, and class have changed over time and are linked to relations of power and political struggles.[19]

Especially problematic is the view that one of these positions is most salient, most crippling, most determining in the lives of oppressed people.[20] This "intersection" model—where gender, race, and class are viewed as vehicles of identity that meet at busy crossroads and some groups of people emerge from the collision more damaged than others— misses the mark in two ways. First, it does not explain how *groups of people* differently assess a situation, assign responsibility or blame, or take collective action. Nor does it provide insight into how *individuals* experience, interpret, and sustain multiple damages or wounds, sometimes unaware of or unable to acknowledge their own injuries. The women's stories shed new light on the social production and reproduction of inequality, especially how people arrive at their sense of personal limits and social standing.[21] Indeed, their stories reveal a complicated web of psychodynamic and political conflicts regarding selfhood; gender-, race-, and class-based identities; types of knowledge; and images and fantasies about authority, dependency, and nurturance—all of which must be taken into account.

SELFHOOD AND SOCIAL IDENTITY

Understanding how the women's life stories are linked to their selfhood and social identities is complicated by the fact that the meanings of these concepts are open to debate. Let me clarify my use of terms. When referring to self-definitions, -defenses and -understandings, I am speaking about psychodynamic processes—how the self is known through others and through patterns of internalized object relations.[22] I view self-formation as being rooted in specific historical and cultural contexts and conditions, as well as in the style and quality of care we experience during our early development—not in innate, pre-formed drives or impulses said to be part of a universal developmental sequence.[23] When referring to social identities I mean cultural processes by which traits, expectations, images, and evaluations are culturally assigned to different groups of people: men are strong, rational, and aggressive; women are nurturing, emotional, and peaceful. Social identities give us a sense of what we have in common with, and what separates us from, others. Social identities are, to borrow a phrase from Judith Butler (1991:14), "sites of necessary trouble" in that we can feel comforted and threatened, liberated and limited, by a particular identity. We both embrace an identity and feel it unnecessarily imposed upon us at the same time.

I see self and identity as co-occurring, mutually reinforcing cultural and psychological processes, and not as fixed entities. While notions of self and identity have come under critical scrutiny, especially in postmodern and feminist texts, their relationship to each other is too often glossed over or ignored. [24] In my view, a sense of self is indistinguishable from a sense of identity. Muriel Dimen puts it this way:

> Self and gender identity inhabit one another so intimately that questions such as these become familiar: If I feel "womanly," am I at my most "feminine"? Or am I feeling most fully "myself"? When I do feel "like myself," does that feeling have anything to do with my female identity? (1991: 337).

The women's stories raise similar questions about the relationship between self and identity and how these two can feel "joined at the heart" (Dimen 1991: 337). For example, when and in what ways did these women feel most "like themselves," and what, if anything, did that have to do with feeling knowledgeable or womanly? When and in what ways did the women feel "like themselves" in school, and what role did students, teachers, and mothers play in these feelings? What other aspects of community, work, or social life were understood by the women to be shaping their sense of social belonging and self worth?

STORIED SELVES

I propose the term "storied selves" to delineate the processes by which the women arrived at their senses of selfhood and social identities.[25] For insofar as the women's stories are *about* the events and conditions of their lives, their stories are also *part of* their self understandings. Rosenwald and Ochberg (1992: 8) use the term "storied lives" to convey the point that "what is told and what is lived promote each other." I use the term "storied selves" to suggest that how a story is told and how people define and defend their selves and identities promote each other.

This notion serves both descriptive and analytic purposes. In the first instance, I use it to acknowledge the women's narrative urgency. I also use it to convey the prominence of a retrospective view, how frequently the women drew upon the past to account for their present social standing. Finally, I use it to highlight the emotional and psychological dimensions of selfhood and social identity. I share Carolyn Steedman's (1986: 12) concern that a "complicated psychology" has been denied or refused to those who are poor and working class.[26] And I agree with her that we need a revised theory of class and gender consciousness (to which I add race consciousness) that is based upon the "secret and impossible" (1986: 144) stories that oppressed and marginalized people tell about their lives. Through the women's life stories we gain insight into the politics and psychodynamics of the social production and reproduction of inequality—how people learn to absorb hidden injuries of race, class, and gender without even knowing it.

When narrating their life stories, the women persistently pit good protagonists against bad antagonists, or good against bad aspects of themselves as actors in the struggle to achieve a visible, worthy, and credible self. Their storied selves draw upon cultural images in which one person or group of people is split off from or set at odds with another person or group. For example, the women's school stories cast middle-class teachers against working-class students, "good" schoolgirls against "bad" schoolgirls, light-skinned black students against dark-skinned black students, and "good" women (as either teachers or mothers) against "bad" women as symbolic antagonists in the struggle for success. The overarching moral of these tales is that school divides female students *within* themselves and *against* each other in the struggle to establish themselves as a "somebody."

I use the concept of "splitting"—the breakdown of the whole person into parts of a person—to interpret the women's storied selves. This concept enables us to examine how tensions within an individual are translated into conflicts between individuals or groups and how both sets of tensions are expressed in the women's personal narratives. I use the term broadly to speak of psychological, cultural, and institutional forces that divide objects, people, ideas, and feelings into oppositions in which one side is devalued and the other is idealized.[27] In a psychological sense, splitting organizes the women's understandings about self in relation to others; it enables them to protect or defend themselves against seemingly irresolvable conflicts or at least give them the illusion of coherence or wholeness in the face of anxieties that these tensions engender.[28] Meanwhile, institutionally speaking, schools are organized in ways that split off and devalue one side of the educational process against another (e.g. the academic being more valued than the social side of student development). Schools split off different kinds of knowledge (common sense versus schoolsmarts, for example) and some people against others (those who are and those who are not teachers' pets). Moreover, these institutional splits encouraged a sense of personal and social limits in the women, and these splits kept them from seeing larger structural forces that impeded their life chances.

OVERVIEW OF THE BOOK

The book opens with a description of the two research settings and my roles and relationships with the women in each (chapter 2). All of these women—black and white, rural and urban, southern and northern—had very clear ideas about knowledge. Knowledge, they felt, was divided into what they called "schoolsmarts" and common sense." But the women in each group defined and valued these two genres of knowledge differently, which shaped their identities and stance towards schooling (chapter 3). When talking about their expectations of the future—how as children they learned that certain aspirations were "unthinkable"—the women expressed distinctive views about who succeeds, who fails, and why. Through their stories about childhood ambitions, we see the historical and institutionally specific conditions that shaped their life trajectories and set the stage for their critical self-appraisals (chapter 4).

The women's stories show that schools shortchange girls in more complicated ways than is currently acknowledged. That the Philadelphia women spoke of their schooling in terms of voice, discipline, and resistance, while the North Carolina women spoke in terms of visibility, access, and ability, tells us a great deal about the effects of school mission and organization on women's education. I also explain how each school context—the urban-bureaucratic and rural-community—produced its own set of student self-understandings, views about teachers' authority and knowledge, and anxieties about learning (chapter 5). The women's vivid descriptions of good versus bad teachers and their persistent focus on teachers' pets highlighted the women's desire for, critiques of, and resistance to school (chapter 6). I analyze these stories for what they tell us about how students and teachers get ensnared by lopsided and unintentionally damaging relationships that can undermine students' sense of legitimacy and self-worth.

Equally important are mother-daughter bonds which have as much hold on the women as do those described with teachers (chapter 7). As the women speak about their conflicts with and regrets and sorrow regarding their mothers, we learn that the organization of school takes for granted the norms of middle-class family life, knowledge, time, and resources, making it appear as if the problem of social inequality and school failure is the result of ineffective, inadequate, "bad" mothers. I maintain that one of the reasons the women's school stories are told with so much passion is because they harbor unresolved feelings toward mothers whom they, at times consciously and at other times unconsciously, hold accountable for what society and school have denied them. Their stories depict schooling as a process that routinely splits into opposites legitimate and illegitimate knowledge, idealized and devalued students, good and bad teachers, and effective and ineffective mothers. Through these processes, the women became acutely aware of the degree to which they and their peers were or were not valued. This, in turn, fragmented their sense of self and social identities. Paradoxically, however, the same forces that pushed them out of school as girls pull them back as women, particularly as mothers (chapter 8).

The women's life stories provide emotional and psychological insight into the effects of class, race, and gender oppression and, in so doing, revise current theories of social reproduction (chapter 9). Their powerful, albeit unformulated, critique of schools as places where young women learn about their relative power and value deepen our understanding of how schools are failing to meet the needs of children, but especially those who are poor and working class. But this need not be so, and I make some suggestions for change (chapter 9). I focus specifically on the institutional, cultural, and psychological barriers that stand in the way of meaningful and egalitarian school relationships because these are the most neglected in school reform debates. Yet, as the women's stories attest, these relationships are what mattered most in their school lives and personal development.

Stories from
the Field

[Two]

In this chapter I take the reader into each research setting and tell some stories that I use as resources for analyzing the women's narratives. These stories of self and other, empathy and identification, conflict and comfort are common to fieldwork, but all too often are kept out of the official record.[1] I view this gap in research storytelling as unfortunate, because the knowledge of fieldwork grows out of and depends upon what happens between researchers and researched.[2] Feminist research strategies tell us to attend to our own experiences in the field and to be conscious of the research process as a relationship.[3] The challenge is to write about what transpires in such a way that readers can decide for themselves the truthfulness, significance, or usefulness of the knowledge that is produced.

THE PHILADELPHIA SETTING

The Lutheran Settlement House Women's Program is located in a Philadelphia neighborhood residents refer to as Fishtown. Once stable and vibrant, this historically white, ethnic, and working-class neighborhood had lost its industrial base and was suffering economic decline and rising unemployment when the Women's Program opened its doors in 1976.[4] The neighborhood had long been neglected by city services. Local residents complained about poor health care; nonexistent child-care facilities; a lack of recreational opportunities, especially for teenagers; increased rates of drug and alcohol abuse; environmental hazards; and a rising crime rate (see Luttrell 1988). In the face of city, state, and federal cutbacks, neighborhood women were taking on new or additional roles and responsibilities to make ends meet. Some women were entering the labor force for the first time, others were seeking more lucrative jobs, still others were taking in boarders or doing piecework at home so they could support their families. Reluctantly, many women were seeking welfare assistance. No matter what circumstances people found themselves in, the integrity and quality of community life was being questioned. In response to these changes, the Women's Program offered a wide range of educational opportunities, a counseling service, on-site child care, vocational training, and a battered women's hotline.

The fifteen Philadelphia women I selected to interview had all grown up in the neighborhood surrounding the Lutheran Settlement House.[5] Most lived within blocks of where they had been born and where extended family members still resided. They ranged in age from twenty-three years to forty-eight and had all attended neighborhood schools during the 1940s, 1950s, and 1960s before school integration. One-third had gone to parochial school, and two-thirds had gone to public school.[6] Five of the fifteen women had graduated from high school, and the rest had left either before or during their sophomore year.[7] They had all moved in and out of the work force as factory hands, clerical workers, waitresses, hospital or teachers' aides. Two-thirds of the women were married at the time of the interviews, although over the course of the study more became divorced single mothers. One woman had never married. All of them were mothers with at least one child still living at home.

The holistic and community-based approach of the Women's Program was crucial to its success. Despite the fact that there were high-school equivalency classes being offered at a nearby community center two elevated-train stops away, and college preparatory classes held at Philadelphia Community College four elevated-train stops away, the women preferred to stay closer to home mostly because they didn't want to feel "uncomfortable" in places they did not "belong."

As will become evident, concerns about not fitting in or feeling at odds with people they viewed as "different" persisted throughout the Philadelphia women's accounts. This was especially the case when speaking about school and their relationships with teachers. Meanwhile, I took note of how often students in the Women's Program classes kept their distance from certain teachers in the program. It wasn't that they didn't like these teachers, I was told; rather, these teachers were just "different." All this talk about difference, often punctuated by the familiar "You know what I mean," made me nervous since I wasn't sure I did know what they meant. And since I too had been their teacher, I wondered how and in what ways the Philadelphia women viewed me as "different." I felt determined to probe this in the interviews.

Mary was especially gracious during our first meeting at her home; she offered me tea and cookies and had bought a small gift for my two-year-old daughter, who accompanied me on this visit. I was feeling particularly at ease as our two toddlers played together. So when Mary started to describe her teachers as having been "different," I took the opportunity to probe more forcefully than I had with others. I asked her to be as specific as she could. First she said the teachers "lived in different neighborhoods—they weren't like the rest of us." When I asked her to explain how the teachers were different, she said, "I saw them as my superiors, I guess. I always saw them as more intelligent. I never saw them as equal." She hesitated and there was a brief silence. I sensed some discomfort—I wasn't sure if it was mine or hers. We both shifted a bit in our seats. After a moment she said:

> I always thought of them (I guess I should say you) [she stopped, looked at me] as being real rich. I just didn't think they were like us. They were from a higher class and must have been real smart to go to college in the first place. I just never felt comfortable with them. But now I know better, I mean they are not all alike. They, I mean, you [she smiled at me and we both started laughing], are not all rich, higher-class people who talk down to students.

This exchange crystallized my own discomfort. I was afraid that the Philadelphia women viewed me as "different" in this way—as a "rich, higher-class person" who would likely talk down to them. In light of their somewhat defensive accounts about why they had felt uncomfortable in school or had dropped out of it, I also worried that they thought I was sitting in judgment of them. When I asked Mary about this, she told me the same thing that Sennett and Cobb's white, working-class male interviewees told them—"not to take it personally" and that she liked me (1972: 42).

As did Sennett and Cobb's interviewee Frank Rissarro, the Philadelphia women often treated me as an "emissary from a different way of life" before whom they "spread a justification of their entire life":

> Frank Rissarro did not so much grant an interview as give a confession. . . . Rissarro believes people of a higher class have a power to judge him because they seem internally more developed human beings; and he is afraid, because they are better armed, that they will not respect him (1972: 25).

Nevertheless, not all people of a higher class deserve to be respected by others, a point that was made over and over again by the women I observed and interviewed. While the Philadelphia women viewed formal education as giving people tools for achieving respect, they, like Frank Rissarro, had a certain "revulsion against the work of educated people."[8]

My fieldnotes and interview transcripts were riddled with references to who was smart and worthy of respect, in what ways, and why. I was puzzling over all this material and why it made me uncomfortable when a particular event, early in the second year of my research, clarified my thinking. Doreen had invited me to her home, where we talked over coffee about the difficulties of raising children. We swapped strategies, confessed inadequacies, and enlisted each other's advice. As we sat in her small, square, brightly painted kitchen, our children played outside on the backyard concrete stoop. The gritty screened door kept slamming as they regularly came in to request snacks or to get help resolving disputes over the toys. We had just settled a dispute over several sand toys when Doreen observed:

> Wendy, your daughter is really bright. Listen to how well she talks. Look, she's even talking about that toy. Tony is older, but he doesn't know half those words. He doesn't talk much—especially when he's playing.

Doreen sounded both congratulatory and somewhat defensive, but I was unsure how to read her remarks. Familiar with Doreen's anxiety that five-year-old Tony was not doing well in school, I felt the need to reassure her (and perhaps myself) about the significance, if any, of my daughter Mikaela's and Tony's different abilities. As I peered through the screen door, I could see my almost-three-year-old daughter struggling to operate a large plastic truck. Tony had moved next to her and quickly manipulated a series of levers, which made the objects he had placed in the shovel drop to the floor. I was amazed by the complexity of the toy and said:

> Look at how Tony figured out how the truck works—it's incredibly complicated. Maybe he doesn't talk yet about it, but he will.

Doreen replied:

> Oh, that just takes common sense. He's good with his hands and figuring out how things work, but he's not smart like Mikaela. Maybe if he had went to daycare. . . .

Interrupted by more requests for apple juice, we left this conversation hanging. For days I felt uneasy about our exchange, unsettled by these distinctions between Mikaela's so-called smarts and Tony's so-called common sense. That Mikaela's verbal abilities had won her the mark of being "bright" and Tony's abilities to "figure things out" had been classified as "just common sense" seemed somewhat at odds with what I was hearing in class and in the interviews. I had often noted the Philadelphia women defend the value of common sense, especially the ability to "make things work," a kind of intelligence they attributed to their fathers, brothers, or husbands, whom they held in great esteem for doing manual labor. Why in this circumstance was Tony's ability to make things work viewed as "just common sense?" Meanwhile, what was it about Mikaela's facility with words, her social and communicative skills, that made her seem "bright" to Doreen?

This exchange was not only intellectually challenging, it also touched me on a deeper, more personal level. For one thing, it evoked my own childhood memories of being told that while I might be doing well in school, I lacked "common sense." This familiar refrain from family members always used to provoke me, making me feel torn about my school accomplishments. In another sense, I identified with Tony, feeling the sting of his mother's comparative and somewhat disparaging remark. But most assuredly I felt uncomfortable with Mikaela's seeming triumph over Tony in the competitive race for respect (otherwise known as intelligence) that characterizes America's class-, race-, and gender-divided society. [9]

There is yet another side to both of these stories. Divided by my own working- and middle-class family roots and loyalties, I found that my conversations with Mary and Doreen evoked in me feelings of envy and guilt about our differences.[10] Put bluntly, I was emotionally bound up in discussions about class. Did these feelings provide insight or distort my ability to narrate and interpret the Philadelphia women's stories and self-understandings? I think both, and one precipitous event confirmed this.

Toward the end of my research in Philadelphia, I submitted a paper abstract about working-class women learners to a regional Women's Studies conference. The paper was accepted, although I felt far from being finished with the analysis. Nevertheless, I knew that presenting some preliminary findings and gathering reactions would be helpful. Two students and two staff members from the Women's Program (two of whom I had interviewed) were also attending the conference as panelists to speak about feminist community-based studies. They all had promised to attend my session to give me moral support.

As I nervously waited in the empty room where I was to deliver the paper, I was grateful to see my four supporters arrive, but no else appeared. My feelings of disappointment and rejection must have been evident when Joanne, an interviewee, said:

> You know, this is exactly why I don't call myself a feminist. Look at this; you say you're going to talk about working-class women learners and no one shows up. If you were talking about Virginia Woolf or women in the 1800s, there'd be plenty of people here.

Joanne's anger put me in touch with my own. I wanted to go home but the women, especially those I had interviewed, insisted I present the paper to them anyway. The paper, filled with their own words, sparked an animated discussion. They said they agreed with much of my analysis; they recognized themselves and women they knew in what I had said. But I sensed they were disappointed or doubtful, and I asked Joanne what she really thought. She said that I told about her life, but I had not told *her* story. I said that I doubted I could do that—only she could tell her own story. She disagreed and said I could do a better job narrating the individual life of each woman I interviewed than the women themselves could. Tina disagreed, saying she didn't want me to write her story; she preferred her experiences being used to illustrate larger points about "working-class women's lives" (her words). We debated this issue but could come to no consensus.

Looking back, this conversation reminds me of Judith Stacey's (1990: 544) account of an epiphanal exchange she had with one of her interviewees: "While everything I reported was accurate, I had not succeeded in rendering her core sense of self. No one could do that she countered, 'you could never capture me.'"[11] Joanne's and Tina's different views about being "captured," as well as my own discomforts about being the "capturer"—a metaphor that bespeaks the problematic politics of representation—lay at the heart of our debate. I also came away from this conversation with more appreciation for the ambiguity of my role as narrator of the women's stories—understanding better that "accuracy" was not the same as "authenticity." Meanwhile, our debate made me an advocate for the notion of a *relational* rather than a highly differentiated *core* "self." What I would write about the women's storied selves would necessarily represent our mutual engagement and exchange.[12]

THE NORTH CAROLINA SETTING

In 1984 I moved to North Carolina. I had a hard time adjusting to the stark racial divisions between white and black. But nothing provoked my discomfort as much as my working at the university, where the housekeeping staff and landscaping crew were people of color and the students, faculty, and administrative staff were predominantly white (with the notable exception of the basketball team). I resented being caught up in social patterns of dominance and deference that were vestiges of a past time I naively thought was over in the New South. Part of my new job included administering a work-place literacy program at the university that offered literacy and high-school equivalency classes to selected members of the maintenance staff who were released from their work duties for four hours a week to attend class. There were four classes of fifteen students, of which I taught two. Over a ten-year period, the program had served close to 200 people, including janitors, housekeepers, painters, electricians, landscapers, and members of the motor pool. I couldn't help noticing, however, that the mainstays of the program were African American female housekeepers.

My first day of class was reminiscent of the Women's Program, except that I was white and everyone else was not. After introductions, Ola said that she hoped I would stay longer than the last teacher, who had only stayed six months. She said all the teachers she had ever liked left before the year was over; she had been "sticking it out" for five years and was getting tired of the teacher turnover. I promised not to leave before the year was finished. Kate asked if I was a "real professor," adding, "We've never had a professor to teach *us*" (her emphasis). With my Ph.D. degree three months new, I was not sure how much of a "real professor" I was. In any case, I was more compelled by the second half of her statement and wondered who *us* meant, though I did not feel comfortable yet to ask her directly.

Ola said she was in school to "better herself"—she was especially proud to announce that her daughter would be graduating high school this year, and her goal was to get her high school diploma alongside her daughter. Others nodded approvingly, and Bessie said she too was in school to "set a good example for my son." Kate said she had graduated high school and attended college for one year before "losing her senses" and marrying; she was in school because she wanted to "become somebody." These parallels between the Philadelphia women and the North Carolina women grabbed my interest, but I felt a new set of qualms about my role as a white, middle-class researcher.

During the first year of teaching, I became acutely aware of myself as a particular kind of white person as the women puzzled over my ethnicity and lack of religious affiliation. For example, Geraldine said she had never met any white person who wasn't Jewish and that still claimed she wasn't a Christian. Lilly speculated that I was of "mixed blood," a cross between one of those Catholic groups (either Italian or Polish) and Jewish. No one could believe I had Irish, "hillbilly" ancestors nor that I had been raised a Methodist, then Presbyterian. I was told I was most unlike *those* white people. Again, I did not yet feel comfortable enough to ask what they meant by "those." Meanwhile, more than a few of the women promised to pray for me and for my return to the church.

I followed the same research protocol as in Philadelphia, surveying present and past program participants about why they had returned to school. In the second year, I selected fifteen women to interview in-depth, and later, when I was no longer a teacher, I observed the women in class.[13]

The North Carolina women I interviewed had all been raised in southern rural communities, although they now resided in neighborhoods close to the university. Most had grown up on tenant farms, and all but two had tended tobacco and picked cotton in their youths. They had all attended school before the 1964 desegregation ruling, often in one-room schoolhouses, and reported sporadic school attendance for reasons I discuss in more detail in chapters 4 and 5. They were all mothers with at least one child still living at home; two-thirds had been single heads of households for most of their lives.[14] These women were all employed as housekeepers at the university and shared similar work histories, including domestic work in white people's homes. Throughout the interviews, they told stories about the tremendous social and political changes in the South that had occurred over the course of their lives and related how these changes had affected them.

Most compelling to me at the time were their stories about working as domestics. In story after story, the North Carolina women recounted in an ironic tone the ineptness or "sorriness" of the "white ladies" they had worked for. Sounding much like the domestic workers Judith Rollins interviewed, the North Carolina women were able to "skillfully deflect the psychological attacks on their personhood" by refusing to accept "employers' definitions of them as inferior" (1985: 212). These stories were told with laughter, and yet I often felt more like crying. I did not know why these stories evoked in me so much emotion. Then one day after a particularly long session with Linda, who had told several stories related to her domestic work experiences, including one where her employer had sprayed her with Lysol, she asked me if I had ever seen anything like what she had described. A long-forgotten memory came to mind, which I shared with her.

In 1963, I was ten years old and my family moved from Chicago to Houston, Texas, for one year. I remember being shocked by the rural and segregated forms of poverty. On a shopping trip with my mother, I encountered segregation firsthand. Needing to use the bathroom, I ventured into territory where I did not know yet that I didn't belong. As I stood at the sink washing my hands, three black women broke into laughter and one remarked: "You're in the wrong place, honey." I said, "But isn't this the ladies room?" This statement generated even louder laughter as another woman said: "Yes, but we aren't ladies." I quickly dried my hands and as I closed the door behind me, I read the sign: "For colored women only." By the time I located my mother in the store I was crying. I told her my version of the story, including my distress about what I viewed as a terrible injustice. Somewhat distracted by the demands of my younger siblings, she calmly replied that this was how it was in the South. I was unsatisfied with her answer, angry that she seemed not to share my strong feelings about this. I proceeded to find the manager of the store to complain.[15] The red-haired youthful manager smiled briefly as I described my outrage about the separate bathrooms. Without so much as an apology or explanation he patted me on the head and said that he would help me find my mother.

After telling Linda the story, I felt embarrassed and vulnerable, as if she were one of the women in the store bathroom. Here I was, years later, still struggling on both an emotional and intellectual level to discern what these women had meant by saying they weren't ladies and what, exactly, this memory meant to me. I was also concerned about how Linda would respond to my story. I knew this story revealed my privileged protection from all the abuses she had just spoken about. Linda waited a moment before speaking and said, "You should tell that story in your book." Then she asked if I had ever been "cared for by a black woman" or if black women had cleaned our house. She asked, didn't I have any stories to tell of that? I explained that my family didn't have domestic servants of any kind. My mother's philosophy was that people should clean up after themselves (or more accurately that women should clean up after men). Linda was surprised by this and explained that "things were different here," and reiterated an earlier statement: "Like I said, some of the white women I worked for were nice and some weren't." Again, this conversation confirmed the value of mutual engagement and exchange in fieldwork. By listening to and exchanging stories with the women, I developed a clearer picture of what it means to define one's womanhood against controlling gender-, race-, and class-based images, including images that I projected onto the women and they projected onto me.

The same can be said about self-definitions in relation to teachers. I learned that my role as teacher vis-à-vis the North Carolina women evoked an altogether different set of comforts and conflicts than those I had experienced in Philadelphia. One particular event highlighted this. As a teacher I always made it a point to meet with each student to evaluate her progress at the end of a semester. For some reason, the North Carolina student conferences felt more taxing than those with the Philadelphia students and I was unsure why. The process itself—students filling out a self-assessment form and talking about their own strengths and weaknesses and me writing a narrative evaluation of their progress—seemed fruitful. But I was never sure whether the North Carolina students saw their progress or that they shared my same assessment of their academic skills and achievements.[16] In one conference, Ola said that she hoped I knew that the reason she came to class was because she "loved me" (her words). She reminded me about how earlier in the year I had called her at home because she had missed several classes. It was not unusual for me to call students at home, so I was surprised that this routine teaching practice had so affected her. As the administrator of the program, I had become aware that certain supervisors made it difficult for their employees to come to class and it was within my authority to intervene if necessary. I thought this might be the case with Ola. However, Ola had explained she was waiting for payday so she could buy a new pair of glasses. She was getting headaches from reading and had not yet been able to afford the new prescription. I had asked if she wanted me to lend her the money so that she would not have to miss class. She did not take me up on my offer, but returned to class the next day (without glasses). During our conference Ola said: "I figured if you cared enough to call me at home, then you must really think that I can do the work. Then too, if you cared enough to call me and to loan me the money, then I should care enough about myself to be in class every-day and not give up on myself. I just never had a teacher to call me like that." She then took my hand and said, "So I am going to keep working at it."

In each research setting my role as "teacher/interviewer" proved to be more significant than I had anticipated. Insofar as the women were willing to talk with me because they knew me as their teacher and we had developed trust and rapport, my teacher role was beneficial. At the same time, this role evoked in them certain experiences with and memories about teachers that were projected onto me as a routine feature of our interview discussions.[17] It was not uncommon for women in both the Philadelphia and North Carolina groups, when talking about their teachers in negative ways, to reassure me that "I was not like that." Meanwhile, as part of this exchange I learned that the women in each group had different concerns about and stakes in their relationships with teachers. Whereas the North Carolina women framed their rela-tionships with teachers in terms of care, the Philadelphia women framed their relationships in terms of conflict, a distinction that will be exam-ined in chapters 5 and 6. The tenacious but different holds that student-teacher relationships have on students' self-understandings and views of school is underestimated in current research about schooling, identity, and social change. I am doubtful that I would have learned as much about this had it not been for my teacher role.

Generally speaking, the women were blind to who I was and held their own fantasies and images about me, as I did of them. This healthy tension between who we are and who we are imagined to be by others is part of all relationships. These tensions can be frustrating and limiting, but they are also what provide us pleasure in making meaningful con-nections with others.

Schoolsmart
and Motherwise

[Three]

Well, I'm not schoolwise, but I'm streetwise and motherwise and housewifewise. I think there are two kinds of intelligence—streetwise and schoolwise. I don't know much facts about things I learned in school, but I know a lot about life on the streets. I guess I someday might be schoolwise if I stick to it long enough. But what I have now, what I know already, nobody can take away. (*Doreen*, Philadelphia woman)

You don't need an education to be smart. I know people who can read and write and do their figures. They are smart but they just never finished school. Like me and my husband. We've learned a lot along the road—in that school of hard knocks. We've got what you call common sense. (*Beatrice*, North Carolina woman)

We are what we know, and, conversely, we are what we think we do not know. In this chapter I chart the similarities and differences in how the Philadelphia and North Carolina women understood and valued two genres of knowledge—schoolsmarts and common sense—and show how these distinctions were both affirming and disabling. In the process, I will reframe the by-now familiar discussion of "women's ways of knowing" so that the racial, class, and gendered links between who we are and what we know can be better exposed and challenged.

Since the pathbreaking work of Nancy Chodorow (1978) and Carol Gilligan (1982), many compelling yet incomplete claims have been made about men's and women's different ways of knowing. This work has generated both awareness of and debate about the gendered cornerstones of knowledge and how it is constructed. Briefly stated, women's ways of knowing have been said to be more relational, oriented more toward sustaining connection than achieving autonomy, and governed by interests to attend to others' needs.[1] Other feminist accounts have invested women with distinctive intuitive and/or emotional capabilities, citing women's exclusion from other ways of acquiring knowledge under patriarchy and locating women's knowledge in the "body," or in female sexuality.[2] Still others have written about women's epistemic advantage in viewing the world more holistically from their particular "standpoint."[3] In contrast, men's ways of knowing are said to center on instrumental reason and abstract rules. Men's knowing is said to be aimed at gaining mastery over nature and is governed by interests to dominate others. By this account, men's social position undermines their ability to see the world accurately.[4]

These theoretical speculations notwithstanding, little empirical work has been done to trace these different ways of knowing; as yet, it seems premature to foreclose debate on the matter.[5] However, if viewed uncritically, such research can reproduce "stereotypes of men and women, flirting with essentialism, distorting the diverse dimensions of human knowing and falsifying the historical record of women's manifold uses of reason in daily life" (Hawkesworth 1989: 547).[6] My concern is that false distinctions between men's and women's ways of knowing may gloss over cultural meanings, power relations, and personal emotions that shape the knowledge women claim as their own. Indeed, by mapping out the women's diversity as knowers and describing the specific material and ideological conditions under which the Philadelphia and North Carolina women constructed and claimed knowledge for themselves, I show how much more complicated these issues are.

PROPERTIES OF COMMON SENSE

The distinction between schoolwise knowledge and common sense first came to my attention in classroom discussions and then even more forcefully in the interviews. Women in both groups brought up the topic of intelligence in response to my open-ended question, "How would you describe yourself as a learner?" Without my prompting, the women discussed multiple forms of intelligence, reflecting on who possesses which form, and why.

Common sense was most often described as a form of intelligence attained *outside* school, a way of knowing that stemmed from life experience and was best measured by people's ability to cope with everyday problems:

> Jim (my husband) considers himself stupid. He's very good at what he does at his job, but he was never good in school. He has a kind of streetsmarts—he's the commonsense type. I don't know, I'm not sure that intelligence can be measured. (*Teresa*, Philadelphia woman)

> Intelligence is knowing how to use what you know—it's knowing how to do things. I think being intelligent means coping with things in life. Even people with high IQs or with college degrees don't know how to do the simplest, everyday things or cope with everyday problems—that takes *real* [her emphasis] intelligence, it takes common sense. (*Mary*, North Carolina woman)

"Real intelligence" (common sense) was said to flourish outside school. According to the women, common sense was not measured by what school authorities could teach you, but by what you could teach yourself or what you learned from the "school of hard knocks." Indeed, as many women pointed out, "real intelligence" stood in inverse relation to and could be corrupted by education or formal schooling:

> I don't think that intelligence has anything to do with schooling. Schools only make you know more. Education is not a sign of intelligence. But people who are well schooled always seem intelligent. I suppose they might not be any more intelligent than me. My husband has this idea that people with a lot of schooling don't have common sense. It is like the more schooling you have the less common sense you have. (*Mary*, Philadelphia woman)

> I used to beg my mother to let me go to school. She would say, "Girl, you have no common sense." Or when I would want to read instead of doing my chores she would say, "You're never going to learn anything like that—you've got to have common sense in this world." (*Lilly*, North Carolina woman)

Common sense has been characterized as "an everywhere-found cultural form," a way of comprehending the world as familiar and knowable (Geertz 1983: 85).[7] By this way of knowing certain things are just given; people with common sense grasp "matter-of-fact" events and ideas simply because they are what they are. Common sense also enables people to handle the unpredictabilities of everyday life. Though common sense is simple, it is not simple-minded. In fact, those without common sense—even educated persons—may find themselves lacking the ability to assess what is true or real. Common sense is also *accessible,* for it requires no expertise, specialized training, or credentials. It is said to be "collaborative," because each generation evaluates the knowledge passed on to it (Fingeret 1983a, 1983b).

The above properties were embedded in the women's discussions about themselves as commonsense knowers. For example:

> I'm the commonsense type. It's just part of the way I am, the way I deal with life and make the best of it. You don't need a degree to have common sense. (*Mabel*, North Carolina woman)

> Common sense isn't something you learn, it has to be there to begin with. It is more to do with experience, knowing how to do things and getting things done. (*Mary*, Philadelphia woman)

Common sense recognizes and validates the knowledge that grows out of life experience—what people have seen and know to be true. Meanwhile, those who appear intelligent (even if they aren't) are viewed as such because they are able to convince people of their truth. Knowing who to believe takes common sense. According to the women, you can assess certain truths more reliably if you know the person or if the person is known by someone within the community. As Barbara explained:

> The people I know have common sense. Like my grandmother. She knows a lot because she's seen a lot. She's seen it all and I believe what she says because she's been there. Like she knows about slavery. She didn't read about it, like all of us young folk.

Since books are one step removed from people's experience, it is difficult to assess the authenticity or validity of information conveyed through book learning. Many of the women would agree with Sadie, who explained her distrust of book learning to interviewer Arlene Fingeret:

> Who wrote the book could put what they want to put there. And my foreparents, they witnessed this. As over the generations they going to tell their children so their children would know. See, the thing what my parents tell me, I believe it's true. A book, you can put in just what they want to (1983a: 23).[8]

To these many properties of commonsense knowledge as being natural, practical, simple, accessible, collaborative, and doubtful of book learning, I add another: Common sense is *self-* and *identity-forming*. It is a cultural form through which the women at once affiliated with some groups of people and defended themselves against others. Common sense, held in such high regard by the women, contains a paradox. It is both a self-destructive and an enabling understanding imposed by gender, race, and class relations.[9]

HOW CLASS MATTERS

Women in both groups persistently described themselves as the "commonsense type" of person:

> I know a lot of people who are very intelligent but they are fruity—I wouldn't want to be one. I have common sense. Maybe I have more intelligence than I'm aware of in some areas, but I am not an academic, learned person, and I don't think I'll ever be. I'm not the professional type. I can work with those kind of intelligent people, but I don't want to be like them. (*Debra*, Philadelphia woman)

> I have just never thought about average people like myself being intelligent. People like me have common sense. (*Dottie*, North Carolina woman)

Common sense was attributed to "ordinary" or "average" people whose knowledge and interests were different from or set against professionals or educated people. Claiming common sense was a way to express a class consciousness.[10]

The affirming side of commonsense knowing came across most strongly when the women described how they solved everyday problems and how common sense was passed on. Family and friends who "know the ropes," who successfully negotiate bureaucracies such as schools, welfare agencies, and hospitals, were viewed as trusted and authoritative sources of common sense. In each example, the women's definitions of common sense validated the actions and adaptations of peers or family members who refused to abdicate authority to people from a "higher social standing" (such as teachers, social workers, or doctors). These professionals, whom they viewed as standing in judgment of working-class people, held knowledge that conflicted with their own values or interests. Claiming common sense against this "expert" advice was a way to assert one's own authority to judge what is "really useful knowledge."[11]

In contrast, the women's views of schoolwise (rather than "real") intelligence were more diffuse. In one sense, being schoolsmart was understood to be an inherited ability (like an IQ). But intelligence was also understood to be socially nurtured. For example, Anne (from Philadelphia) explained that insofar as a person has more schooling, opportunities, and resources, this person is more likely to be intelligent:

> Most people need schooling to achieve their intelligence. Opportunity means a lot. How far you can go with that intelligence. You take two kids who are both intelligent, and one of them has the opportunity to go to college, he's going to be a little brighter than the other guy who didn't have the opportunity, not because he didn't have the intellect but because he didn't have the chance to use it.

Note the important word, "achieve," in Anne's commonly held formulation about intelligence. Unlike common sense, which is accessible to anyone and requires no specialized training, schoolwise intelligence is not accessible—it must be achieved. This is what I mean by saying that the women's views of knowledge were class coded. By associating intelligence with ambition, opportunity, and upward mobility, they could explain or even justify social inequality. Put slightly differently, the women used the notion of intelligence to justify why people end up in the social position they do.[12]

The forms of these justifications varied. One way that the women accounted for their lower social standing was from not using their intelligence:

> Intelligence has to do with how people accept life—how life comes to them and how they deal with it. My boys don't use their intelligence. I don't use half of my intelligence. If I did, why would I be here? (*Doris*, Philadelphia woman)

> The important point is that the system is not working. People's mobility is very limited. People need education in order to get out of the ruts. The system keeps people in their place, in their class. You need intelligence to get out of your place. (*Cheryl*, Philadelphia woman)

When I responded, "I know a lot of intelligent people living here," Cheryl replied:

> Yeah, but if they had more ambition, like me, that's what I'm trying to do here is use my intelligence. Then at least they'd have half a chance of getting out of their ruts.

Another view of the relationship between intelligence and social class was expressed by Edna from North Carolina:

> There are a few people who make it. They're the ones that's blessed or that has intelligence. The rest of us just have to make do.

"Making it," which is associated with ambition and achievement in American society, is a mark of intelligence. By contrast, "making do" is associated with survival (even if against great odds) and is a mark of common sense. Through these split and unequal forms of knowledge, the women came to believe that a certain type of intelligence, not class relations, divides people and sustains social inequality.

HOW GENDER MATTERS

The women's discussion of what counts as "real intelligence" and who possesses it was also gender coded. This code, however, was not expressed nor understood by each group of women in the same way. When talking about people they considered intelligent, the Philadelphia women gave only men as examples. Although they described their mothers, aunts, or sisters as having common sense, only certain aspects of common sense were associated with "real intelligence"—aspects culturally associated with men's work and privileges. This pattern was so striking that I began to wonder about the absence of women and how I might be contributing to it by my questioning. In the remaining interviews I took more time and probed more directly about whom the Philadelphia women considered intelligent. My efforts only served to strengthen the pattern. When Cheryl finished describing her father's and brothers' common sense, what she referred to as "real intelligence," I asked her, "Is there anyone else you can think of that you consider having real intelligence?" She thought for a moment and said:

> Well, I guess you could say my grandmother. She came to this country on her own and worked as hard as any man I know. She raised eleven children on her own after my grandfather was disabled in an accident at work. Yeah, I guess you could say she was intelligent, but I think of her as having a lot of common sense, you know what I mean? Then again, my father had to get his intelligence from somewhere, from her I imagine—it could have come from my grandmother.

Cheryl's grandmother, who "worked as hard as any man," was seen as passing down to others but not possessing her own intelligence.[13]

The most pronounced example of the devaluation of women's intelligence was found in the Philadelphia women's discussion of the "real intelligence" required for manual labor and the ability to "make things work." Peggy and Doris remarked:

> The most intelligent person I know is my brother—he can fix anything. And when you come right down to it, what's more important than being able to make things work? Not everybody can do that, you know.

> Now just because we're going to school and getting educated, we shouldn't forget that people, like my husband, who work with their hands are just as important as college professors and just as smart.

Without exception, the manual ways of knowing that were associated with "real intelligence" applied only to men's manual labor, not women's. Female factory workers were not compared to or noted as being important or as smart as college professors. Nor was women's handiwork such as sewing, baking, or gardening regarded as highly as was men's handiwork.

In the same spirit, the Philadelphia women equated men's self-taught skills with "real" intelligence. Pam and Helen made the following observations:

> My brother is very intelligent—he's self-educated, not school educated. He reads a lot and has taught himself how to play musical instruments. I consider him one of the most intelligent people I know.

> My father is *really* [her emphasis] intelligent. He loves to read everything and is interested in all sorts of things. He graduated high school, but he did really lousy. But he's by far one of the most intelligent people around, and what he knows he taught himself.

Self-taught skills such as helping children with homework were not awarded the distinction of "real intelligence." For example, their mastery of the "new math" skills that they learned as part of helping their children do homework was seen as evidence of "motherwise" knowledge or "problem solving"—the ability to "balance a lot of things, if that counts," not as "real intelligence." Meanwhile, reading the newspaper for pleasure (an activity few women had time to enjoy) was more highly regarded than reading children's bedtime stories. Bluntly put, the common sense associated with women's work, family life, child rearing, and other caregiving tasks counted less (if at all) than the common sense associated with men's work and activities.

Not only did the Philadelphia women value men's common sense more than their own, they described the different ways that working-class men and women acquire common sense. White working-class men were understood to acquire their "real intelligence" through a set of collective, work-related experiences as apprentices, as participants in vocational training programs, or as the sons of fathers whose "craft" knowledge had been passed down from one generation to another. This craft knowledge—the ability to work with one's hands and muscles—belongs to the work group; it is neither individualized nor available from books. It also identifies one as masculine, capable of performing traditionally sex-stereotyped, "manly" jobs.[14] Male craft workers acquire their knowledge and masculine identity through collective expression and public recognition. This contrasts sharply with the intuitive and individualized way that the Philadelphia women acquired their common-sense or motherwise knowledge. As Philadelphia women Anne and Cheryl explained:

> There are lots of things I know—what you might call woman's intuition or mother's intuition. Taking care of a child with a chronic disease teaches you this. You can begin to predict what the doctors are going to tell you and then go home and deal with it on your own. That's common sense; in the end you do what you have to do as a mother.

Common sense is a feeling, really. Like being a mother. You do things that seem right at the time. Nobody ever tells you to do this or do that. Although my sister, she just had a baby, drives me crazy always calling me up, saying, "What do I do?" You'd think she would have a little more common sense than that.

In short, women's common sense was considered a natural part of being a good mother. Lois from North Carolina confirmed this view when she explained:

I was born with it. Now I didn't always use it, like with my boys, but then I was young and running all the time. But you get older, you experience things, you know what's right to do for them and what they need. You're their mother and you stay close to them; you can just feel it.

Women in both groups viewed their common sense as part of their caregiving activities and relationships with others. They emphasized feelings and intuitions, not the thoughts that enable women to "do what you have to do as a mother." This genre of knowledge comes in flashes, often precipitated by an event such as childbirth or divorce. It can also develop over the years, as women (re)evaluate their ability to cope with extenuating circumstances as they care for others. Motherwise knowledge is difficult to universalize because it is emotional, relational, individual, and particularized; it is geared toward meeting (individual) needs. Compared to craft knowledge, which is derived through collective and consensual agreement about the "facts," motherwise knowledge is derived through personal experience, and all too often there is conflict about the "facts."

Insights from feminist epistemologists and psychoanalysts are particularly useful for explaining the gendered construction of knowledge. Just as the organization of women's domestic work makes it impossible to distinguish "love" from "labor," so too in motherwise knowledge it is difficult to distinguish what is emotional from what is objective or rational.[15] Hence the knowledge of care gets conflated with affect, feelings, and intuition, while the cognitive, learned, and thoughtful dimensions of this genre of knowledge go unrecognized. As a result, the hard work, mastery, and collective dimension of how women acquire their commonsense/motherwise knowledge gets masked. Meanwhile, though society may pay lip service to qualities associated with caregiving—sensitivity, patience, empathy, compassion—these habits of mind are relegated to what Lorenne Clark (1976) calls the "ontological basement" of different ways of knowing.[16]

This false division between emotional and objective labor also contributes to men's domination over women. Insofar as "women's work" is organized around the details of maintaining family, business, and community life (women's work as wives, secretaries, nurses, to name a few), men are enabled to pursue more abstracted knowledge and to exercise their power and authority (Smith 1987). Put bluntly, women's work is part of what defines men's rule, making it appear as if men's "reason" and "knowledge" entitles them to more powerful positions.[17]

Just as class relations influence how people understand and claim schoolwise in contrast to commonsense knowledge, gender relations shape attitudes toward rational versus intuitive, objective versus emotional knowledge. These distinctions constrain societal expectations about and women's own belief in their intellectual capabilities. Psychodynamic processes may contribute to this. Alongside the sexual division of labor that values "productive" over "reproductive" work, there is a corresponding sexual division of emotions that privileges autonomy over relatedness. Jane Flax (1987a, 1990) has argued that this division makes it appear as if men's knowledge is autonomous while women's is relational, and that this false split undermines women's claims to mastery and authority. Meanwhile, according to Muriel Dimen (1989: 42), people "try to distance their dependency needs by regarding their longings for love, tenderness, and care as weak, childish, 'womanish.'" This distancing from and devaluation of dependency psychologically prepares people to devalue the knowledge associated with caregiving.

Gendered views of knowledge—that is, the splits between intellect and emotion, affect and cognition, intuition and reason, autonomy and relatedness—fragment the knowledge people can claim for themselves. In this case, the women in both groups were drawn to commonsense and intuition because these forms of knowledge rest in women themselves (not in higher authorities) and are experienced directly in the world (not through abstractions). But both classifications (commonsense and intuition) placed the women in less powerful positions in relation to men and in relation to middle-class professionals (men and women).

HOW RACE MATTERS

The women in each group placed different value on the forms of knowledge held by men and women in their respective communities. The North Carolina women included women as well as men among the people they knew who had "real" intelligence. They did not associate "real" intelligence with skilled manual work, perhaps partly because black men have historically had limited access to the "crafts." Instead, they viewed common sense, most often referred to as "motherwit,"[18] as all-encompassing, mentioning abilities to "make ends meet"; solve family, work, or community disputes; overcome natural disasters (e.g., droughts and hurricanes); and avoid racial conflict. And it was not uncommon for the North Carolina women to identify both male and female kin folk as having such knowledge, even when it applied to the knowledge of child rearing and caregiving. Lois, who earlier in the interview said she was born with her motherwit, went on to add:

> I got my common sense from my momma and daddy. They worked real hard to keep us, and they would always be there to help any-ones that needed it.

For the North Carolina women, motherwit, often renamed "real intelligence," was described in terms of women's abilities to work hard and get the material things they and their children need or want, with or without the support of a man. Bernice and Kate explained:

> I got a sister. I think she is smart, real intelligent. All of them is smart, but this one is special and she do the same kind of work I do (she cleans a bank at night), but she's smart. She can hold onto money better than anyone. It look like anything she want she can get. She bought her a car, this was in the '60s. Then after that she bought her a trailer. She don't buy that many cars, but anytime she or her childrens need something, she can go and get it. But she has a husband that helps her, not like my other sisters or me. Her husband is nice to her and both of them working. But even that [refer-ring to her sister's marriage] takes a lot of intelligence.

> I would say my sister is the most intelligent person I know. She knows how to get what she wants and she has done it on her own, her kids and working; she ain't never been on welfare or nothing.

These claims to real intelligence can in part be explained by the histori-cal significance attached to women's domestic work as part of African American survival and resistance.[19] Understood as central to family and community survival, black women's caregiving knowledge cannot be easily diminished or trivialized. Patricia Hill Collins (1990) makes this point and cites black women's successful efforts to maintain family and community life as evidence of their feminist politics and thought: "The decision to be wife and mother, first in a world which defined Black women in so many other ways, the decision to make her family the most important priority, was an act of resistance" (55).[20]

On the other hand, the North Carolina women also attributed black men's real intelligence to their ability to get black women to do the very things they have sworn they will not do. Lilly and Ola qualified their claims to common sense by describing troubled relationships with men:

> I lose my common sense when it comes to men. I don't know how it happens. They're just so smart getting you to listen to them and what they want. I should have learned that lesson by now, but I haven't—it's just plain stupidity on my part.

> There's lots of kinds of intelligence. It's not so easy to say. And
> sometimes I have it and sometimes I don't, you know, the common-
> sense type. I can get myself into some trouble when I don't. I sure
> need more, but not the kind we get here in school. I mean John,
> you know, he can get me to do just what he wants, just like that.
> And that takes real intelligence, it takes something to get me to do
> things I knows not good for me.

Notice that Lilly and Ola equated men's desires and needs to being
smart, but both women linked their own longings for love to a loss of
common sense. In the end, the notion that (black) men's power lies in
their intelligence or knowledge and not in their culturally sanctioned
license to dominate (black) women, sexually as well as otherwise, was
costly. This notion held the North Carolina women in check, at times
making them willing to accept conditions that (by their own admission)
were not in their best interests.[21]

Another highly valued form of real intelligence was the ability to deal
with racism. Kate provided an example of this capacity in herself:

> I'll tell you what takes real intelligence—dealing with people's
> ignorance. One day I was at the department store, you know,
> maybe it was Belk's. I was getting on the escalator and there was
> this little white boy pointing at me saying to his daddy, "Look there
> at that nigger." Now you should have seen the look on his daddy's
> face: he looked scared, like I was going to start a race riot or some-
> thing. He pushed this boy along trying to get out of my way fast. But
> I know children and they don't mean what they say. He was just
> saying what he hears at home. But people are ignorant, and it
> takes real intelligence to know that it's not that little boy's fault.

> *And how did you get that kind of intelligence?*

> Oh well, you live and learn. You see and watch people. It's a feeling
> you have because not all white people are the same. I sure know
> that 'cause I worked for different ones, you know, taking care of
> their children, and I've seen different things.

Kate's account reminds us of the subtle but persistent evocation of black
bodies as dangerous and the psychic energy it takes to refuse the controlling effects of racist images.[22] Kate's example also reflects Omi and
Winant's (1986) notion of a "racial etiquette" that appears to her as common sense—a natural (and self-evident) part of living and learning as a
black woman in white American society. This knowledge is equally necessary to black men and women. It is collective, learned through everyday interactions *within* black communities and *against* white people's
racism. This knowledge is a particular, not universal, kind in that one
must be black to have real intelligence about the world of white people

who, whether they are understood to be fearful, "ignorant," or racist, can do irreparable damage.[23] Nevertheless, this knowledge is also derived from collective and consensual agreement about what constitutes racist ignorance. It is more like craft knowledge in that it belongs to the group and is not individualized but instead comes about through public/collective experiences and as such is more legitimated in the hierarchy of knowledge. In this way, the North Carolina women were less distanced from their commonsense knowledge than the Philadelphia women. However, it would be a mistake to celebrate the North Carolinians' knowledge claims without noting the hidden costs. While they may value their common sense as "real intelligence," there are few arenas in which these women have been allowed to exercise their power and authority. The psychic and social effects of the denial and repression of African American women's knowledge should not be underestimated.[24]

SUMMARY

In this chapter I have compared how the North Carolina and Philadelphia women understood their own ways of knowing in relation to others'. Briefly stated, all the women held class-based views and values about knowledge in which they split off common sense from schoolwise intelligence, pitting experience against schooling and working-class people against middle-class, educated people. The North Carolina women reminded us, however, that these splits are also racialized—that living in white America requires "real intelligence." Black people who survive and/or resist racism do so because of their common sense or "real intelligence" against white people's "ignorance." Meanwhile, the women in both groups held gendered views of knowledge that divorced intellect from emotion, affect from cognition, intuition from reason, feeling from thought, relatedness from autonomy. Despite this commonality, however, the women did not attach the same value to men's and women's knowledge. In starkest terms, the Philadelphia women overvalued men's knowledge in relation to their own. This was less true for the North Carolina women, but they too embraced a view that men are more powerful by virtue of their knowledge, not their social privilege.

These contrasts reveal that there is no single mode of "women's knowing." Insofar as the kind of knowledge women possess—whether schoolsmart or motherwise—is formed by false oppositions, absences, and denials, women's self-understandings and social identities will be fragmented. While split views of knowledge may enable the women to defend themselves socially, to ward against the hidden injuries of class, race, and gender, these same splits put them in a bind vis-à-vis education. These conflicts come into clearer focus when we consider the women's childhood ambitions.

Childhood
Ambitions

[Four]

My parents they sit down and tell us, you going to be a school teacher. You know how they think. They told us what they wanted us to do, you know, so we wouldn't have to work as hard as them. But we knowed we weren't going to be. 'Cause we didn't have too many school teachers no way. The two schools we went to weren't but one school teacher.

So is that what you wanted to do—to be a school teacher?

I don't know, I guess a school teacher. That's the only thing we knowed. We didn't think about anything else. (*Ola*, North Carolina interviewee)

When I was in grade school they asked us what we wanted to be when we grew up. I wrote that I wanted to be a judge. The nuns got very upset with this and asked me if I had copied it from somewhere. I mean, what little kid from the neighborhood ever thought about being a judge? (*Joanne*, Philadelphia interviewee)

We are what we know and hope for about our futures; we are also what we know not to anticipate or expect for ourselves. This chapter is about how the women learned that certain aspirations were "unthinkable." While I was prepared to ask each woman what she remembered wanting to be when she grew up, not a single woman failed to offer this information on her own accord and in her own animated way. Some women narrated their childhood ambitions as part of their memories of school, and others provided this information in response to my question, "Why are you returning to school?" Their stories highlighted formative experiences through which they defined and defended themselves against others' judgments. Each woman seemed to (re)experience the comparison of herself to idealized and split images of a "somebody" as part of telling her story. This seemed to me a simple, but remarkable finding.

SIMILARITIES BETWEEN THE NORTH CAROLINA AND PHILADELPHIA WOMEN

Grounding their tales in historically specific and emotionally charged terms about what was considered right or inevitable at the time, the women told what they remembered were their life options.[1] North Carolinians Gloria and Bessie recalled:

> The time I was coming along you could do housework, you could baby-sit, work jobs in the back of a kitchen, you know, or you could clean up outside, if you were a man.

> When I got grown up you couldn't find no job nowhere but tending to somebody's babies or cleanin' somebody's house. If you were lucky you could end up like, well, out there like where I'm working [at a university as a housekeeper].

Philadelphians Peggy and Anne explained:

> In the neighborhood there were four choices: you could either be a secretary, nurse, mother, or nun (if you were Catholic).

> When I grew up the choices were clear—either a nurse, nun, secretary, or mother. We didn't think about other things, we didn't know anything different.

Sometimes told as cautionary tales about the risks inherent in childhood longings and sometimes told with a sense of irony, the women's stories unfolded as dramas about who succeeds, who fails, and why. According to the women in both groups, there are those whom we expect will "become somebody" and those who won't. There are people who do the right thing (finish school, get married, etc.) and those who don't (or can't), which explains who gets ahead and why. There are those with brains, ambition, and drive who can make it in school or on the job, while others are deficient and thus cannot expect to succeed. The women explained themselves and their failed ambitions in part as a critique of, and in part as an acceptance of, this shared view of success, how success works, and how social inequalities arise as a result.[2]

The women defined success as the ability to avoid particular kinds of work for which they felt destined. Lilly recalled that as a child she had dreamed of becoming a nurse, explaining that "mostly I knew I didn't want to farm":

> But I really liked going to school and I said a million times I wished that I could have stayed in school like other kids did 'cause I wanted to be a nurse but that didn't work out. Mostly I knew I didn't want to farm. Because we got tired of farming, whenever we farmed on half we always wind up with nothing. We farmed one year and ended up with one hundred dollars apiece and I bought our first refrigerator and record player. But mostly we ended up with nothing. It was hard work—my sister and I we was just working with children, the man wouldn't hire nobody else. We had to go out in the field and prime tobacco, we had to get up on the barn and get on those tills and hang it. We had to set up at night, you know, so the tobacco could dry out in the barn. We had to do all that stuff and, well, we had a hard time then. I knew I didn't want to do that all the time.

Helen hoped to escape factory work and described her fantasy of becoming a secretary in the following way:

> I knew I wanted to be a secretary—which I am and I wish I weren't. I didn't know how crummy some secretarial jobs could be. But my sister was a secretary. I used to see her in the morning go to work and she was all dressed up—she looked real nice. It was either that—and then I had another sister who worked in a factory. She always looked like she was overtired, looked like a bum. I didn't want to do what that one did, I'd rather do what the other one did.

The women's stories about childhood ambitions were narrated "in the voice" and "in the image" of those with whom they identified (family members and peers) and against those who the women viewed as oppositional "others" (school or work-place authorities or idealized peers or coworkers).[3] Consider Joanne's story, which casts the nuns as enforcers of the social oppositions between judges and working-class kids from the neighborhood. Or recall Lilly's story about the race- and class-based antagonisms between the (white) man employer and his (black) child laborers, who were left with "nothing" after a year's hard work. Similarly, Helen's desire to become a secretary was told as part of the symbolic class- and gender-based struggle between manual and mental work, where one sister "looked like a bum" and the other "looked real nice," and it was up to Helen to decide which side she was on. Indeed, one of the most agreed-upon hallmarks of success was the ability to "get dressed up to go to work" or, as Gloria put it, having a job where you go to work "looking like you're a somebody."

What they knew about the future, how they learned not to "think about anything else," and their critical self-appraisals were tied together. Stories about social conflicts in workplaces or schools were bound up with inner conflicts and defensive feelings about standing before judgmental others. In the next section I examine these social and personal conflicts more closely, especially in terms of the differences between the North Carolina and Philadelphia women's storied selves.

THE NORTH CAROLINA WOMEN'S NARRATIVES

> I was wanting to be a nurse, but then we stopped school to help mama out. When she got straightened out I didn't want to go back. I felt like all the kids that we went to school with had moved on. And then when we went back we went back with a younger group. I was ashamed to be so big so I started to work in my first job that I had in a restaurant. And the blacks had to be in the back, had to work in the back. Nobody could see you in the front unless they run short, unless the lunch hour would get busy and they couldn't keep up. Then they would pull somebody black from the back. I started as a dishwasher and helped the lady cook who was in the back. And then one day at lunch time when they couldn't keep up they would pull me out of the kitchen to make hot dogs. I still didn't get out on the floor to clean up, nothing like that. I had to stay behind the counter making hot dogs. All the white peoples was in the front and all the blacks was in the back. And you didn't see the blacks out until it was time for us to leave or if they needed some help. But I really liked going to school and I wished that I could have stayed in school 'cause I wanted to be a nurse.

Lilly's story is typical in that she charts a sequence of events and evokes familiar images that appeared across the North Carolina women's aspirational stories. Lilly's school attendance was limited because of family and farm-work demands, and it became necessary for her to leave school before graduating. She talks about feeling "ashamed" for falling behind in school, a sentiment echoed by those North Carolina women who also were unable to attend school regularly. Lilly then goes on to describe the world of work highlighting the racially split labor market where blacks were relegated to the devalued positions "in the back" and whites occupied the idealized positions "up front." Such divisions not only rendered her work invisible but also disavowed her (black) presence altogether. As Lilly described it, the world of work was organized so that "you didn't have to see the blacks."

The terms for the North Carolina women's storied selves were set by having to defend against racialized images of work, which were historically grounded in the Jim Crow laws of the segregated South. These imposed images were implicated in the women's struggles to become somebody and in explanations for why they failed. Despite their recurrent references to the negative effects of structural or institutional forces (economic disadvantages, racial discrimination, and inadequate school resources and facilities), the North Carolina women noted character flaws and personal traits as reasons for their lack of social mobility. Note that despite Lilly's awareness of the constraints imposed by farm life, school segregation, and poverty, she emphasizes her mother's illness as the reason she fell behind in school and her shameful feelings for having grown bigger than the other children. Later in the interview she talks about how her experiences (especially at work) made her "give up on herself," which she believes was the cause of her "downfall."

Gloria spoke about her thwarted attempts to become a seamstress, concluding that she was "stubborn" and refused to listen to the good advice of her mother, who had pleaded with her not to quit school. Perhaps if she had "more sense" and "more ambition," things would have turned out differently. She goes on to describe the gap between her sewing ambitions and her life as a ten-year-old domestic worker:

I always wanted to be a seamstress. I used to make all my clothes. I would design them myself and I even found me an old sewin' machine someone had thrown out. I cleaned it, greased it down, and got it workin' like it was new. Then I was workin' at the time, since I was about ten years old for a white lady. I started with one of the daughters. You know, just go there and clean up her room and wash out her little laundry. I would go there three times a week. Then I started baby-sitting for her and went on through just like that. I enjoyed it 'cause I was always really wantin' my own money and I knowed if I didn't get out and earn it I wouldn't have none. I worked like that until I dropped out of school 'cause I was stayin' the lot.

What does it mean to stay the lot?

You stayed there all week and went back home on Friday night and then come back on Sunday. I got a baby during the time I was workin' there. There I was taking care of this young white girl's babies (she was not much older than me) while my mother took care of mine. I liked workin' for them, they treated me like one of the family. But it wasn't 'til I left and got my own place that I could take my sewing machine with me, you know, so I could make clothes.

Gloria recalls enjoying her job because she liked earning her own money. Yet the organization of domestic work, in this case "staying the lot," required that she divert her caregiving from both herself and her child to her white employers and their family members.[4] As a result, Gloria's interests had to be subsumed in favor of the demands of the white family, of which she was "treated as part." This familiar notion of "being treated like one of the family" (a phrase more than half of the North Carolina women used to describe their domestic work experiences) is particularly ironic, because it both exposes and masks the ways in which the women learned their social limits. For the North Carolina women, gender- and race-based assumptions about who cares for whom and under what conditions thwarted their ambitions and self-understandings. In the stories that follow, this pattern becomes increasingly clear.

Ella's aspirational story begins with her desire to "get married, have children, and move north." She describes "losing her senses over" a man she met at a church function while he was visiting from New York:

> He came down here from New York, nice and sweet, and I was getting out of the country. I didn't have to work on no farm, I was getting out of the country. So I left and got a good job in New York, to me it was good.

In retrospect she considers her marriage and migration north as a means to escape farm life. Indeed, life was better for her in New York because she enjoyed her job and made new and, in her words, "different" friends. But when she was unable to find adequate child care, she felt forced to return home. The only job she could find was that of a domestic. Her husband, who turned out to have what she called a "bad temper," periodically visited Ella until one day she decided she had taken "one too many beatings" and filed for divorce. She continues her story by describing her many domestic jobs and her difficulties living with her parents in a small rural community, where everyone was "into her business." Ella kept searching unsuccessfully for work not situated in white people's homes and tells this anecdote about getting no respect from her white lady employer:

> We would say if we did any kind of work it wasn't going to be nothing but baby-sitting, that's right, we would say that too. Haven't you heard me tell you how I worked for this lady? I worked for this lady and she fixed dinner for me. Her husband was in a wheelchair and she sat her dog and her husband up at the table and sat me off at a little table in the back [laughing]. I'll tell you something, that hasn't been too long ago. I baby-sat for another lady. Some of the people were nice and some of them were not.

Note how Ella tells her story "in the voice" of her peers—what "we" rural, black girls in the segregated South "would say" about baby-sitting as the only option. Her story also evokes the image of being treated less well than a dog and speaks to the powerful effects of racial segregation and discrimination in learning "not to think about anything else." Still, in her laughter about the white lady's attempts to dehumanize her we see her refusal to be defined by others.[5] Ella presents these opposing sets of voices and images as both a struggle between antagonistic social groups (white and black) and also as a struggle to assert her self and be recognized for who she is. This conflict is one she experienced differently, albeit painfully, with various white employers throughout her early work life (in her words, "Some were nice and some were not"). Ella concludes her interview by saying that she defines a "somebody" as someone who "knows who she is, so she doesn't have to act like she's better than anyone else."

Linda opens her aspirational story by saying that she has always dreamed of owning a small business, especially a day-care center. She explains that her desire to work with children and to instill in them positive self-esteem arises from her work experiences. Her story illustrates the personal effects of being denied human status by her employer. One day before starting her domestic chores:

> We was in the kitchen when she [her employer] came at me with a can of [Lysol] spray. I wasn't going to let nobody spray me. I could feel my hand on the knife behind me on the counter. I might have killed that woman, I could feel the knife in my hand. But I got out of there before any damage could be done. Not all the white peoples I worked for were that bad, some of them was nice people, but then I could never forget. Black people were treated as dirt back long and then.

Linda's final commentary on this event is most remarkable. Relieved that "no damage" had been done, she describes her own remorse at having provided the occasion for being treated with so little respect and value, saying, "I should never have been there in the first place. It is something I will regret for as long as I live."

Betty's aspirational story reiterates this same sense of regretful conflict. She begins by explaining that her motivation to be a social worker was fueled by her encounters with racial oppression and injustice. She recalls feeling torn between her mothers' strategies of "being nice" and her own desires to "talk ugly and defend herself":

> You can't imagine what people got beat out of in those days, how they had to answer to white people. It could make you ashamed to see them take it. But as my mother always say, that kindness don't hurt anybody. You can get more by being easy and kind than you

can by being harsh and ugly. She would say you can get right next to a person being nice, but you can't by being ugly. As ugly as that person talks to you, the nicer you be, that really does something to them. But I didn't see it like that. I wanted my mother to talk ugly to the teachers or to the man whose land we farmed. But see, she didn't do it. She took whatever it was and went on. And that's why I got mad with her. And I regret it. I reckon I'll regret it till I die. But I wanted to do it so—so much so that I wanted to talk for everyone, you know take up everybody's battle. I didn't want nobody thinking I was a coward. But I seen a lot of people being made to be cowards and some of them is cowards and some of them are just afraid they might say the wrong things. They're afraid they will say something that will hurt their own self or get someone else hurt. So that's why I wanted to be a social worker. I wanted to be somebody, that's why I always tried in school and was interested in learning.

Betty's account stresses how she strove to assert herself under oppressive conditions. These conditions further assisted the splitting off and disavowal of those parts of her self (most especially aggression) that were dangerous to self or others. Life-threatening, either-or terms of existence, where one could either be "nice" or "talk ugly," left costly psychological scars, including a sense of remorse for having made wrong decisions.[6] Accounts like Betty's illustrate the social-psychological effects of oppression wherein the "depreciated" self gets, in this case, lived out as guilt and remorse because the "reality and agencies of psychological oppression have been obscured or mystified" (Bartky 1990: 23).

Interestingly, the North Carolina women talked of these events and emotional scars as if they were rooted in circumstances no longer in effect. "There was a lot of worry about back long and then," was a familiar refrain. The North Carolina women talked about current options that they believed were unavailable to them in the past. But despite whatever social progress they thought had been made, few believed schooling would enable them to attain their deferred childhood dreams.

All but two of the North Carolina women told of people they knew who had gotten a "good education" only to find themselves working in laundries, banks, motels, or schools as "housekeepers." Gloria and Betty noted:

I know a lot of educated ones doing work no better than I'm doing now. Then a job is a job. It's nothin' against the job but when you got a little education I think you most likely will try to find somethin' better than cleanin'.

My niece, she has herself a master's, I was there at her graduation. But she's working at a laundry, she's been there some five years. She kept going to one interview after another and she never would get a job. Maybe it was somethin' she said, but you would think that she could be workin' in a place better than a laundry with a master degree.

Discussions about the futility of education persisted throughout the North Carolina women's accounts. The North Carolina women's less-than-enthusiastic endorsement of education can be interpreted in several ways: 1) The women realized that black people don't have the same economic return from education that whites do. 2) It could be argued that their discussion reflects a folk theory commonly held among African Americans about "making it" that does not valorize academic pursuit over other means (Ogbu 1988). 3) Or perhaps they were using an "accounting strategy" to protect against the possibility of being viewed negatively or as having exercised bad judgment regarding their own school decisions (Hewitt and Stokes 1978). 4) Possibly, their views of education were offered as critical insights into the racial and gendered organization of work (Smith 1987). 5) Despite cultural disdain for their work, the women saw value in their housekeeping. Bessie explained that while it was unlikely that anyone else valued her job, *she* believed it was crucial to the scientific advancements made by the professor whose lab she cleaned. These explanations are not mutually exclusive; indeed, they represent the interrelatedness of the North Carolina women's race, gender, and class experiences, identities and consciousness. For all these reasons, the North Carolina women did not fully embrace the dominant view of school as a ticket for upward mobility, nor did they regard school as the primary context or sphere of activity within which their ambitions were formed. The same cannot be said about the Philadelphia women.

THE PHILADELPHIA WOMEN'S NARRATIVES

The Philadelphia women narrated their childhood aspirations by justifying their school decisions and actions, particularly why they had not pursued a college education. Doris's account is typical:

> I always wanted to be a secretary. No, let me backtrack. I guess I always preferred to go to college but the idea that there was no money to go made it that you were going to be a secretary. You knew there just wasn't an option to pick something else. There was one thing definite, I wasn't going to work in the factory.

In recalling their pasts, many stressed that they thought about going to college, but limited finances made college an impossibility. Sallie and Joanne recalled:

> It wasn't that I never thought about college—it was just that nobody around me ever went. We all knew that college was for kids

whose parents had the money to send them. So we just didn't even discuss it.

I remember thinking about college in eleventh grade, but it wasn't feasible. You could sit around and think about it, but it just wasn't feasible.

Moreover, most of the Philadelphia women said that they would not have felt "comfortable" with students whom they perceived as "different," and for this reason they had not gone to college. Pam explained:

I really wanted to go to college, but I would have been with students who were completely different from me. After sixteen years of feeling uncomfortable in school, I needed a rest. Even today I can't walk on a college campus without feeling a pit in my stomach and a lump in my throat.

College represented the unknown, an unfamiliar and potentially unfriendly territory foreign to people they knew and with whom they could identify.[7] As Pam went on to say:

Even though I was in the advanced track, the academic track, I really didn't think about being anything except a secretary. I wanted to stick to something I *knew* I could do.

And what was that?

I knew I could do all the things a secretary does—I had seen my older sister do it. She was great at it and I knew I'd be good at it too. I wasn't sure whether I was college material, I guess mostly because I didn't know anyone else who was.

Pam's account reminds us that it was not simply the financial realities but the passion of her feelings of difference—the pit in her stomach and the lump in her throat—that governed her life decisions.

Peggy, on the other hand, explained that her early job choices had been overdetermined by a class-based system of tracking in her school:[8]

In high school I had signed up for commercial, but I got sent to kitchen practice.

What was kitchen practice?

Being a waitress, cook, chef. That was the worst course in school. There was really the low life in that course.

How did people get placed into kitchen practice?

I think they just went down and said, well this is a poor one and she's not going to do good; she probably doesn't have the mentality. Look at the income, look where she lives, she's not going to amount to anything so stick her in there. Once you got into ninth grade you ran into a lot of problems. It didn't matter how smart you were anymore, they didn't take that into consideration. It was where you lived and how much money you had backing you. There were academic courses where I went to high school, you know English and history and all. Only some of us were put into academic—I wasn't one of them.

Even though you were this really good student in Junior High? [She had made the honor roll every semester]

That's right. You know at the time I just didn't think anything of it. I accepted it. Then afterwards I thought about it, why did that happen? I could have been put into academic. If only I had pushed harder. I remember that I had wanted to become something professional, like a lawyer maybe. I did, I wanted to be somebody when I was younger.

Despite her insight that schools reproduce class inequalities, Peggy ended up finding fault in herself for "accepting it." She went on to add that she could not have envisioned herself in college anyway because she did not believe she was "college material." She wondered aloud about whether life would have turned out differently if she hadn't felt this way or whether she would still have chosen to "stick with what I was good at and people I felt comfortable with."

Other Philadelphia women accounted for their ambitions by rejecting certain school values. Anne's explanation for why she chose to be in the "commercial" and not the "academic" track was not unusual:

We all, all the girls I hung with, all of us were in commercial and we knew what we wanted. We knew what we needed to do to, you know, about life, about getting a job, about being a secretary.

Anne justified her school actions in the voice and image of her peers. As part of the "commercial" track, Anne learned what she needed to know "about life" and, in solidarity with the girls she "hung with," refused the offerings of the academic track.

While they viewed school as a vehicle that could move them up the social ladder, the Philadelphia women persistently gave reasons for rejecting the ride. Recall that Joanne began her aspirational account with her dream of becoming a judge, for which she had been reprimanded in school. She continued by describing her troubled school career in terms of her "bad attitude" toward school authorities and her impatience with petty rules and regulations. Her education was put on hold when, as the eldest daughter, she left school to care for her younger sister, a decision she still takes great pride in; she points to the picture of her sister wearing a high-school graduate cap, thanks to Joanne's support. At this point she describes her atypical work history and travel abroad. After years of "scrimping and saving," she took a trip to Europe, shedding both her clerical and familial duties. Upon her return, Joanne landed a good job as a receptionist in a doctor's office, followed by an even better clerical job in a law firm. She concluded the interview by saying:

> You know, I think a lot of working-class people put professional people with educations on a pedestal. It is like with blacks—if all you see of blacks is that they are trash men, then you think they must all be like that. But I met a lot of professional people—people with more knowledge than me, and maybe more ambition, but they weren't really any better than me. They weren't really any different, even if they were somebody. You know, the thing is, with all the people I met I still married the boy on the corner. I just always felt most comfortable with him. Maybe I had a strong homing instinct, but that's just who I am.

Joanne draws on the image and voice of those "working-class people" with whom she is comfortable, set against the image of professionals on pedestals who may have more status, knowledge, and ambition but who are no "better" than she is.

Her account is typical of how all the women's stories reveal, even as they disguise, the ingrained yet implicit value of upward mobility within American culture. This value is perhaps best captured by Lillian Rubin's observation that we judge people according to how well they "move up or down, not just through" the class structure (1976: 8–9). Perhaps with this judgment in mind, Joanne defends her choice not to "marry up" and casts her decision as a quest for comfort and recognition, an "instinct" to return home to share the company of those with whom she belongs.[9]

Like the North Carolina women's references to being "treated as part of the family," the Philadelphia women's references to seeking comfort among those most like themselves exposes as it masks how they learned their social limits. What is especially ironic about Joanne's account is how she borrows on the same images and ideologies about upward mobility, status, and power that she is attempting to critique. Historically, it is upper-class, white women who have been put on pedestals as cultural and symbolic figures of purity, moral superiority, virginity, and domesticity; since the turn of the century these images and values served to define and consolidate class divisions (Welter 1978).[10] Meanwhile, having been relegated to manual, unskilled labor, blacks became culturally and symbolically associated with "dirty" and undesirable work; these images and values served to justify black people's lowest position in the class hierarchy.

IDEALIZED AND SPLIT IMAGES
OF WOMANHOOD

Whether they discussed their ambitions and self-understandings in light of school or work, women in both groups expressed conflicts about doing "women's work": the Philadelphia women as "secretaries, nurses, mothers, or nuns," and the North Carolina women as domestic workers. The overlapping yet different ways that women in each group framed these conflicts shed light on the combined institutional and psychological forces that shaped their storied selves.

The Philadelphia women's work options afforded them the opportunity to achieve idealized images of femininity as domestic, subservient, nurturant—all the traits of "good" womanhood. These options worked for and against their sense of selfhood, ambition, and power. On the one hand, in their caregiving roles as secretaries, nurses, mothers, and nuns, they could look forward to establishing female bonds with each other through shared work, family, and religious rituals. In the context of a working-class female culture, they could expect to acquire and exercise their own distinct knowledge and authority, albeit in a separate sphere. Their common experiences and camaraderie with girlfriends, sisters, or older female family members generated shared views and values of the work world and a confidence that they "knew what they were good at." As part of their caregiving work, they could exercise their judgments, make choices, and assert their authority. On the other hand, these roles were limiting because they had to suppress their own knowledge in favor of the men (whether as bosses, doctors, husbands, or clergy) upon whom they were dependent and expected to be subordinate.

As domestic caregivers in white peoples' homes or as service workers in institutional settings, the North Carolina women anticipated a different set of conflicts. While they were afforded fewer opportunities to achieve idealized images of womanhood and lacked authority and power in the face of their white employers (men, women, and children), this domestic service work was less about "who they were" and more about "what they did for a living." Meanwhile, historically viewed as acts of resistance within African American communities, the North Carolina women's caregiving skills and knowledge were seen as sources of power and were more highly valued by both themselves and their communities (Davis 1971; Jones 1985; Stack 1974). Nevertheless, the North Carolina women struggled to define themselves against controlling images and myths about black women (Collins 1990). Their storied selves were shaped as counterpoints to idealized images of women as clean, domestic, and married—that is, "good" women. They built the stories they told upon the hard, dirty, and tiresome jobs they sought to avoid, the difficulties they faced raising children, and the pain associated with being separated from their children.

In light of these idealized split images of womanhood, it is not surprising that women in both groups mentioned nursing as a childhood aspiration. No doubt the history of nursing and the varied avenues through which poor and working-class women have been able to enter the profession (as hospital aides, LPNs, RNs, and midwives, for example) provide a clue to this common goal. Just as important, however, is that nursing builds on symbolic and idealized images of women as clean, white (as in their uniforms), nurturing, and subservient, while simultaneously promising professionalization and better pay than other types of women's work. These converging factors made nursing an aspiration through which women from both groups could construct a bridge between available opportunity structures and ideologies about what "good" or "ideal" women should be and their own desires to "be somebody."

The women's contrasting discussions of motherhood reflect the gap between opportunity structures, and cultural ideas about who they were supposed to be, what they were supposed to want, and what they could expect for themselves. Recall that the Philadelphia women cited motherhood as one of four life options they could anticipate, but it was not mentioned by the North Carolina women. For the most part, the Philadelphia women spoke about motherhood in the context of marriage and domesticity. Indeed, their experiences reflected this more conventional nuclear family structure: more Philadelphia women than North Carolina women married as a result of a teenage pregnancy, and more were able to stay at home to raise their children (especially during the preschool years) while being financially supported by their husbands. Only one Philadelphia woman had never married (compared to five North Carolina women). This is not to say, however, that their family lives or their experiences as mothers had been more stable, happy, or settled—only that in terms of expectations and myths about the "traditional family," more Philadelphia than North Carolina women fit the cultural ideal. This point was driven home by many Philadelphia women who talked about youthful illusions, especially in terms of romance and marriage; most agreed that they did not want their daughters following in their footsteps. Two Philadelphia women reflected on their experiences:

I started going with Bob. All the girls thought I was so lucky. I really wish I hadn't fallen in love that young. You know we all dreamed about white picket fences—a little house with flowers and staying home with the kids and all. You know, typical *Father Knows Best* family. We just had no idea that those things don't work out. Funny, my own family wasn't like that. My dad lost his job several times and my mom supported all of us, but that's how we thought it would be.

I keep telling my girls and hoping against hope that they will listen to me—don't get married as young as I did, you need to take time for yourself and get skills to support yourself before settling down. Don't be in such a rush to get married and have kids—there's plenty of time for that. I'm not saying I regret the choices I made, only that maybe I wish that I had had more choices to make when I was younger.

In contrast, the North Carolina women discussed motherhood as part of, not separate from, their work lives. Indeed, their discussions of motherhood were woven into descriptions of work and kin relations, wherein they reflected on their feelings about being "good" or "good enough" mothers. Several shared their grief and sorrow for having been forced to live apart from their children. Geraldine cried as she described sending her two children off to live with her mother when they were ages three and five.

I'll never forgive myself for that. Only one of my children I kept for any length of time. That one there [She points to the picture on her television]. That is my biggest grief.

The North Carolina women who had been able to raise their children alone or in nuclear families did not view this outcome as either expected or ideal but rather as the result of circumstance or chance. Still, it was an aspect of their womanhood for which they felt split and unresolved.

Regrettably, one consequence of idealized images of womanhood is that individual women are held responsible (by others and by themselves) for being in a social position in which they are devalued and treated with little respect. This is what the women are accounting for in their stories: their places in a society where some women count as "somebodies" and others don't. In this sense, Helen's "choice" between the sister who worked in the factory and "looked like a bum" and the other sister who went to her secretarial job looking "real nice," and Linda's experience being sprayed with Lysol by her employer, are both variations on the same gendered theme. The women protected themselves from or defended themselves against these social conflicts and negative self-valuations by splitting. Let's take the case of Helen. By splitting off the "bad" aspects of herself (being unattractive, looking like a bum) and projecting these aspects onto another (her sister the bum), she was able to ease her own anger (yet another "bad" aspect in women) about her limited life options and the demands placed on her to be attractive in the first place. This social defense left Helen feeling false, in her words, untrue to her "real self," who doesn't "judge people by how they look but by how they act." Or consider Betty, who felt torn between her "good" mother (who advocated kindness rather than anger toward her oppressors) and her own "bad" self for wanting to be aggressive and speak up on her own behalf. As a consequence of this splitting, she was unable to appreciate the fullness and richness of both her own and her mother's subjectivity. Betty suffered from this fragmentation and her irresolvable regret toward her mother, even as it fueled her prideful and lifelong commitment to education and community service, where she has become known for taking up the cause of people who have been wronged.

Cast in either/or terms, the women's stories pit good and bad, attractive and unattractive, clean and dirty, black and white women as symbolic antagonists in the struggle for success. These splits promote women's participation in varied institutions of womanhood—e.g., motherhood, marriage, caregiving, and the illusory world of heterosexual romance—none of which are defined in women's best interests. And, as some feminist scholars have noted, when women assess themselves and others according to these split and idealized images, their potential collective resistance is held in check (Matthews 1984; Palmer 1983).

SUMMARY

By juxtaposing how differently the North Carolina and Philadelphia women narrated their childhood ambitions, we learn three important things. First, there were inextricable links between educational, work, and family opportunity structures and the cultural values and expectations that the women in each group appropriated in their self-definitions and ambitions. Second, their ambitions were bound up in split, idealized images of womanhood and "somebodiness," which operated at both the psychological and social levels. Finally, we learn that women in both groups felt compelled to answer for their devalued place in American society. But whereas the Philadelphia women stressed why they, as individuals, had rejected upward mobility, the North Carolina women stressed why they, as a group, had been rejected by white society.

Five

Storied Selves
and School Mission

Tell me what you remember about being in school.

What I remember most about school was that if you were poor you got no respect and no encouragement. (*Joanne*, Philadelphia woman)

Back a long time ago when I was going to school, and I can remember just as good as elementary school—if your parents wasn't a doctor, a lawyer, or a teacher, or someone you know, high, then the teachers would look down on you. That's right. And they wouldn't, they just wouldn't, you know, well, they would class you as a nobody. (*Cora*, North Carolina woman)

Joanne and Cora responded to my open-ended question, with these "abstracts" of their school experiences.[1] Despite their different educational experiences, the women told similar stories about being "classed as nobody," "looked down upon," and treated with "no respect and no encouragement." Their stories portrayed school as a place where they attempted to establish at least the image of a worthy, legitimate self, a place where they defined and defended themselves against teachers and other students who "looked down" at them. Their stories provide critical insights into schools as arenas of struggle where selfhood, identities, values, and knowledge are contested and where only certain students garner respect as a "somebody." But whereas the North Carolina women narrated their school struggles according to issues of access, ability, and (in)visibility, the Philadelphia women recounted their struggles according to issues of discipline, authority, and voice/silence. In this chapter I discuss how these distinctive struggles, self-definitions, and defenses emerged out of each school context—one rural-community and the other urban-bureaucratic.

DISCOMFORTS, DISCONTENTS, AND DIFFERENCE

While each woman had her own unique set of school memories, not one woman I interviewed said she had felt comfortable in school. This universal feeling of discomfort was attributed to class differences, especially between teachers and students. Class differences—most often described in terms of what parents did for a living—served to explain (if not justify) why certain students (whose parents were "somebodies") were "smart" and received support from the teachers, and why teachers were, in the women's words, "superior." Regardless of whether the women liked or disliked a particular teacher, they viewed teachers as "different" from themselves and their families.

For the Philadelphia women, these differences were most often expressed in geographic terms. Teachers were outside "the neighborhood" but said to live in close-by suburbs where, according to the women, different kinds of relationships were fostered between people, particularly family members and neighbors.[2] As Eileen remarked, the suburbs produced people who

> just don't know about certain things. You know, where I grew up, everybody in the neighborhood knew everything about me, who my mother was, what my father did, what we were doing on a Friday night. I had relatives everywhere and they kept me and my sisters in line; we couldn't do anything without everybody knowing about it. The teachers, they didn't know. I guess you could say I liked that about them, but then again, they didn't care to know much about us.

Teachers were viewed as having different concerns, life styles, activities, and opportunities, not all of which were thought to be beneficial to family or community life. Doris characterized teachers' lives in the following way:

> You know, teachers are married to lawyers and doctors. They're worried about different things, things like nice clothes and what country club they're going to belong to. They have children, it isn't like they didn't know about children, but their children are differ-

ent, like they assume their children are going to college, but they don't expect our kids are going to college. Then again, there's a lot that goes on in college that isn't so great for kids.[3]

While the Philadelphia women drew upon suburban-urban distinctions to talk about class, the North Carolina women drew urban-rural distinctions. Thirteen of the fifteen North Carolina women explained that their teachers were different because they "came from the city." More than half told stories about how their parents were reluctant to deal with teachers or take part in school activities because of their "country ways" or their inability to read or write. Cora recounted a childhood incident that she said remains a source of pain and sadness in her adult life:

'Cause I was going to say that my parents, they was well, decent people. But they couldn't read and write, you know what I mean. And they was clean peoples, they never got in no trouble. They never did nobody no harm or nothing. But they just couldn't read and write and they was honest and hard working. And when they would go to PTA meetings, well naturally I would have to go along to try to explain to them what's going on so they could, you know, and they tried their best to do whatever was right. And them teachers said things that, but just because they had no profession they looked down on them and they looked down on me too, you know. And then, back then wearing home-made dresses and things, I wasn't dirty or raggedy but I just wore home-made clothes that my mother would make for me because they only made but so much you know. And like if I want to participate in a play the teacher would pick all over me and get somebody else.

How did the teacher do that, exactly?

Well, you see we would be sitting in the classroom in elementary school and the teacher would say, "We're going to have a play." And she would read out the parts. If you raised your hand and somebody else behind you or either on the other side of the classroom that's mother or father was in professional business, well they got the part that they raised their hand for. If you were the only person that raised your hand, in fact I was the only person to raise my hand for a part, then the teacher would probably give it to me. But then she would tell me after school, "Be sure you get that, learn this part, be sure to get the right costume." And you know, everything like that. She would tell me so much so that I would be hating that I raised my hand for the part. And I'd have to go home and talk to my momma and see if they can squeeze out enough money for the costume. And then one time my momma went to ask the teacher for if she could kind of describe a little bit the way that the costume she wanted me to have so she could make it. And the teacher was kind of rude to her, so much so that it kind of hurt my feelings. Then my momma told me, "If you really want to be in that play okay, but I wouldn't even bother." But I didn't really understand. I was only in the third or fourth grade. I didn't quite understand what my momma said, "If you really wants to be then I will go back to her again and get some understanding about it." It gave me sort of an inferiority complex 'cause I saw how the teacher was talking to my momma. I loved her and I just didn't want nobody to be hurting her feelings.

This story illustrates how social differences between teachers, parents, and students were lived out and felt. Cora's perception that the teacher was anxious that Cora might not learn her lines and that her mother would not provide the right costume, confirmed Cora's sense of discomfort and difference. Most importantly, the teacher's remarks reinforced in Cora a sense of her social limits and the degraded value of "country ways." For her, school—but particularly the teacher—had thrown into doubt not only her intellect but also her manner of deportment, style of dress, and speech, so much so that she wished she had not raised her hand in the first place—that she had censored herself.[4]

Whereas the Philadelphia women described their teachers as (imagined) "others" who had different concerns, values, and life styles from their own, the North Carolina women described themselves and their parents as being the (rejected or shameful) "others" who felt like they did not belong at PTA meetings or inside schools. This contrasting sense of self/family in relation to school carried over into the women's approach to adult education.

In classroom settings, I observed that the Philadelphia women expressed discernible *fears of making mistakes*, while the North Carolina women held *mistaken fears* about their intellectual capabilities. Each approach, in its own way, undermined each woman's sense of herself as schoolsmart. A persistent and overriding concern of the Philadelphia women was whether they were meeting teachers' expectations and providing the "right" answers. It was difficult for them to suspend this preoccupation—to allow themselves to move from asking "did I do this right" to consider "what makes this a right or a wrong answer." Meanwhile, their anxieties found the greatest expression in classes that were less traditional, designed with participatory, experiential, or collaborative learning opportunities and tasks. Alone and in groups they worried aloud as to whether such classroom assignments were "serious" or whether as students they would measure up to teachers' demands.[5] In contrast, the North Carolina women were quite willing to suspend judgment about what and how they were learning—sometimes to a fault. They did not question the purpose of assignments and seemed especially to appreciate (and enjoy) opportunities for more untraditional and

engaging classroom tasks. Rather than worrying about their answers—
as the Philadelphia women did—the North Carolina women focused
their anxieties more on themselves as learners. They seemed preoccu-
pied with whether they were capable of doing the work at all, and as a
teacher I spent a good deal of time finding ways to confirm for them their
own skills.[6] It was as if they were fighting themselves over their own
abilities, so they sought out teachers' reassurances that they could learn.
By contrast, the Philadelphia women seemed more embattled with the
course material and often viewed it as an extension of the teacher, for
whom they needed to "get it right."

Despite these differences, women in both groups had struggled to
assert their selves. Sociologist Philip Wexler (1992) has observed a similar phenomenon. He argues that schools are organized (sometimes
unintentionally) in institutional and pedagogical ways to "attack" students' selves. In response, students strive to "create a visible, differentiated and reputable self" as their primary activity in school (132).[7]
Indeed, students' attempts to assert a self (or at least an image of a self)
and to have this self image be recognized and valued by others is what
life in school is all about. At the same time, different school contexts
mobilize the attack on students' selves in unique ways. Wexler's ethnography of three urban American high schools (defined as "working-class,"
"professional middle-class," and "urban underclass") illustrates how
each context produced its own set of student self-understandings. In the
next section I examine the contrasting set of self-understandings as
expressed by the North Carolina and Philadelphia women.

ACCESS, ABILITY, AND
THE STRUGGLE TO BE SEEN

The North Carolina women framed their stories about school in terms of
issues of access and ability. Their stories featured problems attending
school, inequities in school resources, and anxieties about "giving up,"
"falling behind," or being "slow learners." Often described as a luxury or
special privilege, school was enjoyable for those able to attend. As Ola
explained; "We loved going to school. We enjoyed it, it was all we had to
enjoy sometimes." The North Carolina women said school often served
as a welcomed opportunity to escape chores and family responsibilities,
such as taking care of siblings, farming, doing laundry, or cleaning. As
Lois emphasized, school was reserved for rainy days when they were not
needed on the farm:

> Most times we were working on the farm and we wouldn't go
> to school nothing but rainy days, no way. Sometimes daddy would
> let my younger brothers and sisters go, but not me, I was the
> oldest.

The women also stressed the difficulties students faced in just getting to school—long, arduous walks, bad weather, and the threat of racial violence along the way. For example, Ella explained that she was nine years old when she started school because her parents feared for her safety during her five-mile walk to get there. She told of how she and her five-year-old brother had been harassed by a group of white children who had the privilege of "being carried" by bus to their white-only school just one mile away. Louise explained that she started school at the age of eight when her teacher offered to pick her up in the mornings. Jackie remembered that by the time she and her siblings got to school their hands were so cold that it took them half the morning to warm up. Lilly explained that because she and her sister were required to help their mother with the wash in the morning, most days "we just never made it." Because irregular attendance made it hard for them to keep up with the demands of school, most North Carolina women described doubts and anxieties about their school performance. As Louise recalled:

> What I remember most was being tired. By the time we got to school—there was no bus long and then for black childrens—the morning was half over. We be missing how the teacher told us to do the work, or were just too tired to think.

Teacher-student relationships were profoundly affected by the routine demands of rural poverty. The North Carolina women's accounts highlighted the problems black teachers faced in one-room schoolhouses, which had little or no heat and inadequate supplies, and where they were expected to educate forty to fifty children of many ages and grade levels. Perhaps most striking in this light were the North Carolina women's descriptions of teachers who had taken "special care" of them. Stories about teachers fixing hot food, bringing them clothes, and acknowledging their family/work responsibilities and demands were common. Not surprisingly, these descriptions echo the writings of black teachers of the time who found ways to pass on schoolwise knowledge despite untenable conditions.[8] Unable to neatly separate out children's daily survival needs from their intellectual needs, these teachers concerned themselves with poverty, lack of transportation, and the harshness of farm work. They inspired students to persist against overwhelming odds.

The North Carolina women's self-definitions in school were also shaped by the all-pervasive reality of racism. Drawing on metaphors of visibility to describe the effects of racism, the North Carolina women's accounts were charged with painful memories and stark images of alienation.[9] The women spoke of feeling invisible both inside the classroom as darker-skinned children and outside the classroom as black children who were routinely "passed by." Ola's story is but one example:

When we were little there was no bus for black children. Everyday we be walking to school and watch that big yellow bus drive by. It would stop right up in front of us to pick up the white childrens. And when we were little, this is the truth, a white person, if you were riding on the road, you know down the highway, and you was in front of them, that white person would run you off of that road to get in front of you. They didn't care. And then one time daddy had all his little childrens in the car, I don't know where we was going. Anyway, a white man come up, and daddy had to pull over and if he hadn't a went like that, the white man probably a killed us all. My daddy just pulled over to the side and let him go right on by. I remember we used to stand over on the side and watch all the white childrens pass right on by to school.

Lilly described how her (black) teachers "looked over the top" of dark-skinned children:

We really had a hard time in school cause if we know something, like if I go home and do my homework and really learn something and really get into it, we go back to school the next day. Then the teacher start asking about the lesson, getting us to go to the board and asking questions, we sitting and raising our hands and they would just look over the top of us. Now, all the little dark-skinned childrens, the teachers didn't take up no time with them. All the little light-skinned kids, teachers would take up time with them. And I got, [pause] I had went so far I just got tired. I had got to the place where I didn't care if I learned anything or not.

And Geraldine talked about black students' invisibility within the entire educational system, how no one noticed (or cared) whether black children attended school:

Long and then nobody cared if black children went to school. There were no officers coming around to see if you was in school.

Struggling to make themselves "seen" left the North Carolina women with little energy for their own creative, intellectual, and emotional development in schools.

A "culture of dissemblance" and a "self-imposed invisibility" characterize African American women's responses to such denials, according to historian Darlene Clark Hine:

Because of the interplay of racial animosity, class tensions, gender role differentiation, and regional economic variation, Black women, as a rule, developed and adhered to a cult of secrecy, a culture of dissemblance, to protect the sanctity of inner aspects of their lives. The dynamics of dissemblance involved creating the appearance of disclosure, an openness about themselves and their feelings, while actually remaining an enigma. Only with secrecy, thus achieving a self-imposed invisibility, could ordinary Black women accrue the psychic space and harness the resources needed to hold their own. (1989: 915)

Kate's story about the resources and strategies necessary for her to "hold her own" in school is especially telling. To protect herself from students' taunts about her clothes and "country ways," she found a secret spot "where nobody else was around" to eat her lunch:

I would go behind the gym or go behind the building or go to a classroom where nobody else was around and eat my lunch. It would never have gotten out except for my biology teacher. He happened to see me one day going into a classroom. I thought I was in there by myself and I pulled out the jelly biscuit. He was standing at the door looking at me and I didn't know he was 'cause he was looking through the glass on the door. And getting back to biology class, we was dissecting a frog and I couldn't quite get it 'cause I was so fat. I was fat and my fingers were clumsy. He spoke up right there in front of the class, everybody was listening to him and he says, "Doyle, you could dissect that frog if you would leave off eating all those biscuits. And you wouldn't be so big and fat." And everybody in class laughed and I tell you, I hated to go into class after that. And sometimes I would tell my mother that I had forgot my lunch, but I wouldn't forget, I was just too ashamed to carry it, the brown bag. If he had never told them about me carrying biscuits [pause] but they [the teachers] looked down on me.

There were recurring incidences, like Kate's, where the North Carolina women's bodies were publicly scrutinized (and self-scrutinized) regarding size and shape, skin color, and hair.[10] Narrating with a sense of urgency about the wounds inflicted, the women gave repeated examples of students who "picked on" them and teachers who added fuel to the fires. Indeed, each North Carolina woman recalled at least one event when she had been publicly shamed or humiliated in school.

The North Carolina women experienced school as an assault on their selfhood. Geraldine explained how she got along despite these public insults and attacks:

In the classroom I got along most of the time, I knew the lesson and stuff like that. But she [her teacher] would always be saying that was I dumb or something like that. Maybe that come from me having kind of a stutter, and she said from that. In front of the whole class she would talk about me. But I kept on and told my momma I wouldn't let it get me down.

In such stories the women told of being shamed by their teachers for things related to being poor (having raggedy clothes or no shoes), having "country ways" (bringing brown bags with biscuits), or not being able to attend school regularly. Indeed, Beverly explained that she dropped out of school so that her new baby could one day attend school without shame:

> And when I had my son I said, I don't want him to come up poor, go to school half ragged and everything. And then at that time white people liked for you to work in their houses so I told momma, "I ain't going back to school cause I want my son to wear nice clothes, you know and all, to school too."

Public assaults were often absorbed by the women as evidence of their limited or stunted abilities, what they called being a "slow learner." Most telling was the finding that all the North Carolina women chronicled their school stories according to whether they were passed onto the next grade or "kept behind." Because they attended one-room schoolhouses or schools with only a few rooms, I asked how they knew what their "grade" level was. Even without age-graded classrooms, standardized tests, or formalized report cards, the North Carolina women perceived that they had been judged by some rational, performance-based set of standards to which they had not measured up. They internalized these standards and explained the moral behind their failure: they had been "slow learners." Gloria summed up what more than half the North Carolina women said was their problem in school:

> My problem was that I was a slow learner. I didn't catch on the way the other childrens did. I was always behind trying to catch up; the teachers didn't take up no time with me. Except in third grade with Miss Johnson. She was a good teacher and she made sure that I stayed up with the class.[11]

Alongside images of themselves as invisible or slow, the North Carolina women also noted that school held little promise for them. It did not offer upward mobility, and, as Ola explained, schoolwise knowledge was deemed unnecessary for their work as women:

> Long back at that time we didn't have nothing to go to school for. All of us, like a bunch of girls would get together, we'd say, "What good is going to school? We's out here on the farm so we ain't going to do nothing but stay out here on the farm and have babies, farm, and keep house." You can do that, you can learn that from momma and daddy. You don't need to go to school for that, to stay out on the farm or to baby-sit and clean house for white peoples.

Barbara justified why she had dropped out of school:

I decided I'm just going to give up my education so [my son] could get his. 'Cause education didn't mean nothing to me back then, it didn't lead to nothing. Now I see that we both should probably have went on to school, but I just made sure that he went to school and graduated.

DISCIPLINE, AUTHORITY, AND THE STRUGGLE TO BE HEARD

The Philadelphia women framed their stories about school around the issues of discipline and authority.[12] This emphasis emerged most clearly as they described school as "boring," "routine," or a "farce." They attributed their school problems to teachers who were more interested in order and discipline than in teaching anything of interest. In Doris's words:

Everything was just like routine. Every day we did the same thing over and over. The teachers weren't interested in teaching us; they were there to keep order.

Their accounts focused on school's arbitrary rules and the harsh discipline of teachers.[13] Without any prompting, all fifteen Philadelphia women provided detailed anecdotes about unfair or unnecessary restrictions on both their bodies and their minds. Their frustrations were expressed repeatedly in the common refrain that teachers "treated us like children, to be seen but not heard." They saw teachers as overly attentive to and/or restrictive of student's behavior and personal style (clothing, hairdo, makeup) while at the same time "ignoring" students' problems. Tina and Mary recalled:

Well, I was used to making money, being on my own. But they treated me like a child. The rules were ridiculous. You had to read what they wanted you to read. Your dress couldn't be too short, you couldn't wear too much makeup, your bangs couldn't be too long— there were rules for everything. Things were very regimented and rigid—they treated us like children.

When I went to school you wouldn't have dreamed of telling a teacher how to do some thing or making a suggestion about anything. The teachers just didn't respect kids and their ideas. They bothered you about talking in class or being a problem in class, but they couldn't be bothered if you had a problem, like you didn't understand something or you couldn't concentrate.

The importance of order and discipline extended beyond the classroom, as Peggy and Doreen described:

What the nun said was rule. If a nun hit you, then you deserved it. In some families if you told your parents that a nun hit you, then you got hit at home because obviously the nuns were always right. But in my family if I told them a nun hit me they could understand why I was upset, but they would never challenge it. [14]

I had an attitude toward authority even when I knew I would get in trouble in school and then again at home. In those days the teacher called your parents and you got it twice—once at school and then again at home. Parents didn't think to challenge the teachers. There was no discussion about why you were in trouble; if the teacher said it was so, it was so.

Teachers' authority and discipline constituted a backdrop against which the Philadelphia women either established a voice or were silenced. Indeed, the metaphor of voice pervaded their accounts as they told stories about struggles to "control my mouth," "speak my mind," and "tell the teacher off."[15] This "attitude toward authority," as twelve of the fifteen Philadelphia women put it, was viewed as a character trait that had interfered with their academic success. Their "bad attitude" explained why they were not "suited" for school. Those women who described themselves as good students felt forced into silence in order to achieve:

I learned at a young age to button my lip. You couldn't win with the teachers; they hated fresh-mouthed kids, so . . . [long pause]. My sister couldn't put up with it and she didn't do well, I guess you could say it was more my style to take it, so I did real well in school.

It could be said that the Philadelphia women's preoccupation with these issues rested on unresolved images and expectations of what power and authority should be. Perhaps their resentment of being "treated like children" was a projection of their feelings about parent-child relations onto teacher-student relations, (I examine this possibility more in chapter 7).[16] In another sense, their resistance to teachers' authority and discipline (their attendant "bad attitude") seemed to anticipate future work places, where future employers would also demand obedience and discipline.[17] On yet a further level, their complaints about "being treated like children" (especially in high school) and their quest for a voice indicate an implicit critique of school. The Philadelphia women felt at best muted and at worst silenced by schooling practices that they said ignored the exigencies of poor and working-class people, *particularly women's roles as caregivers*. That these explanations are interrelated will become clear in chapter 7. For now I want to emphasize the class- and gender-based nature of the Philadelphia women's critique of school.

Teachers' middle-class conceptions of childhood simply did not correspond to the demands working-class girls faced, as Anne and Doreen's remarks illuminate:

> I had a lot of responsibility for my younger brothers and sisters. I accepted it at the time. I used to baby-sit at the age of ten, but now that I think of it, I was really young to be doing all that. In the first grade I had to wake my mother up to let her know I was ready to go to school. Everyone I knew came from big families—we were all used to a lot of responsibility.

> I remember going shopping for clothes for my brother and sister when I was twelve. My mother just didn't have the time 'cause she was working hard to support all of us by herself.

The Philadelphia women worked hard and at young ages to keep themselves and often their families together, taking care of siblings, preparing meals, shopping, and cleaning. Most had held a job during their high school years. Despite its centrality and importance in their everyday lives, school undermined the knowledge, value, and authority of their caregiving. Joanne said that she never expected school (or her mother, for that matter) to encourage her. She had her own views about her caregiving role when she dropped out of school at sixteen:

> My mother worked as a waitress for sixty-five cents an hour and raised three children without any assistance. She just really didn't have any time to encourage us much. But I also worked since I was fifteen—I was very independent and I didn't expect to get any encouragement, especially from the teachers. I had to be very responsible, not like a child in school. When my mother died my sister was only thirteen and I took care of her. I'm very proud that she made it through school and graduated, even if I didn't.

Joanne's story was not uncommon in that she took pride in her mother's and her own self-reliance and caregiving (which she later defined as common sense). Yet she knew not to expect validation of these skills or knowledge in school. More often than not, school penalized working-class girls for their responsibilities at home and rewarded "good girl" behavior and traditional middle-class femininity, an image of women as domestic, tranquil, attractive, and financially dependent.[18] School denied the reality and legitimacy of working-class femininity, an image of women as independent, hardworking, responsible caregivers.

The Philadelphia women viewed school as causing a conflict between teachers' demands and those of family and friends. Debra described herself weighing the following choices:

> I didn't really want to be a smart kid in school. I don't know— maybe it was the friends I hung with. If I did something too good,

they would look at me funny. They thought, why are you doing that? You don't have to do that to get through.

So you didn't want to look like you were trying?

Mostly I didn't want to try too hard for the teachers.

Debra portrayed the girls "she hung with" as being opposed to teachers and school values. This conflict is similar to Anne's discussion of why she chose the "commercial" rather than the "academic" track that I described in chapter 4. Sounding much like the girls in Michelle Fine's (1991) ethnography of an urban high school, the Philadelphia women spoke of being trapped by dominant school values and traditions that did not fit their circumstances, needs, or desires.

Regardless of their resistant stance toward school, both Debra and Anne expressed concern about the personal costs of "mouthing off" toward teachers. There was much at stake in their school actions for which they felt compelled to account. These inner dialogues and dilemmas fueled the women's sense of narrative urgency. Debra spoke emotionally about certain regrets when she said:

It was crazy the way they treated us as if we were children. We did everything adults do and we had a lot of experience under our belts. It was as if we were supposed to pretend like we had nothing to do except come to school every day and be good little girls. I guess we also thought we knew more than they did so we didn't have to do the school work. The girls I hung with, we all thought we had one up on the teachers.

What did you know more about?

Getting by in life. We knew how to get over on the teachers. We all thought we were so smart. Now that I look back at it, we were all wrong. [19]

Tina's account of dropping out of school serves as yet another example of the Philadelphia women's conflicted relationship with school:

I didn't even consider going back to school when I found out I was pregnant. All those restrictions and all those hang-ups, I thought, I'm having a baby and I'm going to not go to school and be a kid anymore. It was like my adult statement.

So you wanted the baby?

Well, the baby wasn't planned. But I wasn't going back to school. No way. I took the books and dumped them in a corner someplace.

Tina resisted the discipline of school and asserted her autonomy and independence by making what she calls her "adult statement" (again the metaphor of voice). From Tina's perspective, her pregnancy was not the problem; school was.[20] Pregnancy and motherhood offered her an opportunity to escape the disciplining force of school (as did Anne's view of work as a way to escape what she called a "prison"). In every case, the women saw themselves as opposing school authorities *and* laying claim to "what matters most in life." Nevertheless, these resistances had their own costs insofar as they drew on dominant gender ideologies, including the familiar but false dichotomy between "good" and "bad" girls that characterizes female sexuality and power. On the one hand, Tina's "problem with authority," her "mouth," and her sexual activity defined her as a "bad" girl. Yet, her impending marriage and motherhood not only made her more of a "good" girl but also put her in an enviable position with the "girls she hung with":[21]

> I remember in the beginning that my friends used to come visit after school and talk about how much fun it must be, taking care of the baby, buying cute clothes and all. We lived with his mother then and it wasn't so easy, but they didn't know about that part of it. Still, it was better than being in school.

Ironically, Tina's decision to drop out of school in order to resist one "regime" of discipline and authority (school and teachers) rested on accepting a different "regime" (family, husband, mother-in-law).[22]

According to Tina, she would not, in retrospect, have made different choices. Yet she does view her current participation in school as a way to convince her daughters that they need not make the same choices she did:

> Part of why I'm in school now is to show them (her daughters) that they have options and that they can finish school before they decide to get married and have kids.

In the end, the Philadelphia women's view of school kept them from acknowledging the full range of their abilities. The false yet clear split between what they "knew" and what school wanted them to know fragmented their self-understandings and compromised their claims to knowledge and power. To resist the discipline of school and assert a visible, differentiated, and worthy, female, working-class self, the Philadelphia women took on gender-based ideologies that were self-limiting. These ideologies located women's sources of knowledge and power in traditional female domains such as sexuality, marriage, and motherhood. As part of their assertions, the Philadelphia women split off (and denied, devalued, or repressed) their abilities and desires for intellectual or academic mastery.

In contrast, the North Carolina women did not view school as posing the same set of conflicts. Even though school held little promise and had at times assaulted their senses of self-worth and social valuation, the

North Carolina women were more willing to immerse themselves in school values, knowledge, and authority. They were less concerned with who knew more, teachers or students, but more concerned with who was allowed to learn or who was capable of knowing, who had access and who was denied. The authority or legitimacy of schoolwise knowledge was not at issue in the North Carolina women's school struggles. At stake was their own legitimacy as school students.

EFFECTS OF SCHOOL
ORGANIZATION AND MISSION

How do we explain the women's different versions of school? In large part, by the differing missions of the schools they attended. Each context organized the relationships among self, identity, and knowledge differently, which helps to explain the women's contrasting stance towards school.

Writing about how gender relations vary from one school context to the next, Elisabeth Hansot and David Tyack (1988) provide a useful characterization of the rural-community and the urban-comprehensive school. In the rural-community school, *age* and *cognitive proficiency* organize instruction, whereas in the urban-comprehensive school, *gender* organizes the curriculum. In the 1920s, "progressive" school reform sought to design the urban-comprehensive curriculum to address the presumably different needs of boys and girls. Educational reformers worried about how high schools were separating students by class, yet these same reformers tended to see gender differentiation as both natural and desirable. Whereas the explicit goal of the urban-comprehensive school was to prepare students for adult occupations, fashioned primarily around the needs of industry, the implicit effect was to replicate in the school the sexual division of labor that students would be expected to accommodate as adults. Thus, according to Hansot and Tyack, gender gained greater "institutional salience" in the urban-comprehensive schools, even as school practices worked to obscure this salience. Moreover, the increased importance of gender depended upon the rigid institutional boundaries that separated family, work, and school. The urban school system was large and bureaucratic, no longer analogous in either structure or operation to families, churches, or community life, and school was often experienced by students as being separate from, if not hostile to, these other parts of their lives (as we saw in the Philadelphia women's narratives). By contrast, the boundaries of family, work, and rural-community school life were more fluid, experienced by students as "part of a seamless web of community contexts, each interwoven with and legitimating the other" (Hansot and Tyack 1988: 752).

The urban-bureaucratic school was set apart from, rather than integral to, other institutions that prepared students for their future roles and responsibilities. Furthermore, students in urban-comprehensive schools were forced to negotiate different gender expectations in the transitions from family to school to work. Hansot and Tyack offer the following example: a young girl might find that in school she did the same work as boys and was rewarded in the same way for her efforts. But when she entered the work force and found that her opportunities were limited and that she was not rewarded in the same way as her male counterparts, she was forced to somehow make sense of the discrepancy. How she did this and negotiated changing gender practices and meanings was not simply the result of personal insight but was also governed by historical, cultural, ideological, and institutional forces.

In this light, let us consider how each school context generated divergent practices and problems for the women to negotiate. Consider the Philadelphia women's view of school as both stemming from and answering to the urban-comprehensive school's organization and mission. Organized around the requirements of industry, the urban-comprehensive school emphasized the obedience and discipline required in working-class jobs as it prepared students to enter a sex-segregated labor force (Bowles and Gintis 1976). The "commercial track" and the "kitchen practice" were part of this preparation; girls learned clerical or waitressing skills, while boys learned a skilled trade in "shop" classes. I suggest that the Philadelphia women made sense of this school organization in *class* more than *gender* terms. For example, to explain why they chose the commercial track, the women spoke about class-based antagonisms between teachers and students and between schoolwise and motherwise knowledge to account for their "choices." Their explanations pit their middle-class teachers—for whom they did not want to "work too hard" and with whom they did not share the same life concerns or values—against their peers, with whom they shared common interests, knowledge, and authority about how to "get by in life." School fostered this antagonism by splitting off as unequal "academic" from "vocational" (i.e., the commercial or clerical track and the even more devalued "kitchen practice."

The Philadelphia women also made sense of the boundaries between schools, families, and work places and the discrepant gender expectations of each in *class* terms. Recall that the women resented their middle-class teachers for refusing to acknowledge the multiple responsibilities of working-class girlhood, and thus they rejected school as a way to claim a voice (i.e., knowledge and authority) about family life and its demands. These class-based understandings of school worked against the Philadelphia women's ability to see how gender inequalities organized school, families, or work places. This was the case for Tina, who said she rejected school (and its restrictions) in favor of marriage and motherhood. Admitting that family life was not as easy or romantic as she had anticipated, it was still "better than being in school."

In contrast, consider the North Carolina women's views of school as both stemming from and answering to the organization and mission of the rural-community school. Organized as part of the fabric of black rural life, these schools produced a different set of issues for the women to negotiate. For example, the rural school did not track students according to gender, nor were the gender practices in school much different from those on the farm, in families, or in church. The North Carolina women identified with their black female teachers, even when these teachers mistreated them.[23]

This identification with teachers, however, was made problematic by the "racial uplift" mission of the black rural-community school. During the time when the North Carolina women attended school, black middle-class female teachers assigned to rural schools were committed to a mission that "equated normality with conformity to white, middle-class models of gender roles and sexuality" (Higginbotham 1992: 271). Exposed to the domestic-science movement as a way to promote the moral betterment of rural blacks, these teachers sought to correct black country ways, including speech, appearance, behavior, dress, and etiquette, which they viewed as impediments to social mobility not only within black communities but also within white society.[24] This model contrasted sharply with the vocational model and thus generated different and complicated relationships between female teachers and their students. Recall that the North Carolina women spoke with shame and humiliation about the school's mission to correct country ways. Moreover, they interpreted the school's mission in race- and class-based terms, angrily citing how black teachers invoked the "intimidation of color" as they "passed over" darker-skinned students or failed to encourage students whose parents were not professionals.[25] They were less aware that teachers invoked traditional, middle-class styles of femininity as part of the uplift mission, remembering with fondness those teachers who had made them "feel special." Yet by buying bows and dresses for those girls who, because of poverty, could not attain a traditionally middle-class, feminine image, these teachers unwittingly encouraged in the women a sense of their lower social standing and a devalued sense of self.

Whatever their goals, the efforts of black, middle-class teachers were undermined by racism and segregation that signaled to rural black children, but especially those living in poverty, that they were worth less than white children.[26] Whatever schoolwise knowledge black students could claim would not be recognized by the larger white society, nor would it provide them with occupational mobility, regardless of gender. By organizing instruction around age and cognitive proficiency at a time when regular school attendance was sporadic, if not impossible, for girls as well as boys, the rural-community school promoted the view that individual ability accounted for school success more than anything else.

Admittedly, such school organization was not intended to undermine black students' beliefs in their academic abilities. Yet the North Carolina women's narratives speak to the unintended consequences of institutional practices. In light of school segregation, the racial uplift mission, and class and color conflicts within black rural communities, not to mention damaging racist ideologies about blacks' inferior intelligence, it is not so surprising that the North Carolina women came to see themselves as slow learners.[27]

The mission of both school contexts was limited insofar as it only prepared students for what educational philosopher Jane Roland Martin (1985, 1994) calls "productive" rather than "reproductive" processes. Since the turn of the century, schools have split off the knowledge of the work place and the public/political spheres of life (most often associated with men) from the knowledge that comes from the areas of family, private, and emotional life (most often associated with women). Schools purportedly teach students such values as property rights, justice, freedom, and equality, which support political and economic development, while ignoring values such as empathy, nurturance, and sensitivity, which support personal growth and development.[28] Hidden or evaded in the curriculum are the skills, knowledge, and values that have to do with "taking care": everything that comes from knowing about and caring for human bodies and relationships.[29] These habits of mind are considered natural, not something to be learned and practiced by either girls or boys in school. As a result, schools promote a narrow view of citizenship, one that privileges the ethics of work and public life over the ethic of care.

This split school mission also teaches girls that their future work as women will not be recognized or valued. Moreover, it serves to silence what girls already know about the world. This silencing drives girls' knowledge "underground," fragments their self-definitions, or causes them to develop a split consciousness about what really matters in their lives.[30] School's split institutional mission had especially negative consequences for the women I interviewed, because the material conditions of their lives required considerable investment in caregiving knowledge. As girls, they were called upon to carry out the demands of family life and its survival, demands that neither school context directly acknowledged or rewarded.

In summary, I attribute the women's contrasting self-understandings of being (in)visible and voiceless and their different concerns about access, ability, discipline, and authority to the organization and mission of each school context. I do not offer this explanation as a complete account but rather as a corrective to explanations that ignore the important role of school missions in shaping selfhood, identity, and knowledge claims. There is more to the story, especially in terms of just how lopsided and adversarial the struggle was to attain at least the image of a "visible, differentiated, and reputable self" in school. These struggles are brought into bold relief by the theme of good and bad teachers and teachers' pets, to which I now turn.

Teachers and
Their Pets

[Six]

I made the honor society in high school. But that was really because of Mrs. Smith. She liked me and recommended me to the selection committee. She took me on as her student and it made me feel smart. She must have thought I deserved it, even if I wasn't, you know, even if I wasn't as intelligent as some of the other kids. (*Peggy*, Philadelphia woman)

I did well because the teachers liked me. I don't know if I am any smarter than anyone else. I certainly didn't work much at it. But if the teachers liked you then you got along better in school. I think you learned more too. Like my husband, he didn't get along well in school, the teachers didn't like him, and so he never thought he was smart, in the school sense I mean. (*Mary*, Philadelphia woman)

I would never have learned to read if it hadn't been for Mrs. Williams. I was in fifth grade and still couldn't read because no one cared if I could; maybe they thought I couldn't learn. Then came Mrs. Williams and she just said, "You can do this, I am going to see that you learn to read." And she did.

How did she do it?

Well, I guess you could say she cared about me, she believed that I could learn so she didn't take no for an answer. If I said I didn't know a word she worked with me until I figured it out. (*Bessie*, North Carolina woman)

The women's stories cast teachers as all-important in determining students' development and academic achievement. They expected teachers to stimulate students' interests, bring out individual talents, and inspire students to succeed, despite numerous obstacles. Meanwhile, without exception, the women attributed their academic achievements, such as passing a grade, learning to read or write, or making the honor roll, to a "good" teacher and her influence. Not one woman claimed her achievements in school to be her own, but rather, in each case, believed success to be the result of a relationship to a particular teacher.

It was striking to me, especially as a teacher, that so many years later teachers remained such key figures in the women's assessments of and claims to their own abilities and knowledge. To have liked a teacher (and for her to have liked you) meant not only enjoying but also having done well in the subject matter. Sallie recalled:

I never could stand math until I had Mrs. Hill. She was nice to all the kids and made the work so much more interesting. That was the only year I can remember doing well in math, and that was because I liked Mrs. Hill.

Conversely, disliking a teacher (and her disliking you) could mean forfeiting one's own interests. Peggy's account represents many I heard:

I used to be good in history, I guess because I loved to read about things that happened long ago. But then, I had Miss Waters and I lost all interest. She was one of those picky teachers where you had to do everything exactly her way; she had her own way for you to write your name, date, and all at the top of the page. If you didn't do it right, she marked you off. I stayed away from history classes after that.

What about reading about history, did you continue to do that?

Not really, I guess I got into other things that I thought I was good at.

In other words, the women conflated their academic interests and abilities with their relationships with teachers.[1]

What is important, if not so obvious that it gets overlooked, is that the women took it for granted that their teachers were *women*, especially during grammar school. This assumption was made clear by the women's references to their women teachers as simply "teachers" and to men in these positions as "men teachers"—something akin to "women lawyers." That teaching is defined as "women's work" is a bedrock of American education. Yet the hidden effects of this cultural assumption and institutional arrangement on student self-understandings has been minimized by feminist theorists and all but ignored by the so-called critical pedagogists.[2] In this chapter I trace the women's subjective ties to and conflicts with their teachers that were expressed through the themes of good and bad teachers and teachers' pets. I show how these ties and conflicts shaped the women's self-understandings and social identities.

"GOOD" AND "BAD" TEACHERS

The Philadelphia women viewed their teachers at worst as cruel authoritarians and at best as benevolent dictators. "Good" teachers were those who did not abuse their authority; they were seen as benign, strict, and all-knowing. The Philadelphia women expected "good" teachers (which were noted much less frequently than "bad" teachers) to be fair and treat all students equally, demanding obedience and academic performance in return. Most importantly, "good" teachers won this distinction because they commanded respect and hard work from students. In retrospect, many of the Philadelphia women, like Anne, expressed gratitude for a teacher's disciplinary demands:

> You know, at the time I didn't appreciate Mrs. Higgins. She was tough, but fair. She didn't play favorites, she terrorized everyone equally with her rules and regulations. But she made sure everybody turned in their work and that we learned. I guess you could say she really cared about her students. We didn't like her, but by the time we left her classroom we knew our multiplication tables and could spell anything.

These "good" teachers inspired student's performance and school compliance through rigid rules (though fairly enforced) to show that they cared about students.

Believing that a "good" teacher viewed her work as more than a job, many Philadelphia women fondly regarded those teachers who expressed genuine concern for children. These teachers "weren't in it for the money"; their work was viewed as an expression of their womanly or motherly interest and commitment to children. Mary was not alone in her gendered description of teacher's work:

> My favorite teachers were in grammar school. Mrs. Rose was my third grade teacher and you could tell that she really loved children. She wasn't in it for the money or anything, she just liked being with children. I don't think she had any of her own children, so I guess you could say she was making up for it by teaching us.

Sallie described her teacher, Miss Fulton, who would routinely invite student "goodies" to her beautiful home. Sallie believed that, as a single woman with no children, Miss Fulton's "maternal instincts" were fulfilled by her profession. In these cases, the criteria for being a "good" teacher were based on her care and concern for children, an extension of women's "natural" caregiving skills.

In the end, then, these "good" teachers exerted their authority by virtue of their femininity (defined as a naturally nurturing quality) rather than by the power invested in them by the school. These "good" teachers inspired students to learn out of love rather than fear. Still, the Philadelphia women more often than not cited teachers like Mrs. Higgins (the egalitarian terrorist) as "best" over ones like Mrs. Rose or Miss Fulton (teachers as surrogate mothers).

In contrast, the North Carolina women's definition of "good" as well as "best" teachers were those who "took special care" of black, rural students. As I've already mentioned, these teachers bought children clothes and shoes, "carried" students with no transportation to school, prepared hot meals, lent books or invited children into their homes. Ola remembered:

> Some days the teachers, they would fix us hot milk. And they give us warm beans. But they would give us something hot and we enjoyed that; we loved those teachers who fixed us good hot food. I believe they was the best teachers we had.

These "good" teachers saw to students' basic needs, demonstrating the importance of what Nel Noddings (1984) and others have termed "an ethic of care."[3] Several North Carolina women remembered teachers buying them clothing so that they would not feel embarrassed or uncomfortable in school. As Bessie explained:

> Miss Price, she was my best teacher. She was my third grade teacher, and she took a liking to me. She bought me dresses and shoes, even ribbons for my hair. That's when I got interested in school, in learning. She was good to me, she made me feel special so I wasn't embarrassed to go to school.

"Good" teachers like Miss Price made sure students were not shamed or ridiculed by others. Ola tearfully recalled her favorite teacher, Miss Washington, who had protected her against the taunts of the other children:

> The other childrens picked on me and my sister, so much so that I took to staying inside during recess. Miss Washington, she was nice to me, letting me help her wash the blackboard and all. She started bringing me books to read. I got to reading them so fast, about three a week. Then one day me and my sister were coming into school late from tending tobacco. One of the childrens grabbed at

my book in the yard and before I knew it I was on top of him, angrier than you can imagine. Miss Washington marches out to the yard and says, "Ola, now you know that ain't ladylike, even if he did deserve it." She picked up the book from the dirt and handed it to me. She said, "You'll be needing another one by tomorrow, I reckon." Her books meant everything to me.

Ola remembered Miss Washington invoking the importance of "ladylike" behavior. This value construct noted in the previous chapter was an implicit part of the racial uplift mission. This (middle-class) school value notwithstanding, Ola felt that she could defend herself from assaults on her person in school because Miss Washington had given her the means through her special care, attention, and, not unimportantly, her books.

The North Carolina women distinguished between the teachers they called "sticklers" (those who were more concerned that "we crossed all our t's and dotted all our i's than if we had shoes on our feet") and "good" teachers who responded to children's survival needs. Interestingly, while valorizing teachers' caregiving efforts, the North Carolina women still pitted emotional/social against academic concerns. Teaching rational academic skills (crossing t's and dotting i's) was understood to be in competition with teaching students to feeling good about themselves.[4]

Countering the effects of "good" teachers were the "bad" teachers, who undermined students' legitimacy and feelings of self-worth. Again the women in each group used different criteria for defining what made a teacher "bad." The Philadelphia women described as "bad" those teachers who used cruel and unusual punishments to enforce order and discipline. They gave vivid accounts of teachers who used paddles to punish children who misbehaved or made academic mistakes. They described teachers who threatened children, promising to tie them to chairs or put them in closets. Jeanne and Helen provided the following examples.

What do you remember about school?

Well, there's not a whole lot to say. School was not very interesting. It was boring and the teachers were crazy. In the fifth grade the nun put a bar of soap in my mouth for talking. My mouth broke out into a terrible rash.

I remember this one teacher who used to tie the kids to the chair if they got up without asking for permission. One day this kid had to go to the bathroom and Miss Hoyt said he had already gone too many times that day. He started to get up to go and she stormed over to tie him in his chair. No sooner had she tied him up, he was peeing all over himself. The teachers were not interested in teaching us anything, they were there to discipline us.

"Bad" teachers were portrayed as fearsome, dominating, militaristic in their rigid enforcement of arbitrary rules. According to the Philadelphia women, such teachers demanded obedience over achievement in the classroom and in the learning process itself.

In contrast, the North Carolina women described as "bad" those teachers who publicly ridiculed students for their "country ways," speech patterns, clothing, or physical size. They experienced these teachers not as fearsome but as shaming figures who reminded them that as black children they need not (or could not) be educated. Meanwhile, still vivid in the women's minds were those "bad" teachers who preferred light-skinned children and neglected those, including themselves, who had darker skin.

These different versions of what made a teacher "good," "bad," or "best" can be explained in terms of school context and mission. Each school provided a different context for teachers to exercise their authority and care for students. In one sense, black female teachers in rural schools exercised more autonomous authority in an isolated one-room schoolhouse than did their urban counterparts who were directly supervised by (male) principals. Meanwhile, black female teachers exercised their authority as part of a more integrated school-family-community context and set of interwoven relationships. Teachers who prepared hot food and so forth as part of everyday school life were part of a tradition of black women caregivers whose efforts in families, churches, and community organizations contributed to racial survival. These teachers promoted the value of women's work and their authority even if they embraced false dualisms between the academic side and social side of schooling.

These more permeable boundaries between school, family, and work set the stage for the North Carolina women to develop specific conflicts individuating themselves and separating their skills from those of the teachers. Put another way, the rural-community school context, with its emphasis on embeddedness and connectedness and its (maternal) authority relations, tipped the balance in the differentiation process toward a denial of self. For inasmuch as the North Carolina women felt connected to and cared for by their teachers, they also experienced anxiety about their autonomy as learners. Ironically, the more the "good" teachers made them feel special, the more the women became convinced that they couldn't learn on their own. Beatrice remembered:

> Miss Wright, she was my third grade teacher, she must have told Miss Parker how to treat me and all, because Miss Parker she was nice to me too and took up a lot of attention with me. But the next year I got this teacher who didn't care about me one bit. I had been doing real well, learning, reading, and spelling, and then I just gave up on it, you know, like I couldn't do it or nothing.

Ola felt the same way when Miss Washington left the school. In the absence of her favorite teacher, Ola found a bit of reassurance and protection in the books she had been given, just as teachers' more common gifts of dresses and hairbows (so prominently featured in the North Carolina women's school accounts) helped other women see themselves in a better light.[5] Yet these objects regulated black rural girls' senses of self in complicated ways. At the same time that these objects served as forms of self-protection, they also reinforced the white, middle-class image of "good" schoolgirls.

In contrast, the explicit mission of the urban-comprehensive school was to prepare students to meet the needs of industry. As already noted, this school context organized teacher-student relations around the obedience and discipline required in working-class jobs. This rigid, bureaucratic, and strongly bounded institution recalls Waller's (1932) image of the school as a fortress set apart from, if not potentially threatening to, family and community life. These bureaucratic authority relations, coupled with schools splitting off academic skills over emotional relations, limited teachers' caregiving practices.

The urban school context set the stage for the Philadelphia women to undervalue teachers' maternal authority and knowledge. Teachers who exercised their authority through love and care were fondly regarded, viewed as "motherly." But teachers who exercised their authority through the school's regulations and rules and who instilled fear held more sway in the women's minds. Meanwhile, the urban-school context tipped the balance in the differentiation process toward a denial of the other. Recall that the women accounted for their failure in school by citing their "problems with authority," not their unmet needs for care or nurturance by the teachers. "I always was in trouble"; "I always had a mouth"; "I just had to speak up"; "I always had to speak my mind"; "I could never keep my mouth shut." This chorus bespeaks their efforts to assert themselves against a real and imagined other.

This is all to say that within the urban-bureaucratic school context, teachers were more easily blamed and viewed as other. Within the rural-community school context, teachers were more easily idealized and viewed as extensions of self. Hence, each group of women came to understand the struggle for a "differentiated, worthy, and reputable" self in different terms. The Philadelphia women understood their conflicts in terms of autonomy and voice, while the North Carolina women understood theirs in terms of dependency and (in)visibility. These tensions were also evident in the women's different storytelling conventions: the Philadelphia women favored absolute adverbs (always, never) as well as the first person singular (I . . .) to describe their relations with teachers. In contrast, the North Carolina women's use of language de-emphasized the self as an actor in favor of the teachers: "Miss Parker, she was nice to me; Miss Price, she took a liking to me; Miss Washington, she was nice to me, letting me help her; the teachers, they would fix us hot milk. . . ." Psychodynamically speaking and in terms of self-definition, this speech pattern indicates greater omnipotence of object, and less differentiation of the self in relation to the other, who makes things happen.

In both school contexts, however, teachers were not viewed as fully human. The women's stories reveal deep-seated images of maternal love, care, and power that at once blame and idealize teachers as maternal figures for their central role in children's development and growth. These myths operate on both the cultural and psychological levels, affording teachers (and mothers) tremendous power and influence, while masking the social reality that most teachers have little control over the conditions under which they care for and instruct children. Through these myths, larger social problems that attenuate student learning and development (such as hunger, homelessness, violence, abuse, and so forth) are made to appear the responsibility of individual teachers rather than of public or school policies.[6]

The women sought to explain their school experiences in terms of the perfect teacher—the teacher who cared about her students, made all children feel special, attended to daily survival needs, and successfully passed on schoolwise knowledge. In projecting their fantasies about the perfect teacher, the women came to attribute their own school successes or failures to a teacher's style, personality, or encouragement, and they depended upon teachers to simultaneously protect them from the "real world" and to prepare them for it. The women's split views of teachers as either good or bad drew critical attention away from other important social and political forces that mitigated against the students' well-being, growth, and development. Meanwhile, by seeing teachers as all-powerful (whether as adversaries or allies), the women may have protected themselves from their own conflicts, especially those related to a sense of separateness and autonomy that are said to characterize girls' self-formation and development (Chodorow 1978, 1989). In this light, it could be argued that the women's tendency to split their teachers as good versus bad was, in part, a way for them to protect themselves from the need, albeit painful, to separate and individuate in the learning process. This "reflexively self-denying split of self" from teacher (who was a fantasy) may partially account for the ambivalence, discomfort, and exclusion felt by the women.[7] Even as the women treated teachers as larger than life, all-knowing, or all-caring, they denied teachers' complex subjectivities as well as their own.

TEACHERS' PETS

Tell me what you remember about being in school.

What I didn't like about school, the teachers they all had their own pet. If you were a pet you had it made, but if you weren't they didn't take up no attention with you. Everybody knew that the teachers treated the kids who were dressed nice and all better— the teachers all had their pets. (*Louise*, North Carolina woman)

I wasn't encouraged much in school, mostly the teachers didn't think much of me. They didn't think much of my background, I guess you could say. I wasn't the teacher's pet type, you know the kind that got picked to stand in front of the line or to pass out paper or pencils. I suppose the teachers didn't think I had promise or was going anywhere. (*Anne*, Philadelphia woman)

One way to experience the self as worthy of a teacher's respect and attention in school was to be chosen as a "pet." Discussions of how teachers chose certain students as pets; how the women felt about having been a pet (or not); how they felt about others who were chosen; and how the pet contest affected their school achievement were found across all the women's accounts.

Women in both groups gave numerous examples to show that teachers favored girls over boys in school. Nevertheless, the women did not view teachers' gendered preferences as benefiting all girls equally. As many recalled, to be chosen as pets, girls had to be "pretty or cute," but mostly they had to be "good."

The teachers liked the girls better. But then I think it was easier for my brothers in school because nobody expected them to be quiet. But I couldn't keep my mouth shut, talking all the time and I was loud, too, so the teacher, she didn't care too much for me. (*Barbara*, North Carolina woman)

I was Miss Tough Girl. I was a real bully and a troublemaker. A lot of us played tough, but you couldn't be too tough or you would stand out in class. The teachers didn't treat the girls as rough as the boys—I guess because girls aren't supposed to be as bad as boys—anyway I was pretty bad. (*Doreen*, Philadelphia woman)

Considerable research documents teachers' differential behaviors toward boys and girls and the negative effect on girls' school achievement.[8] While this research confirms the women's perceptions that teachers behaved differently toward boys and girls, it oversimplifies the social learning that goes on in the classroom. For example, most educational theory and practice implicitly assume that teachers direct gender socialization in the classroom, but we know little about how teachers react to boys and girls who deviate from expected gender roles—for example, girls who are *tough* or *loud,* as several of these women described themselves.[9] Moreover, we know little about how girls from different classes, races, or ethnic backgrounds interpret teachers' differential and/or preferential treatment or which strategies they use to evoke certain responses in teachers.[10]

According to the women I interviewed, not all girls have (or think they have) the same opportunities to look, act, and be treated as "feminine" or as "teachers' pets." (All girls, do, however, desire to be treated as such, which I discuss later in this chapter.) "Good" girlhood is problematic rather than given, an accomplishment not easily achieved. For example, to be chosen as a female pet, girls had to comply with traditional, middle-class femininity, which for some women was either unrealistic or impossible:

Life was rough on the streets. You couldn't go around being Miss Priss and stay alive. So I got tough and teachers didn't like me. (*Anne*, Philadelphia woman)

I didn't have no frilly dresses with lace and skirts and all. I was worried about soles on my shoes. There were lots of days I didn't go to school because I was just too ashamed of my clothes. (*Geraldine*, North Carolina woman)

I mean if you didn't have cute ringlets, an ironed new uniform, starched shirts, and a mother and father who gave money to the church, you weren't a teacher's pet and that meant you weren't encouraged. (*Joanne*, Philadelphia woman)

While teachers preferred attractive, smart, and—most important—*good* girls, being good wasn't always the best way to defend themselves against physical or emotional assaults. It could be risky to be *good* when children unmercifully picked on others or when life got rough on the streets. Sallie from Philadelphia described the rewards of being good when she spoke about Miss Fulton, who invited "goodies" to her home:

The goodies were smart kids—they liked smart girls. But you also had to behave and act like a lady if you were going to get invited to their place. I used to imagine myself having tea at Miss Fulton's but I never got asked.

Sallie's conflicted feelings about Miss Fulton—her envy and resentment toward those who were chosen as pets—were echoed by many women I interviewed. Such unresolved inner conflicts about the pet contest differed for the Philadelphia and North Carolina women.

The Philadelphia women described themselves as having to make hard choices about whether they would pursue being a teacher's pet. As Debra explained:

I remember one girl used to act in a real cutesie way and the teacher would be so impressed. I didn't like the teacher and I didn't like the girls who acted like that. I just wouldn't be cutesie like that—not even if it did impress the teacher.

Debra reasoned that if the teacher chose you as a pet, you risked losing friends; other kids would be jealous. And even if you did act "cutesie" and "sit like a lady," you knew it was an "act" rather than the real thing. Helen talked about this dilemma in a way that split her true self from a false one:

> I was a teacher's pet so I got by pretty well. [Laughing]

> *A couple of other women have laughed just like you when they described themselves as teachers' pets. Can you explain this?*

> Because you know you are and it's uncomfortable. I mean either they like you or they don't, but when I was a kid I guess I was a smooth talker. I was real cute and learned how to bat my eyes, look cute, sit like a lady, and boy, the teachers really ate that stuff up. I guess I felt bad because I felt like I had conned them, like it wasn't really me who they liked.

The choice to become a teacher's pet, to represent one's self falsely in order to win the teacher's approval, was not a happy one. Those Philadelphia women who were chosen as pets and were successful in school described their achievements with guilt or discomfort. As Helen continued,

> I used to feel so bad for my sister. I mean, I didn't even have to study and I got A's. The teachers liked me cause I knew how to win them over with my smile. But my sister, she worked so hard and didn't get anywhere. I couldn't feel too good about how I was doing when she was having such a hard time.

Others who wanted to be pets but were not chosen expressed wide-ranging feelings, including wistful desire and a sense of rejection. But most (eleven of the fifteen Philadelphia women) said that they had forgone the opportunity to be a teacher's pet, mostly because of their "bad attitude" toward authority and their inability to keep "their mouths shut." It wasn't that they fully rejected the prospect of being a "nice" or "good" girl in other realms of their life, but their "bad attitude" did not fit the requirements of teacher's pet status.

The North Carolina women, however, did not seem to have choices about being a teacher's pet. As dark-skinned women, they saw themselves as disadvantaged in the contest to win the teacher's approval and affections. They did, however, observe that lighter-skinned girls were offered the chance to compete. As Gloria explained, some girls were always "putting on the dog" to get the teacher's attention. In response to this competition, the women expressed many emotions, including a profound sense of betrayal. Gloria recalled:

What I didn't like about school, the teachers they had their own
pets. Like if you were light-skinned, you had it made. But if you
were black [she emphasized this word], they didn't take up no
attention with you.

All the North Carolina women referred to the role that skin color played,
emphasizing that teachers' pets were cute, good, smart, higher class,
and "what we used to call 'yeller,' back then." They described how
teachers "passed right over," "looked straight through," or "looked over
the top of" darker-skinned children. As Gladys added, "I suspect it was
'cause them teachers were yeller, too."

Mary Helen Washington (1982: 208–17) notes that this "intimidation
of color" surfaces as a recurrent theme in the lives and literature of
black women. She also writes that "in almost every novel or autobiography written by a black woman, there is at least one incident [of] the
dark-skinned girl who wishes to be either white or light-skinned with
'good hair'" (1975: xv). Bessie told of a light-skinned childhood acquaintance, Dorothy, whom Bessie resents and envies to this day:

You know, if you come to school dressed real nice, you know with
one of them ruffle dresses, little bows and stuff on your hair, looking real neat, the teacher would take up time with you. Something
that she would tell her, she probably wouldn't tell me. Like this girl,
her name was Dorothy. She was the teacher's pet. She had light
skin, pretty black hair, she came from a wealthy family, you know.

What was it that made her the teacher's pet?

I believe it was her lighter skin. And then the clothes she would
wear. And the teacher would have PTA meetings, and my mom she
never went to no PTA meeting or nothing like that. I reckon that
showed the teacher you wasn't interested in your child. So that was
that and the teacher wouldn't take up no time. But she took up time
with Dorothy with her light skin and pretty black hair. [11]

How class as well as color distinctions impacted black girls' school
chances and achievement is explored in the life history of Mamie Garvin
Fields (1983). She describes how members of the same family with
lighter skin color received greater educational recognition and
resources. Growing up in a middle-class black community in Charleston,
South Carolina, in the early 1900s, she recalls:

When I was a little girl, I recognized that there was a difference,
because my brother Herbert used to tease me and call me black—
"blakymo"—although he was as black as I was. It used to make me
so mad I would almost fight him. He would say, "Well, we are the
black ones and they [their siblings] are the light ones. They can do

this and that." We used to joke this way, but it wasn't all joke either. One reason why I didn't go to our private school for Negroes in Charleston was that, back then, honors were always given to mulatto children, light-skinned half-sisters and brothers, grands and great-grands of white people. It didn't matter what you did if you were dark. Used to leading my class up through elementary school, I hated this idea, so I began to say I wanted to go somewhere else. (1983: 47)

The North Carolina women's position in the color line, combined with their lower-class status, disadvantaged them in the teacher's pet contest. For them, the pet contest served as an everyday reminder that they were not worthy of competing for social mobility.

TEACHERS' PETS: ILLUSION, POWER, AND DESIRE

The women's stories alert us to the ways in which school divides students against each other along the fault lines of gender, race, and class. The women understood that it was not Dorothy the person but Dorothy the light-skinned, middle-class, traditionally feminine, black girl who became the teacher's pet and therefore succeeded in school. It was not Helen the person, but feminine, cute, and obedient Helen as a "type" that accounted for her school achievements. Through these gender, race, and class divisions and antagonisms, the women in both groups came to view teachers as emissaries of dominant and oppressive values, passing on schoolwise knowledge according to interests that were in conflict with the women's own.

Thus the women's interpretations of the teacher's pet contest served to corroborate what they already knew about social divisions. These interpretations were complicated, if not conflicting. In one sense, the women's positions in the teacher's pet contest provided a venue in which to critique school values and knowledge. By refusing to become a pet and/or rejecting the terms of the pet contest, they learned useful, if limited, arts of resistance. But the women's understandings of the teacher's pet phenomenon also served to mask women's collective power, particularly that of the "bad" girls who chose not to compete or were not chosen as pets. Likewise, it masked black students' collective power. The light-skin/dark-skin dichotomy falsified race relations, making it appear as if teachers' individual prejudices, rather than institutional racism, undermined black students' success. The sanctioning of lighter-skinned blacks as smart and successful learners at the expense of darker-skinned blacks served to divide black students against each other, undermining their collective knowledge and power. At the same time, the light-skin/dark-skin dichotomy falsified gender relations, making it appear that only the color line, without patriarchal impositions, pitted the black, rural, female students against each other.

Similarly, the split between "good" girls and "bad" girls functioned as a method of social control, a way to get girls to regulate themselves and others. It also masked gender inequalities in the classroom, for despite the fact that women in both groups viewed teachers' pets as having knowledge and power, closer scrutiny reveals this to be a distortion, if not an illusion.

Greer Fox (1977) provides a useful analytical framework in which to unpack the illusory power of the pet. She explains three strategies typically used to regulate women's behavior and constrain their freedom. The first is *confinement*, the most familiar example of which is the *purdah*, or seclusion, associated with, although not limited to Arab-Muslim cultural practices. The second is *protection*, which involves regulating women's access to the world through designated protectors such as male kinsmen, older female relatives, or family friends (the chaperon is a structural feature of the *protective* pattern). Finally, and of particular relevance, is *normative restriction*, embodied in the value constructs of "good" or "nice" girl and "lady," which serve as standards and goals for feminine behavior. Fox cautions that while normative restrictions appear to allow individual women the highest degree of direct and independent participation in the world, this may be illusory. Whereas the confinement and protection strategies rely on external agents (such as the veil, the harem, the chaperon) to enforce control, no obvious external agents enforce the value construct of "good" girl, where the control is internal—self-control through the internalization of values and norms.

What is particularly misleading about the "good" or "nice" girl value construct as embodied in the teacher's pet phenomenon is that goodness or niceness is an achieved (not ascribed) status. Wealth and distinguished family background are not necessarily sufficient for "ladyhood." Indeed, this lesson could be drawn from the racial uplift message promoted by the black teachers in rural-community schools—that proper ladyhood could be achieved through the right manners, clothes, and speech patterns.[12] But, according to Fox, the guise of democracy in normative restriction (that niceness or ladylikeness is an achievable ideal) ensures continual compliance: "because every woman can learn to be a lady, every woman is expected to act like one" (1977: 809). Meanwhile, the appearance of nonrestriction and noncontrol of the "good" girl value reduces the likelihood of resistance. Those who comply are said to be guaranteed safe passage in the world. Those who don't are seen as "getting what they deserve."

> The not-nice woman becomes the target of ridicule, ostracism and psychological punishment directed not so much at her behavior as to her person. The group withdraws its approval from her and

attacks the worthiness of her self; it negates her moral existence as part of itself, and by so doing it absolves itself of the responsibility for the fate of its "unworthy" members. (1977: 817)

Who gains by the "good" girl value construct as represented and lived out in the teacher's pet contest? It would be simpleminded to suggest that only boys benefit, gaining more freedom of expression and attention (although empirical research does lend credence to this point).[13] More important, how are we to explain the tenacious resonance of the teacher's pet theme across all the women's stories? There are ideological and psychological issues that require attention if we are to appreciate the full force of the pet contest and why women might want to compete in it.

The women understood the relationship between teachers and their pets as a form of patronage, whereby teachers chose individual students to be theirs to "own." The pet's ability to succeed thus depended on her patron, the teacher. According to the terms of this relationship, the patron promised support, encouragement, and praise in exchange for the pet's productivity and achievement. Additionally, the association was understood to be a unique, one-to-one alliance between a particular teacher and a particular student (your pet cannot also be my pet). As a result, the women learned to view knowledge and power as *personalized* and *individual* rather than *collective* or *social*. Moreover, this personalized and infantilized image as the teacher's pet (the human pet being an infantilized person) connoted an affective bond. Being someone's pet suggested an emotional or even erotically tinged bond between pets and their owners (as in the common expression, "petting").[14] However, the relationship between teachers and pets was charged with deception, which diminished the pet's sense of self and worth, as women attested. Girls participating in such associations were seen or saw themselves as presenting a false self to attract the teacher's attention. Moreover, because a pet's achievements and school knowledge were gained through such deception, their accomplishments were viewed as suspect. Put somewhat differently, the women who could not perform as a pet felt *un*recognized by the teacher, while the women who had been able to perform as a pet felt *mis*recognized by the teacher. Both cases were unsettling to the women's identities as learners.

The women's description of school as a teacher's pet contest also illustrates the complexity of female objectification—how the experience of being or not being a desired object, a pet, was both distressing and pleasurable. We can interpret the teacher's pet phenomenon as part of subject/object splits that are gendered. As Muriel Dimen writes:

Subjects, in our cultural and intrapsychic representations, are men. The subject says, "I want." The subject, "Man," desires. Since men represent authorship, agency and adulthood, women as adults are expected to be subjects too. At the same time through splitting that occurs equally on cultural and psychological levels, women are also expected to be objects ("object" here meaning not the intrapsychic representation of persons, as psychoanalysis uses the term, but "thing," as the vernacular has it). As inanimate things, women are represented to be without desire, to be the targets of the subject's desire. If subjects want, objects are there to be wanted.

Women, then are expected to be both, the subject and the object. The development of femininity is, therefore, a compromise, almost, you might say, a compromise formation. It is the process of learning to be both, to take yourself as an object and to expect others to do so too, and all the while you know that you are a subject (1991: 343–44).

We could say that the teacher's pet contest is part of this compromise formation. Part of the pleasure that a pet derives from her situation (and that others may envy) is the enjoyment of being both a desiring subject and a desirable object at the same time.

Let me summarize what we learn from the women's stories about teachers' pets. First, being a "teacher's pet type," like being the "commonsense type," was self- and identity-forming. By identifying with one side or the other of these split images of femininity, the women at once accepted and rejected certain school values, styles, and kinds of knowledge. Second, through the teacher's pet contest, the women revealed what they had been told and what they had resisted about their own lack of social worth relative to men and to other groups of women. Third, the split images of femininity (bad and good/black and white/light skinned and dark-skinned) that defined the teacher's pet contest reinforced the dominant message that women's power lies in their attractiveness, desirability, and submission more than in their intellectual capabilities or collective identities and interests. Fourth, the teacher's pet contest divided women from each other and thus reduced the possibility for effective resistance. Finally, the teacher's pet contest was enviable or appealing to the women because it enabled girls to be both subjects who wanted and objects who were desired.

My narration of the tale of teacher's pet would be incomplete without a self-reflexive word. During presentations of this material to varied academic audiences (who, generally speaking, have had successful school careers), I have encountered a range of strong reactions. It was often the case that an audience member would publicly defend herself or privately confess to me her guilt about having been chosen as a "teacher's pet."[15] But one exchange was especially provocative. At a women's studies faculty seminar, a colleague noted what she considered to be a lot of "animus" toward teachers' pets in my presentation. She asked me to comment on this and on whether I myself had been a teacher's pet. Somewhat taken aback by her directness (and admittedly unsure of the meaning of "animus"), I replied with a qualified yes. I could recall one particular teacher who had treated me as a pet, but many others who had not. It has taken me some time to appreciate and not defend against my colleague's question, searching my own memories about my changing position in the pet contest and resentful and shameful feelings about it, as both a complicit and injured party.

In the end, what bothered the women I interviewed (and me) most about teachers' pets was that some students were chosen to be special at the expense of others—a fundamental betrayal of trust in the student-teacher bond. Teachers' pets enhanced the hold of teachers and certain students on their privileged social position (whether age, gender, race, or class based), so the contest became a ritual celebration of social injustice. That student-teacher bonds evoke both conscious and unconscious self and object images and desires that are full of social and psychological complexity, seems crucial to acknowledge as being part of women's paradoxical relationship to schooling. I address yet another set of images and desires in the next chapter about mothers.

Schools and Mothers

[Seven]

I could not be sure whether for the rest of my
life I would be able to tell when it was really my
mother and when it was really her shadow
standing between me and the rest of the world.
—Jamaica Kincaid, *Annie John*

In Jamaica Kincaid's coming of age
novel, *Annie John*, we learn about the powerful attachment and painful
separation of daughter from mother. Told in the voice of a still-young
woman struggling with her ambivalence about her mother's love and
betrayal, the novel reminds me of the Philadelphia and North Carolina
women's narrative urgency to do the same. Images of maternal caregivers (both in real and fantasy terms) were ever-present in the women's
school stories, casting shadows over their self-understandings. Indeed,
my request for their school stories proved a catalyst for each woman to
reflect on and critically appraise herself in relation to the woman who
had raised her. Fathers rarely entered the women's school stories except
for the degree to which they encouraged or discouraged their daughters
to attend school.[1] Some women described fathers, uncles, or grandfa-
thers who insisted that they behave properly in school or finish their
homework, but no one described her father as being part of the daily
ongoing life of the school. Nor did any of the women speak about their
feelings about their fathers in relation to teachers.

The primacy of mothers in the women's school stories is not so surprising when we consider the gendered organization of school. A sexual
division of labor is built into the American educational system as its

working assumption and in a way that (re)produces class inequalities.[2] Alison Griffith and Dorothy Smith put it this way:

> The institutional order of the school requires particular activities to be accomplished within the home, a work organization usually managed and coordinated by mothers. At the primary educational level, an overtired or hungry child is unable to keep up with the morning's teaching program. In the later grades, a child living in a crowded space, who has limited time and resources has difficulty completing homework assignments. Where mothering work does not conform to the generalized requirements of schooling, or to the particularities of the classroom, it appears as inadequate mothering due to incompetence, or social deprivation. (1987: 87)

The women's stories draw on what Griffith and Smith call "the paradigm of the ideal mother constructed in relation to her children's schooling." This ideal mother is part of a mothering discourse that matches middle-class resources, time, and knowledge.[3] Mothers who for whatever reason don't fit the ideal (especially poor and working-class mothers) are exposed to the hazards of "guilt, invidious comparison, and anxiety," especially when children do not behave or perform in ways that fit the classroom order (1987: 97–98).[4]

The women's stories illustrate the extent to which they measured their mothers and themselves according to what Griffith and Smith would call the intersecting discourses of mothering and schooling. But what struck me more than their discursive practices were the women's emotionally charged images and ambivalent feelings about mother and self.[5]

MOTHERS' RELATIONS TO SCHOOL

> My mother didn't encourage us much, she didn't have the time. She worked two jobs, she couldn't go to PTA meetings or nothing like that. I guess she was interested, but she didn't get involved. (*Mary*, Philadelphia woman)

> You know how the teachers think about kids whose parents don't show no interest. My mother never went to a PTA meeting or a parent conference. I guess you could say she wasn't interested. But don't get me wrong. I love my mother more than anything and she raised us up good, but I don't believe she was interested much in school. (*Beverly*, North Carolina woman)

Whereas the women spoke about their teachers as "good," "bad," and "best," they described their maternal caregivers according to three types: the *uninvolveds*, the *school back-ups*, and the *school antagonists*.[6] These types are not meant to be binding; for example, mothers could be uninvolved at one point, and then later serve as a back-up to teacher's authority. But for the most part, the women's stories cast their mothers' actions as coherently organized around one of these three relationships to school.

UNINVOLVED

The highest proportion (thirteen of the thirty women—six Philadelphia and seven North Carolina women) viewed their maternal caregivers as *uninvolved* in school. They gave many reasons for this: some women explained that their mothers worked more than one job and didn't have time, while others said "country ways" or lack of education inhibited their mothers' school involvement:

> The teachers liked the children whose parents were involved in the school. My mother didn't go to PTA meetings or parent conferences. She couldn't read or write and I reckon that she thought it was the teachers' job to teach us. I mean that was what they were getting paid to do and they (the teachers) knew how to do it, she wasn't supposed to know. (*Louise*, North Carolina)

> I would say that some of my problem in school was because my mother just wasn't involved. She really had no time so I don't blame her. But I remember thinking how come my mother doesn't go to meetings like the other kids' mothers? (*Pam*, Philadelphia woman)

Over half the women who described their mothers as uninvolved (for whatever reasons) believed that this had negative consequences for them as students. As Debra explained:

> I suppose the fact that my mother didn't get involved in the school told the teachers that she wasn't interested so why should they be? I'm not saying it was her fault, I love my mother, but then again, I'm sure it didn't help me that she didn't show much interest in my education.

Most of the women I interviewed believed that maternal involvement and interest corresponded with teachers' attentiveness and student success. Of the close to 200 women who took part in this study through short, semistructured interviews about why they were returning to school, 88 percent believed that contemporary problems in the schools were due in equal measure to teachers and mothers who were apathetic or uncaring about children's needs.

Still, the women who described their mothers as uninvolved said they did not blame their mothers, even if as children they might have been resentful or disappointed.[7] Betty, from Philadelphia, who recalled feeling especially disappointed that her mother showed no interest in her school success, offered the following explanation:

My mother never once looked at my report card, and you know I
was getting all As. She had lots of things on her mind at the time,
you know she didn't have an easy life. Then again, nobody had
much of an easy life when I was going to school. Things are different nowadays. I mean I wouldn't think of not looking at my children's report card.

I asked Betty how she thought things were different back then. She
responded in great detail about her mother's laborious life working in a
factory; her father's drinking, gambling, and bouts with depression; and
how, given these circumstances, she couldn't expect her mother to be any
more encouraging than she had been (what about her father's encouragement, I wondered to myself). Betty described the effects of her childhood as "character building," viewing life's adversities as challenges she
has been able to overcome. She explained that this philosophy of life is
currently being eroded by social policies (particularly welfare) that fos-
ter dependency rather than self-reliance. Providing her children with a
safe, stable home environment has been a hard-earned achievement "by
anybody's standard." Still, in her adult life the times are different because
new standards have been set for raising children. Paradoxically, while
these standards are better for children, life is much more dangerous. In
her view, child rearing requires more parental interest, involvement, and
supervision than in the past, and so to compare her more attentive caregiving to her mother's would be unfair on her part.

BACK-UPS

Eleven of the thirty women (five North Carolina and six Philadelphia
women) spoke of their mothers as *back-ups* to the teachers. These mothers carried out the demands of school at home in multiple ways: by pun-
ishing children who behaved badly in school; by supervising homework
every night; by pressing uniforms and starching white shirts; by attending parent meetings; and by working extra jobs to provide school
clothes. More than half of the women who described their mothers
in this way regretted that they had not been more appreciative. While
not always viewing family-school alliances in entirely positive terms,
the women stressed their benefits in the long run. Mary, from North
Carolina, explained:

I believe my mother spent more time up at that school than she did
working. Everyday they be calling her up to school about one of her
childrens and everyday she be telling us, "If I got to come up there
again you won't need to worry about the next day." One time she
told me she would kill me if I didn't stop acting up. That made me
settle down for a while. I might not of finished seventh grade if she
hadn't said that. But my temper was bad and the teachers they
looked down on me; it made me so mad.

Helen, from Philadelphia, noted the difference between her own and her mother's alliance with school:

> My parents were not interested in whether the teacher was right or wrong. There was no point in explaining to my mother why I had flunked a test or why I had skipped school. She made up her mind according to what the teacher said. We didn't discuss anything about it. I'm not like that with my kids. I listen to their problems in school and I decide whether I think the teacher is being fair or not. In those days parents took the teacher's word, whatever she said. I guess it wasn't all bad—at least we all learned the basics, not like so many kids now who have such bad discipline problems that they don't learn anything in school. You can't expect teachers to teach kids discipline, they have to learn that at home.

Philadelphian Sallie spoke not only about her mother but also about other (female) caregivers who supported and allied themselves with school:

> My mother was up early every morning getting things ready to send us to school. She made sure we cleaned behind our ears and looked nice everyday. If she found out about any of us causing trouble then we didn't hear the end of it. You know, I believe that the problem today is that most mothers don't care about their kids. But in those days mothers knew what their kids were doing. And if your mother found out you were messing around, well then everybody else knew it too. My grandmother and my aunt (they lived on our block, my mother's mother and her younger sister) would say, "We hear that you have been doing this or doing that in school. You better shape up."

Several women remembered the force of their mothers' negative reactions when, as adolescents, they had announced their plans to drop out of school. Gloria, from North Carolina, recalled:

> When I told my mother that I was going to drop out of school she told me "over my dead body." Of course I didn't realize at the time that she was right. Anyway, I was determined to quit and my mother said, "Okay, but only if you have a job." So I got a job and she signed the papers.

ANTAGONISTS

Only six of the women characterized their mothers as *antagonists* to school and teachers (three Philadelphia women, three North Carolina women). Their stories featured mothers as triumphant over teachers who treated children unfairly, harshly, or abusively. As advocates, these mothers took up their daughters' sides when school disputes emerged.

Ola remembered her mother confronting a teacher for being prejudiced against darker-skinned children:

> I remember there was this one teacher and she didn't do nothing for black students. I kept telling mama that my teacher wasn't calling on me, that she was passing right over me when I would sit and raise up my hand. I told her so that I think she got tired of hearing about it. So she went on up there to school and she told the teacher she had better be paying more attention or she was going to get me transferred out of her classroom.

And then what happened?

> Well, the teacher, she did start calling on me. She had told my mama that I was quiet and didn't talk much anyway and my mama told her maybe she had better get me to do more talkin' if that was the case.

Two of the Philadelphia women told stories of their mothers challenging the teachers' choice of punishment. In both cases the teachers were nuns who had used particularly harsh measures:[8]

> I had been getting in a lot of trouble, and they were making me stay for detention after school and clean up. But then one time the nun hit me across the face and I went home with a bruise that looked like I had walked into a door. My mother asked what had happened and I told her the nun had hit me for talking in class. My mother marched into the Mother Superior's office and said she wasn't paying for me to get hit by the nuns. Most mothers wouldn't have done that—what the nuns said was rule for most parents in those days. But I guess she thought a bruise like that was going too far.

Similarly, Doris's mother defended her daughter. When Doris's mouth broke out in a rash from soap the nun had used to punish her for talking in class, her mother warned the nun that "she wasn't allowed to lay another hand on me, no matter what I did. That was my last year in Catholic school."

These two women spoke admiringly of their mothers, but others expressed some ambivalence or doubt about taking an antagonistic school stance. Pam, from Philadelphia, reflected:

> It is a real problem. My son comes home all the time in trouble in school for speaking up against the teacher. I tell him that he just can't do that, he has to respect authorities. But at the same time I am proud that he is speaking up. I guess my mother had the same problem with me. She would encourage me to speak up for myself, and then when I got into trouble she would yell at me.

Cora, from North Carolina, expressed some resentment for what she considered her mother's unrealistic demands that she get the teacher's attention:

> I used to come home with homework and I couldn't do it, mostly I couldn't understand what I was supposed to do. My mother would sit down with me and say, "Well, what did the teacher say she wanted?" I would explain how she [the teacher] didn't take up no time with me so I didn't know what to do. My mother would say, "You gotta raise your hand until she calls on you. You can't just sit there. You gotta make her take up time with you. I don't want to hear you tell that she didn't take up time with you tomorrow."

Eventually, Cora's mother confronted the teacher for being prejudiced against darker-skinned children. But the result was not positive; in Cora's words: "The teacher had it out for me and I just fell further behind."

Regardless of whether the women characterized their mothers as uninvolved, back-ups, or antagonists, the women's experiences in school were subjectively tied to their mothers' feelings and actions toward teachers.[9] This is a simple but remarkable finding that sheds light on how daughters become emotionally caught up in the intersecting discourses of mothering and schooling.

SELF IN RELATION TO MOTHERS

> A belief . . . that women or mothers are powerless is both a social analysis and a powerful motivator of guilt and inhibition, of a need to repair and not to move ahead of mother. Guilt and sadness about mother are particularly prevalent preoccupations and as likely to limit female autonomy, pleasure and achievement as any cultural mandate. (Chodorow 1995: 540)

The women's stories were tied together by their social analysis of motherhood and psychological preoccupation with it. They expressed mixed emotions ranging over guilt, anger, abiding love, shame, disappointment, sadness, and resentment. Oftentimes they shifted from one emotion to another depending upon the incident they recalled. The women spoke in strikingly similar ways about their mothers even though their stories were unique. In their descriptions of marginality, exclusion, or resistance at school, the women looked to their mothers for protection or comfort; and it was their mothers whom they tried not to blame for their childhood disappointments. Most concluded their stories by affirming their gratitude toward their mothers.[10]

A persistent sadness and regret, what Nancy Chodorow (1995: 534) calls "weeping for the mother," punctuated the women's stories. In telling their stories, the North Carolina women were more likely to weep for their mothers' subservience to white employers and to the teacher's demeaning manner, while the Philadelphia women were more likely to weep for their mothers' subservience to or neglect by husbands. But these differences were overshadowed by the women's shared sadness for the harsh conditions of their mothers' lives—conditions of farm or factory life, racism, dominating family members, poverty, unemployment, intrusion and neglect by social services, all of which attenuated their mothers' acts of love and recognition.[11] Regardless of their differences, the women were torn between gratitude and frustration toward mothers for not having met their deeply felt needs for recognition.

Some women expressed anger more than sadness, while others focused more on their ambivalence or guilt.[12] Ola remembered crying for herself and her mother:

> I couldn't go to school much because my mother was having childrens so much so that I had to stay out of school and help her. I used to hate to see her get pregnant again, me knowing that I wouldn't be going to school much that year and her getting more and more sad. I used to cry myself to sleep about that, thinking about her and me not going to school. I'm not saying that I don't love my momma, we's very close, but her being pregnant so much was hard on me.

Ola's sorrow is echoed by other African American women who have written about their childhoods. For example, Ann Moody (who came of age at the same time as Ola in the rural South) writes about the costs of her mother's repeated pregnancies:

> Again Mama started crying every night. . . . When I heard Mama crying at night, I felt so bad. She wouldn't cry until we were all in bed and she thought we were sleeping. Every night I would lie awake for hours listening to her sobbing quietly in her pillow. The bigger she got the more she cried, and I did too. (1968: 46)

Joanne held back tears as she described the difficulties her mother faced raising three children with little help from Joanne's father. Coming to terms with the difference between idealized versions of maternal love and her own demanding and often troubled real mother was difficult:

> It is hard for me to believe how much responsibility I had as a child. I can remember fixing my own breakfast in grade school while my mother stayed in bed. I used to wish I had one of those mothers who came to school with cookies and all that kind of thing. But I was at home fixing my own breakfasts and dinners for me and my brother and sister. I'm not saying that I expected my mother to do more than she did, she worked hard raising us, and she couldn't be

expected to do any more than she did. But to be honest I wish it had been different, you know?

Both Ola and Joanne later explained that in retrospect, even though they might have wished for more attention and affection, their mothers' physical care and mere survival were acts of maternal love.

Kate struggled with her guilt toward her mother, seeing herself as having been formed by, even as she battled against, her mother's teachings, modeling, and values. She told about one particularly injurious school incident that in her words still "has a hold" on her and for which she feels tremendous regret about having, in her view, harmed her mother. As she began to tell her story, Kate asked me to turn the tape recorder off, saying that she still had some "strong feelings" about the event, especially regarding her mother. After turning off the tape recorder I moved from the chair to the couch. Kate observed this unintentional move on my part and said she appreciated my moving closer so that I could better "hold her story" as she "let go of it." Upon finishing her story, Kate said she wished we had taped it. We agreed that I would return the next week to record the story so that she could "listen to it every now and again."[13]

I was struck by the gripping image of her story as something she or I might "hold"—the story as an object of her inner life that she carried in her head, an object she invested with projected images of her mother. In a sense, Kate's story was like a transitional object, helping her to move past but still hold onto her mother.[14]

Kate began her story by chronicling the events that led to her exclusion from the school's honor society. To take part in the induction ceremony, students were required to wear special clothing, shoes, and a cap. Kate knew her parents could not afford these items, so she asked the principal if she could wear clothes and shoes that she already owned. Kate could not stop crying as she described watching the principal remove her name from the poster board commemorating the honor students.

> Well I guess, the principal said to my mother that we could borrow the things. But my mother never did let us borrow anything and she never let nobody borrow anything from us. You see, 'cause she just believe that we should get along with what we got. And whatever we have we should make that good. There was other childrens too the same way, but they was lucky enough to borrow the clothes and they never confronted the principal. I was the one, I reckon, I was the odd one. I should never have said anything [crying again]. And then my mother, if she'd a pursued it a little bit more, instead of letting it go on and keeping me out of it [crying]. She told me, "Anything else, I promise you I will," 'cause she saw I was hurting. For graduation she paid for my cap and gown, you had to rent that.

> She told me that she regretted it, but I just wanted her to talk up
> and tell the principal what was right. I acted ugly towards my
> mother and I shouldn't have. I regret it to the day now that I think
> it over.

Kate admired her mother's values about and success at being self-
reliant. But at the same time, she was pained by her mother's subservience to the principal's authority. Kate struggled to resolve her
ambivalence and talked about how this dilemma continued to resonate
in her own dealings with people who tried to subordinate her. How could
she free herself from feelings of guilt and sadness toward her mother?
How could she understand rather than blame her mother for not speaking up for what was right? How could she reduce the hold of this story so
that she could view herself in relation to (m)other in new ways? Years
after the incident, Kate re-evaluated her mother's decision without
resentment or anger but still full of regret, viewing her mother's subservience as, in part, a costly act of maternal love.[15]

Patricia Hill Collins (1990) discusses the many difficulties black mothers face in raising daughters who must learn to be strong in the face of
oppression. She cites many compelling accounts of African American
women's retrospective evaluations of their mothers' acts of maternal
love and sacrifice, which as children, they were unable to appreciate.
Lilly told her story with more ambivalence than those reported by
Collins. After her father's death, Lilly's mother suffered from what Lilly
called temper spells and was unable to serve as a source of encouragement or confirmation for her daughter's school achievements. As a
result, Lilly said she looked to her teachers, whom she felt ignored her
needs because she was dark-skinned. Years later, Lilly still grappled
with torn feelings about an incident in which she felt denied a sense of
her own rightful (and hard-earned) achievement:

> We was in the 4H club. You know, we did sewing and cooking. We
> did everything they normally do in 4H club, but we also wrote little
> stories. They was going to give a program in the auditorium in
> Raleigh one year. And we had to write a story about the first thing
> that we had made. I wrote one on this dress that I was going to
> make and I read it to the class. Well, they gave mine to the peoples
> who would go through them to accept the ones that were going to
> be on the program. And they took mines and took my sister's too.
> That morning I got up and was all excited. I got all dressed to go
> and momma was going to cook. I was to crack a bowl of eggs for
> her but I dropped them all. So we didn't get to go to the program.
> So I got out of 4H. I didn't care too much about wanting to be in it
> no more. Well I, [long pause] maybe if the teachers would have
> really took up a lot of time with me I could have continued. I think

things would have turned out better, you know, if the teachers had got me to continue.

Lilly was reluctant to talk about her feelings toward her mother, but she confessed that, like her mother, she too suffered from "temper spells" that had impeded her happiness and success in life. Lilly, however, had sought treatment (she was diagnosed as being depressed) for her spells and related headaches, treatment which had proven effective. She described her social worker as a "life saver" and said she felt badly that her mother had not been afforded the same.

Helen, from Philadelphia, also struggled with ambivalence toward her mother, whose decision not to enroll her in a school for "bright kids" was still cause for resentment.[16] While she made it a point to say that she no longer blames her mother, she said she continues to feel bad when she gets angry:

> When the teacher called my mother and told her that I should go to a different school that was for bright kids, my mother said she wasn't going to let me transfer to a school so far away from home no matter how much better it was. She said she didn't feel it was safe. It is not that I blame my mother, but I'm sure my life would be different if I had gone to the other school. It took me a long time to get over that, I still feel bad when I get angry with my mother, but I think she could have encouraged me and things might have turned out better for me. But then I didn't push either, I was worried about not having friends at the new school and I didn't want to leave my old friends.

When I asked Helen why her mother thought the school was not safe, she explained, matter of factly, that it was in a predominantly black neighborhood. Aware of Helen's activism in a multiracial coalition of parents lobbying for a new high school, I asked her if she had ever considered that the effects of racism had impeded her schooling.[17] She thought for a moment and then replied, "I just never thought about it that way, but I guess you could say that."

In another case, Tina recalled an incident that touched off strong feelings that she (like Helen) wished she didn't harbor toward her mother. During the spring of her freshman year, as a scholarship student at a prestigious Catholic school for girls, she was called down to the Mother Superior's office to explain why her tuition had not been paid. Worried about asking her mother for the money, Tina decided to make up a story about how she had been thrown out of school. Recalling the incident was painful for Tina, and she said angrily, raising her voice:

> Why did you have to make me remember all this? [She shut off the tape recorder.] I don't like to think about my mother like this, but how could she not have known about the tuition bill?

I felt threatened by her anger and guilty at the suggestion that perhaps I was responsible for her strong feelings.[18] I quickly said I was sorry for having upset her and that I knew how much she cared for her mother. But as I started to put the tape recorder away, Tina stopped me, saying, "I need to get this off my chest." She turned the tape recorder back on and proceeded to describe in vivid detail several childhood disappointments. Tina said she was proud of the ways she was like her mother, especially her self-reliance and stoicism when dealing with life's hardships. She had learned from her mother how to "get by" and "get on" with her life, not to "cry over spilt milk." Under her mother's tutelage, Tina had learned to split off and defend against certain emotions, particularly feelings of sadness about a loss, because "dwelling on things never helps anyone."

Tina's story echoed one told by Carolyn Steedman of her own South London working-class childhood and her relationship to her mother, from whom she learned that "tears are cheap," that it is important to "'get by'; the phrase that picks up after all difficulty," because "no one gives you anything in this world" (Steedman 1986: 1–2, 31). As Steedman's story unfolds, we learn that there are costs attached to "'getting by' without empathic mothering" (196), a point that Tina, as well as many other women I interviewed, would affirm.[19] At the end of our conversation, Tina noted that it was she who was expected to be empathic toward her mother and not the other way around. She said she can't imagine her children protecting her in the same way she protected her mother. For this she remains upset, but resolved that she will "make things different for her own children."

DEFINING A SELF BY
SPLITTING THE (M)OTHER

In most contemporary versions of child development, the mother-child bond is understood as necessarily conflictual, generating deep-seated ambivalent feelings within the child toward her maternal caregiver. Conventional wisdom holds that in the course of development, children must learn that they cannot always have what they want, and that it is a mother's duty to teach this hard lesson of life. Children are more or less expected to express both loving and hateful feelings toward maternal caregivers who stand in the way of their desires. While each culture has its own social rules and conventions about what these denials will be and how they will be enforced, all children are said to experience loss, exclusion, and the sense of being cut off from what they desire.

Psychologically and in terms of self-definition, the child's first and essential exclusion is from the mother. Analysts point to varied cultural and psychological tools that children use to form a differentiated self. For example, the cultural representation of mothers as benevolent

and/or destructive (the wicked stepmother and the good fairy god-
mother) speak to children's simultaneous love and rage toward their
maternal caregivers.[20] From a somewhat different perspective, Melanie
Klein (1975) has argued that from early infancy, the child splits the
mother as "good" or "bad" as a way to deal with opposing experiences of
gratification and frustration. As a necessary part of a healthy development, the child seeks to repair feelings of guilt for having harbored
destructive fantasies toward the mother. Or as Margaret Mahler (1975)
argued, children develop fantasies of evil maternal figures or project a
"bad" mother image onto another caretaker to protect themselves from
their destructive feelings toward their own mothers. From still another
perspective, Freud theorized that in order to maintain a view of mother
as sexually pure, children learn to project their sensual feelings onto
another. In the case of men whom he diagnosed as having the
"mother/whore" syndrome, these feelings were projected onto a
degraded object (Suleiman 1988: 28). For all these theorists, healthy
development requires reworking the split images of (m)other into a
holistic picture so that the child emerges with a stable sense of self and
an ability to relate meaningfully to others.

Early mother-infant interactions are filled with both the joys and
pains of mutual recognition. From the mother's perspective, the baby
comes from her, yet is unknown to her; multiple emotions accompany
the moment when I recognize you as my baby who recognizes me.[21] This
recognition entails a sense of loss that you are no longer inside/part of
me; you are no longer my fantasy of you; we are no longer physically and
psychically one; I can no longer take care of you simply by taking care of
myself. According to Jessica Benjamin (1988), many mothers put this
side of reality out of consciousness, declaring the child a "dream" child;
taking care of the child is viewed as part of taking care of oneself.[22]
Meanwhile, the child's early experience of mutual recognition with the
mother is wrought with similar conflicts and emotionally charged
images and fantasies. Children experience pleasure, anxiety, and fear as
well as the fantasy that, even though I am no longer part of you, you will
still take care of me, anticipating and fulfilling my every need. The child
also puts aside certain realities about mother's subjectivity, declaring
her as omnipotent, fearsome, and/or perfect. Meaningful differentiation
occurs when both parties can move between realities and fantasies
rather than settling into one or the other; when both mother and child
can sustain rather than resolve these doubled images and emotions
about self in relation to other.

From this perspective, then, learning to differentiate self from
(m)other occurs in relationship. The child grows into a functioning
human being by learning to distinguish between self ("me") and the
(m)other ("not-me") and by learning to view the (m)other as a separate
being with her own interests and activities that sometimes diverge from

what the child wants at any particular moment. This shift toward the (m)other as distinct and a subject in her own right, having an existence apart from the child's own needs for gratification, involves some conflict and struggle. Indeed, recognizing the (m)other as a subject is possible only to the extent that the child is not dominated by urgent needs or by mother's own sense of exclusive subjectivity. [23]

Given that women are assigned the responsibility of early caregiving, they become for children the "other" or object. According to Nancy Chodorow (1989: 104), insofar as we understand child development and the process of differentiation from the viewpoint of the "infant as the (developing) self, then the mother will be perceived (or depicted) only as an object." She goes on to explain that this view of the self-making process changes if we accord mothers their own selfhood:[24]

> From a feminist perspective, perceiving the particularity of the mother must involve according the mother her own selfhood. This is a necessary part of the development process, though it is also often resisted and experienced only conflictually and partially. Throughout life, perceptions of the mother fluctuate between perceiving her particularity and selfhood and perceiving her as a narcissistic extension, a not-separate other whose sole reason for existence is to gratify one's own wants and needs. (Chodorow 1989: 104)

The women's stories about their mothers in relation to school reflect this personal conflict, which is bound up with cultural images and expectations about mothers, often referred to as the "myth of maternal omnipotence," to which I now turn.

THE MYTH OF MATERNAL OMNIPOTENCE

Cultural beliefs about women's "natural" talents for caregiving are said to be part of the social organization of families (Benjamin 1988, 1994; Chodorow 1978, 1989; Chodorow and Contratto 1982; Dinnerstein 1976; Johnson 1988) and are built into the marketplace, where service work is predominantly done by women (disproportionately women of color) who, as providers, are expected to feign caring (Hochschild 1983; Tronto 1989).[25] The regrettable effect of these myths is that women are divided against each other and, ultimately, against themselves. Women are said to internalize controlling cultural images about "good" mothering, learning to judge themselves and other women based on how well they measure up to an externally defined ideal (whether defined as the domestic "cookies and milk" kind of mom, the "super strong, self-sacrificing" kind of mom, the career, super-woman kind of mom, etc.).[26] One of the most pernicious outcomes of the idealized image of women as naturally nurturing, all-loving, and all-knowing mothers has been the division of women along class, race, and marital lines. Poor and single women have historically suffered for their inability to abide by idealized norms of motherhood, often losing their children to so-called child-saving agencies because they appear not to be all-loving or all-knowing about their children's best interests (Gordon 1988). Meanwhile, the ability of white, upper middle-class women to achieve the maternal ideal has been set at the expense of other women as mothers and their children.

Obscured by these myths, images, and fantasies is the reality that women mother under situations and circumstances that are not of their own choosing, nor within their (individual) power to change.[27] The myth of maternal omnipotence makes it appear that individual women are solely responsible for what happens to children. As a result, the politics of caregiving go unchallenged. In Valerie Polakow's words, "The ideology of mother care and *attachment* has effectively served to conceal and rationalize a public policy of *detachment*" (1993: 40). In the next chapter I explore how this myth both inhibited and fueled the women's education.

The Push and
Pull of School

[Eight]

When Margaret arrived in my class in Philadelphia, she read at a fourth grade level, which is considered "functionally illiterate." During her placement test she said that she hated the term "adult illiteracy," but acknowledged that she fit that classification and that she was pleased to be enrolled in a "pre-GED" class.[1]

Margaret explained on the first day of class that as a child she had had a neurological problem that had caused her facial muscles to relax on one side. This caused her speech to blur, and she had been placed in special education classes where she was taught "basic life skills." "They thought I was retarded and didn't belong with normal kids. My mother didn't want to say I was retarded, but she told me not to expect to graduate. She said a diploma doesn't prove you're smart, only that you went to school." At the age of thirty-eight and with her speech still slightly impaired, Margaret was pursuing her long-time dream of getting a high school diploma so she could show her two children, husband, and mother that she was "worth listening to."

A year later, Margaret took the first of the five tests that comprise the high school equivalency (GED) exam and passed by two points. She was proud to have taken the test with the rest of her classmates, saying it made her feel like she was a "normal" student. But she had not done as well as she had hoped. She confided to me that maybe her mother had been right all along. I was surprised by her self-doubt. As her teacher I was amazed at the progress she had made. I knew that, as a special education student, Margaret had not been exposed to much of an academic curriculum and certainly not to high-school-level coursework. Moreover, like many of her classmates who had been out of school for two decades, just meeting the demands of regular homework and preparing for exams was a daunting task. In my view, her greatest obstacle was her conviction that she was "retarded." I asked Margaret if she would consider being tested for learning disabilities and, after several months of cajoling, she agreed. (Unlike most of the women in the program, Margaret had health insurance that would cover the costs of these tests.) I hoped that the test results would enlighten us both about how to continue with Margaret's studies.

I accompanied Margaret to the high-rise Center City building where she was to be tested, and returned with her the following week for the results. The psychologist began by saying that there was no question that Margaret could get a high school diploma—her IQ score confirmed that. He went on to explain that she did have some short-term memory problems, which could account for her reading comprehension and math difficulties. He suggested tutoring to complement her classroom work and said she could improve her scores by taking the exam untimed. He pointed to a poster of famous men (Einstein was featured) who had what he liked to call "learning differences" similar to Margaret's. He hoped that nothing would interfere with her learning goals now that she could put her anxieties about being "retarded" to rest.

Throughout the meeting I kept an eye on Margaret, who remained silent. Even when the psychologist asked her directly if she had any questions or concerns, she did not respond. I was surprised by this and wondered how she was taking what I considered to be the good news. As we stood to walk out I noticed that she was fighting back tears. She wept in the lobby and as I reached to comfort her she grabbed hold of me. She cried quietly and I felt her body shake. Her raw emotions took me off guard. Finally, she said:

> I can't believe that for all those years my mother believed I was retarded. I didn't really have to go to that school, I never had to go. All those years, I thought, [long pause and more tears] all those years are wasted and I'll never have them back.

On the trip back to her house, Margaret talked about her troubled relationship with her mother, which had been exacerbated by Margaret's return to school. Margaret thought her mother was threatened by her attempts to get a high-school diploma because it would prove her wrong. But now she reinterpreted her mother's lack of support. Perhaps her mother had doubted the school's view of her as retarded but had been unable to challenge the authorities. Perhaps

Margaret's return to school and her success had reminded her mother of her inability to advocate for Margaret when she was young. Margaret feared that if she related what the psychologist had said, it would make her mother feel worse about the past and, consequently, about Margaret's going to school now. Margaret wavered between blaming and understanding her mother. How could she hold her mother responsible for "knowing what only the psychologist is trained to know," and yet "how could she not have known the truth about me?"

Margaret's relief to have tested in the normal range was overwhelmed by frustration, pain, and loss. The future looked just about as bleak as the past. Her mother had recently suffered a heart attack and, needing Margaret's daily attention, was to move in with Margaret's family. "I guess I really can't tell her anything now," Margaret concluded. "Her heart is bad and this could really kill her. It will be easier for me to not tell her than for her to hear about it."

This tragedy tells us a great deal about both Margaret's and her mother's relationship to school and how they learned about their personal limits and social standing. Although Margaret had always longed to be recognized as "normal," she still did not hold school officials responsible for misdiagnosing her medical condition or for labeling her in such a way that her education had been impeded. During her sixteen years no teacher or school official had noticed the full range of her capabilities.[2] It was as if she took it for granted that a working-class child with disabilities would be marginalized, cast off by the school system. Instead, and even though she tried hard not to, she blamed her mother for her lost childhood and opportunities.

After Margaret's mother moved in, it became increasingly difficult for Margaret to attend class, and she was unable to find a tutor whom she felt she could trust "not to talk down" to her. Her adolescent children got into trouble at school and with the law, which drained her emotionally and financially. Only her husband kept encouraging her to continue her studies.[3] Margaret decided to quit the program; the "time was not right." Focusing on her diploma now would be "selfish."

Margaret coped with the news of her intellectual abilities by splitting herself. In one sense, Margaret could be said to have set aside a newly discovered part of herself, her intellect, in favor of her more social side, the side with an interest in relationships and need to maintain them. She often talked about this social, caregiving side of herself with pride. She was a good mother and a good waitress, despite people's persistently harsh judgment of her. She was proud that she had married, was successful in getting her children through school, and had earned the respect of many of her neighbors for being generous (she often loaned people money when they most needed it). She described this part of herself as actively supported by members of her family, sometimes at the expense of her own needs and desires. Margaret characterized her relationships with her mother, husband, and children in terms of only what they needed from her, not also what she needed from them. Interestingly, when faced with the very real possibility that she could develop another side of her self, such as her intellectual mastery, Margaret's guilt and fears about others—especially her mother—held her back. She worried that her mother would reject her if she worked to actualize "the truth" about herself. She also feared that by acting on her desires she might destroy her mother. Insofar as her feelings and needs were at odds with those of her mother's, she felt inhibited (and perhaps protected) from experiencing an integrated, "authentic" sense of self.[4] Above all, Margaret's limited sense of her own agency and authenticity, her inability to realize her potential, was tied up with her conflicted feelings about her mother in a way that denied the injustice and inadequacies of her schooling and the damage it caused her. Her mother may have been *a* problem, but she was not *the* problem, and this Margaret was unable to perceive.

Of the many Philadelphia and North Carolina women I interviewed, Margaret's experience was unique in degree but not in kind. The others too had been taught about their personal limits and social standing in schools that had failed to recognize their potential. They too harbored unresolved feelings about mothers and teachers whom they sometimes knowingly and sometimes unknowingly held accountable for what school and society had denied them. They too felt torn about competing sides of themselves and questioned whether and in what ways they were "schoolsmart." Like Margaret, they viewed a high school diploma as proof against that which school had made them doubt: that they were "worth seeing or listening to." And, like Margaret, they experienced as threatening, if not bad, their desires to be visible and to have a voice. More often than not, they too characterized their educational goals as "selfish," or worried that the time was not right for them to act on their potential. Meanwhile, they faced the same set of obstacles as Margaret— economic, social, familial, and personal—obstacles that only a few of the women I interviewed would be able to overcome.

Margaret's experience was typical in yet another way. Narrating her life story, she emphasized and took pride in the social side of herself, the part of her that enjoyed and depended upon relationships with others. Indeed, this social, relational side of women's selfhood framed how the women narrated their childhood ambitions, school decisions, and current reasons for returning to school. Recall, for example, Joanne's decision to leave school so her siblings could graduate and Beverly's decision to quit school and go to work so that her son could attend school in clothes that would not bring him ridicule or shame. This social side also framed the women's "common sense," which they defined and valued in terms of how well they were able to care for others. This narration of women's capabilities is not surprising; it is an aspect of women's self-hood that society praises. It is what women learn that makes them appealing, but, as the women's life stories attest, it is a costly lesson.

The women's stories illustrate that they often felt conflicted in their efforts to establish or sustain relationships. The problem was not that they had relational needs or that these needs took precedence over others. The problem was that the repression or thwarting of other needs (e.g., to be autonomous, aggressive, or intellectual) extracted such a high price from them. Indeed, women in both groups spoke of their "social selves" as being partial, if not at times false.[5] This was especially evident in their descriptions of teachers' pets—how girls would falsely represent themselves to gain teachers' approval. Recall, for example, Helen's discomfort in being a teacher's pet, how she felt she had "conned" the teachers into believing she was someone she wasn't. Indeed, the ability and/or willingness of some girls to represent themselves falsely as "good" and "feminine" was what the women resented about school as a pet contest. The problem with this false representation of self is that it divided women against each other and internally against themselves.

The women's stories also highlight the harsh conditions under which their social selves were formed, conditions that all too often presented the women with false or self-negating choices. For example, recall how Kate and Betty from North Carolina talked about their unresolved feelings toward their mothers, whom each viewed as presenting a false sense of self (i.e., being nice) in the face of discrimination. Or consider Linda's remorse and self-blame for having taken an aggressive stance toward her white employer who had treated her with so little respect. Conditions of oppression, abuse, and material deprivation served to fragment the women's selves, making it difficult for them to achieve a sense of their authentic or best self. These conditions assisted the psychological splitting off (in part disavowing and in part protecting themselves from) those aspects of themselves that were deemed socially unacceptable or threatening to others.

These same conflicts about different aspects of women's identities fueled the women's return to school. And, once again, in narrating their life decisions, the women stressed their social selves. They left school to attend to the needs of others and now they returned to school to do the same—to be a good role model for their children. The overwhelming response to my question, "Why are you returning to school," was the general statement "to better myself." Of the 200 women with whom I spoke, 80 percent added that they were returning to school to become "better mothers."[6] More often than not, being a "better mother" meant being better able to meet their children's educational needs. To be a good role model for their children was the most common reason the women gave for returning to school. As Joanne put it:

My mother thinks I am crazy for coming back to school; she doesn't see the point and thinks I should be home with my kids. I try to explain that my going to school is good for my kids; I'm being a role model for them and I feel good about that.

If they were not taking the lead by being a role model, at the very least they did not want to be "left behind" by their children or to feel small in their eyes. Many women confessed to feeling inadequate, unable to help their children with homework assignments. As Louise said:

Sometimes I say that I am too tired or have a headache, but the real reason is that I'm afraid to show her that I don't know. I could handle the work when she was in grammar school, but now, she's way beyond me. Maybe we will graduate high school together—wouldn't that be something?

Conflicts such as these remind us once again of the tenacious and damaging links between schooling and mothering discourses.[7] That the women saw themselves as key to but inadequate for the successful education of their children is one of the most insidious and effective mechanisms regulating and reproducing social inequality. Part of the day-to-day dynamics of class transmission through education is that individual mothers are blamed, and they in turn blame themselves for the institutional failure of schools to educate disadvantaged children.

These dynamics are insidious in two ways. First, a child's successful schooling *should* depend upon a great deal more than the efficacy of any individual mother. That is the promise of public education. People are quick to recognize that schools, by themselves, cannot be expected to meet the intellectual, social, and emotional needs of all children, especially those who are poor. But neither can individual mothers meet all these needs. As long as the responsibility for monitoring children's schooling rests on individual mothers and is not shared across family and community members, school officials, and teachers, as well as social service agencies of all sorts, then working-class and poor children's school success will be compromised. Second, this focus on each individual mother's responsibilities for her children's education encourages women to view their own educational goals as "selfish." As Doris admitted:

I guess you could say my reasons are selfish—I have always wanted to get my high school diploma. I just don't feel complete without it. You know, when my girls were little, I put myself on the shelf. Now that they are old enough, I can think about doing some things that I need to do for me. But mostly, it's for them.

To put one's self on the shelf, like a book that perhaps one day one will have the time, permission, or even the obligation to read, is a fitting metaphor for these working-class women's relationship to school.

Lessons from the Women's Stories

Americans are said to lack class consciousness, with the overwhelming majority identifying themselves as "middle-class." Those who have not yet moved into the middle-class can aspire to do so because it is believed that individuals who work hard enough, who are ambitious and skillful can rise above all obstacles. Once referred to as "American exceptionalism," the contemporary version of this notion is illustrated by the Nike advertisement that calls upon Americans to "just do it."[1] This celebration of freedom, individualism, and the quest to "become somebody" is coupled with a pernicious cultural ignorance and denial of social inequalities, violence, and structures of domination. In this way, the American elite is able to convince those who aren't that status, privilege, and power are of little or no significance. Indeed, their ascendancy as rulers depends upon the appearance that color, class, ethnicity, and gender do not determine who counts as a "somebody" or who attains the American dream.

How is this accomplished? The women's stories point to the crucial role of *schools*. Their accounts show that schools divide students into persons of different types—for example, those who were and those who were not teachers' pets. School denied but at the same time protected certain students' unearned advantages related to class, gender, and skin color in ways that made the women doubt their own value, voice, and abilities. Their stories stress the formative, painful, and enduring effects of this school denial and self-doubt. Insofar as the women were degraded by teachers and school officials for their speech, styles of dress, deportment, physical appearances, skin color, and forms of knowledge, they learned to recognize as "intelligent" or "valuable" only the styles, traits, and knowledge possessed by the economically advantaged students. Their testimonies equate teachers and other students' cultural capital with the following distinctions of privilege: forms of knowledge and ability validated by school; white, middle-class feminine behaviors and appearances (e.g., submissiveness, obedience and attractiveness that won the pets approval from the teachers); light skin color; and urban or suburban mannerisms and styles of speech. Most important, the women viewed those who possessed such cultural capital as entitled to their superior positions. That the women continued to feel diminished or subordinated when in the presence of those with greater social standing, such as teachers, doctors, and social workers, and also with the men in their lives, is testimony to the powerful role of school.

We learned that the women found creative ways to survive school's degradation and disdain—what Bourdieu and Passeron (1977) refer to as "symbolic violence." Some women survived through silence and self-imposed invisibility and others by speaking up against teachers or developing an "attitude toward authority."[2] In some cases the women refused the logic of school, as when certain Philadelphia women refused to act "cutesie" or to censor themselves and when the North Carolina women recognized as "real intelligence" their abilities to outwit or endure the effects of white racism. In other cases the women accepted school's logic as valid, for example, when the Philadelphia women joined the commercial track, saying that they "knew what they were good at" and that secretarial work was the best means to apply their skills or when the North Carolina women embraced the label of "slow learner"—a label they adopted despite an awareness that infrequent and interrupted school attendance as well as poverty had stalled their learning. In both cases, the women sought to protect and defend themselves against the injurious judgments of other students, teachers, and school officials.

We learned that the Philadelphia and North Carolina women coped differently with school's symbolic violence, and these differences can be explained, in part, by each specific school context and mission. That the Philadelphia women were torn between asserting and censoring their *voices* reflected the arbitrary and authoritarian modes of discipline that characterized the urban school context and its mission to prepare students for working-class jobs. The urban high school, with its class- and gender-based tracking system, identified the Philadelphia women as members of the "commercial track" or "kitchen practice," whose failure or success depended upon their obedience to teachers' authority. And if they spoke up and complained about the future that they had been persuaded they faced, they were told that it was their "choice" to enroll in that track to begin with.[3] Meanwhile, the Philadelphia women did not look up to their white, middle-class, female teachers. These teachers disregarded, ignored, and/or punished them for the family and work demands they shouldered as working-class girls. The school mission split off and devalued the very skills and qualities necessary for working-class survival, specifically those skills related to caregiving. As a result, the Philadelphia women could not fully embrace schooling as a way to establish knowledge and authority about what mattered in their lives.

By contrast, the North Carolina women felt torn between asserting and censoring their *visibility* and this reflected the effects of racial discrimination and violence, coupled with the school's racial uplift mission. The rural-community high school was more a part of family and community life, and this allowed the North Carolina women to integrate school values and knowledge into their feminine identities. Moreover, the North Carolina women identified with their black female teachers, even those who, as emissaries of racial uplift, showed disdain for students and parents who had "country ways." Their relationships with teachers were mixed with feelings of love, dependence, shame, and rejection. They fondly remembered those "good" teachers who had taken special care of their needs and expressed bitterness and resentment toward those "bad" ones who had failed to encourage them either because their parents were not professionals or, worse yet, because they were darker-skinned. At the same time, and despite the efforts of some "good" teachers, the overarching message they received from these racially segregated schools was that young, black girls were not worth educating. In their eyes, white society (not the rural schools the North Carolina women attended) had slated them for work as domestics; as young girls they had realized that education would not alter this fate.

Women in both school contexts were willing to place the blame for their school failure on certain "bad" teachers, but they were also prone to idealize the "good" teachers. They attributed any sign of their school success to a teacher who had taken a "special interest" in them, who cared for, defended or protected them, sometimes in ways that their own mothers had been unable to do. Unpacking these stories of teacher omnipotence and the women's mixed feelings toward their mothers illustrates how schools promote social inequalities in unseen ways.

Their stories drew upon a world of women—teachers, mothers, daughters—who were judged and who judged themselves according to how successfully they met the demands of school. These judgments and the range of emotions they evoked—anger, guilt, defensiveness, sorrow, gratitude, love, vulnerability—were integral to the women's interpretations about why they ended up in the social position they did. Such judgments and emotions continue to underwrite the myth of meritocracy—that anyone who is raised well, who is loved enough and feels good enough about themselves—can rise above the hardships imposed by poverty, racism, and sexism. Mutually reinforcing cultural images of and personal longings for the perfect caregiver keep people from realizing the full scope and impact of social inequality.

The women's stories expose the gendered organization of school with its structural, but hidden reliance on *ideal*, not real, women. This gendered arrangement directs people's attention toward the qualities of the caretakers and away from the conditions under which children are (and are not) cared for and educated. This unseen but profound dimension of injustice in our educational system comes at great cost to women. Being unable to be both schoolsmart and motherwise is but one example of this cost.

I have stressed the psychological defense of splitting which has the weight of cultural images behind it as key to how the women survived school's symbolic violence and resolved their conflicts related to school. Images that divided and privileged some groups of people against others (the somebodies" and the "bums," the "good" and "bad" schoolgirls) were often projected onto others as a means to shore the women up or to protect them from feeling vulnerable. Following the lead of the women themselves, I have focused on conflicts between their "true" and "false," idealized and devalued feminine selves in school, and the recurring, embattled comparisons that the women made between themselves and other female students as well as their mixed feelings about their teachers and mothers. Such splitting was assisted by specific institutional arrangements that divided labor, knowledge, and people into opposite types and conferred the dominance of one group over another: the class-based division of manual versus mental labor; the racially segregated workplace that put the "blacks in the back" against the "whites up front"; and the gendered mission of school that fosters "productive" over "reproductive" knowledge while setting "manly" traits of reason against "womanly" traits of emotion. These institutional splits fragmented the women's self-understandings and conferred dominance of one side over other sides of themselves, impeding their development. These are important, if partial pieces of the picture of how identities are shaped in and through schooling in ways that undermine working-class women's education.[4]

These conflicts expand and complicate explanations for how schools shortchange girls. Despite the obstacles that schools present to young women's developing selves, schools still outpace other institutions in encouraging girls, regardless of race or class, to express, if not fully realize, their intellect, ambitions and autonomy. I suggest that by returning to school the women were asserting (even if unconsciously) those elements of their identities that are still most forbidden for women. As such, their desires and actions should not be minimized, nor should they be perceived as having uncritically embraced the myth of meritocracy. In my view, this was the deeper meaning and the more radical significance of the women's educational pursuits. Having been encouraged to stifle the development of some aspects of themselves for the sake of others, these women returned to school to regain the visibility, voices and autonomy denied them.

GENDER, RACE, AND CLASS
IDENTITIES AND STRUGGLES

The women's interpretations of their lives illustrate how race, class, and gender direct and deflect one another; indeed, this is the drama of their tales. A striking feature of this drama is the way in which the Philadelphia and North Carolina women differed in their explanations of why they failed to attain the American dream. Whereas the Philadelphia women emphasized why they, as *individuals*, had rejected upward mobility (either through education or marriage), the North Carolina women stressed why they, as members of a *group*, had been rejected. This individual/group distinction points up the importance of identifying the conditions under which people feel the need to highlight their individuality or their group membership as they seek recognition and respect in the world. Knowing more about these conditions could deepen our understanding of identity politics.

The women's stories show that they arrived at different identities through their participation in schools, families, communities, and workplaces. There was no single context that determined or set into stone these identities. Rather, each context, organized with its own goals, structures, modes of control, and regimes of authority, gave rise to the women's overlapping, yet distinct ways of seeing themselves in relation to others. For example, the North Carolina women arrived at their identities and self valuations in subordination to and resistance against several communities—the larger white racist community; the "urban," "professional," and middle-class community of blacks who "looked down" on them because of their "country ways"; and the community of black men who could get them to "lose" their "(common) senses." Meanwhile, the Philadelphia women experienced a similar phenomenon. In solidarity with other white, working-class women, they arrived at their identities in subordination to white, working-class men, whose "common sense" they invested with more value than their own. They also defined themselves and their knowledge against the authority of white, middle-class, female teachers who overlooked the contributions that the Philadelphia women had made as girls to working-class survival. Women in both groups arrived at their gender, race, and class identities through contested *community* as well as *individual* relationships.[5]

We also learn that the women's stories, views, and actions cannot be framed in either/or terms, as evidence of either resistance or compliance. For example, consider the North Carolina women's experiences as domestic service workers—their refusal to accept mistreatment, as well as their self-blame about being in a position where employers could treat them "like dirt." Or consider the Philadelphia women's "attitudes toward authority" and their decisions to drop out of school as both a rejection and an acceptance of their destiny as "secretaries, mothers, nurses, and nuns"—choices they did not regret but hoped their daughters would be able to avoid. Casting these understandings as "false consciousness" would not do justice to the full scope and meaning of the women's experiences of social inequality.

These stories illustrate that identity formation and struggles are about the personal choices people make, the doubts they express, the strategies they devise, and the efforts towards self-transformation that they take—what R.W. Connell calls the "practical politics" of personal lives (1987: 61). The practical politics of identity are grounded in and compelled by specific and situational contexts, not in some set of essential traits and attitudes. And this contingency is what fuels the possibility for social change.

STORIED SELVES: TOWARD A MORE UNIFIED UNDERSTANDING OF STORYTELLING, IDENTITY, AND SOCIAL CHANGE

"If I know anything, I know how to survive, how to remake the world in story," writes Dorothy Allison (1996: 4), a working-class, white woman born and raised in South Carolina. She writes about the power of storytelling to save lives; how, by telling how she survived years of childhood sexual abuse and domestic violence and listening to others recount the same, she has regained a sense of self-worth and value. Her book, *Two or Three Things I Know for Sure* expresses the same sense of narrative urgency found among the Philadelphia and North Carolina women in this study.

I have used the notion of *storied selves* to highlight this urgency and to acknowledge the women's desire to tell the story behind their survival and to account for their lack of social mobility. My other reason for using this notion has been to convey how cultural and personal images about credibility, value and power were bound up in ways of which the women were unaware and that served to keep existing power relations intact. My analysis of the women's stories has featured their persistent use of split, idealized, and devalued images of themselves and others as one way to illustrate how a "piece of the oppressor" gets "planted deep within each of us" (Lorde 1984: 123).[6] How these pieces of the oppressor—racism, sexism, elitism—take hold in varied ways, with varied force, and with varied costs attached for individuals requires a more unified analysis than currently exists of how selves and social identities are formed at both the personal and cultural level.

Three elements are necessary for developing such a more unified approach: 1) linking psychodynamic with structural processes; 2) taking an open, experiential, and bottom-up model of selfhood and social identity that allows for contradictory tendencies within the self, between self and others, and among members of overlapping communities; and 3) stressing the relational, reciprocal, and mutual sides to the process of identity formation and change. The women's stories show that selves and identities are mutually reinforcing processes— not fixed entities, essences, or categories. They became who they were not by learning a one-dimensional message that they were either working-class or middle-class; manly or womanly; white or black; schoolsmart or motherwise. Rather, they arrived at their senses of themselves by absorbing and attempting to resolve the mostly false oppositions between these categories. This conflict was made especially clear in the women's presentation of the "teacher's pet" contest. The choice between being a desirable object in the eyes of the teacher was at odds with being a desiring "subject" in their own eyes. The women's efforts to reconcile these oppositions, to feel whole and "true" to themselves, to be recognized for all sides of themselves in a society that routinely divides and privileges some people over others, fueled their desire for change.

Their stories also show that they became who they are not only by being "regulated or transformed *by*" an other, but also through "active exchange *with*" an other.[7] That people with power can impose themselves and their views upon less powerful people cannot be underestimated. But what people make of these impositions is subject to revision and change. This imposing, regulating view of identity formation was prominent in the women's stories about teachers whom they cast as all-knowing, all-powerful others. At the same time, the women's quest for mutual recognition—to be seen for who they were in their own right, as persons with complex motives and abilities—propelled their return to school.

Through the women's storytelling, we learn that life stories are about self-understandings and social identities; that these life stories are shaped by multiple structures of domination; and that life stories are shaped by the desire for mutual recognition. But there is a fourth, more visionary lesson: that telling life stories can provide impetus and direction for new ways of being and acting in the world. George Rosenwald writes about what might be considered a "better" life story, one that allows "new living action." He says:

> The "better" story is never cheaply bought. A narrative will lead to new actions and new narratives to the extent that it was hard won.

> The truth of a narrative is therefore not representational and not
> pragmatic but dialectical: the narrative is true in that it enshrines
> the toil of undoing repression and social perplexity— both forms of
> routinized suffering. (1992: 286)[8]

"Better" stories recognize forms of oppression and routinized suffering
that keep people stuck. "Better" stories also clarify power relations and
the costs of alternative actions. Many of the women I interviewed could-
n't give up the idea that their educational goals were "selfish," doubted
their intellectual capabilities, or viewed their desires for voice and visibility as bad. These self-doubts were forms of routinized suffering that
diminished the women's selves and limited their social actions. At the
same time, by returning to school, many women learned new things
about themselves, oftentimes making for a "better" story. Experiencing
school as an adult afforded for some the opportunity to re-visit and re-
interpret past feelings of powerlessness and inadequacy in the face of
teachers' authority. By becoming part of a classroom community where
life stories were exchanged and valued as part of the learning process,
the women often discovered that a person's story was too similar to be
dismissed as idiosyncratic, forcing other women to rethink how they had
arrived at their own sense of personal limitation and self-blame. Being
able to tell their stories to an audience that listened in new ways and
with different expectations freed many women to speak of secret or
forbidden longings (things considered "selfish"). Speaking not to husbands, children, or mothers—but to each other—many women came to
see these longings in a new, more positive light. A smaller number of
women achieved the goals they set out for themselves. For example,
Philadelphians Peggy and Joanne obtained their GEDs and enrolled in a
local, four-year college. Each eventually earned a college degree and
found a job related to her interests. Ola, from North Carolina, received
her GED on the same day that her daughter graduated high school. She
has become an important figure in her church, no longer afraid to
"speak up in public." Louise also earned her diploma and decided to take
early retirement from her job at the university. She is now attending
classes at a local community college, taking business courses so that she
can open a small business of her own.

   I do not mean to suggest that narrators' lives are automatically
improved by telling "better" stories. Telling "better" stories is a political
act which depends upon a community of supportive listeners, people
who can hear the stories in a way that is not blaming or discrediting.[9]
The American labor, civil rights, women's, welfare rights, and gay and
lesbian movements are all examples of political and cultural contexts
that have enabled and legitimated the telling of better stories. But the
exchange of such personal storytelling is risky; it creates anxiety
because, in telling our stories, we open ourselves up to feeling vulnera-

ble, to being rejected or devalued. Still, by choosing to believe that our story has value, we feel entitled to other people's respect. If we invest our stories with value and if they are well received by others, then we feel better about ourselves. Storytelling is Dorothy Allison's "cure for bitterness."[10] This is why "better" stories matter—they can make a difference in our personal lives and in our politics.

IMPLICATIONS FOR FEMINIST RESEARCH AND REFORM IN EDUCATION

Having listened to adult women call up the vivid details of their schoolgirl memories of being made painfully mindful of their class, color, and gender; having watched these women struggle to recover from emotional wounds and to let go of feelings that maintain a hold on them; having heard these women regretfully reflect on their mothers as an inevitable part of their school story and to hear them tell of their own determination as mothers to make a difference in their children's lives—having heard all this, I am not willing to give up on American public schools. I am not willing to accept what I consider to be a widespread cynicism and lack of imagination about what public education can and should be. If these women haven't lost faith in schools, in the power of education to change lives, then neither should we.

These stories have convinced me that there are no simple solutions, no quick fixes or easy answers for ameliorating social inequalities, domination, and symbolic violence in schools. Nonetheless, their stories point to paths that might be fruitful to explore and locations where advocacy might be most persuasive, and in this spirit I draw the following implications for educational research and reform.

ACTIVIST ETHNOGRAPHY

Before we can develop a fully informed and inspired platform for educational reform there is much more to learn about how students' selves and social identities are formed and transformed in different school settings. I believe that comparative ethnographic research holds much promise toward this end. The task, as I see it, is for educators to become activist ethnographers, in the broadest and best sense, systematically and empathically observing and documenting what children are doing, listening to what they are saying, and probing what they are feeling despite school practices that conspire to distort, mute, or silence what they know and have to say about themselves and the world around them.

Teachers who are already skillful participant observers can make use of their observations and the knowledge generated by other school ethnographies to inform their teaching methods. I am not suggesting that teachers take on an additional role, but rather, that the work teachers already do should be defined in new ways. The ethnographic "learning" and "doing" described by Shirley Brice Heath (1983) in her comparative study of a black and a white, working-class, southern community is an excellent model. She found that, with suitable information and a willingness to work collaboratively, teachers were keen observers and analysts of children's cultural practices, ways of speaking, and learning. These teachers were better able to recognize and validate the different language codes, knowledge, skills, and values children brought to the classroom, and this had a positive effect on students' achievement in school.

There are pockets of experience across the nation where teachers successfully broker among home, community, and school cultures in ways that enable children to acquire schoolwise knowledge and to decipher "codes of power" (Delpit 1995). We need to know more about these exemplary teachers and their successes, what choices they make, and what facilitates their work.

RETHINKING SCHOOL RELATIONSHIPS AND SUCCESS

The women's stories remind us that what is most memorable about school is not *what* is learned, but *how* we learn it. Unspoken and unresolved *emotions* (a taboo subject among most educators) and the ethical and political dimensions of relationships make a difference in the learning process. The women's memories about being or not being a teacher's pet; the scars left from having been publicly shamed; the fierce defensiveness and protectiveness they felt toward mothers who had been treated with disdain by school officials; the fond attachments to certain teachers who had treated them with special care—all these relationships and feelings profoundly shaped the women's identities, self-appraisals and self-valuations as learners.

The women's view of school as a series of embattled relationships compels me to agree with Frederick Erickson (1987:354) that the "politics of legitimacy, trust and assent" are key factors in ensuring children's success. Their distinct but overlapping versions of school as a "teacher's pet" contest is an especially telling illustration of the subtle ways that school can betray students' trust and legitimacy. Taking heed of these stories might lead some teachers to become more sensitive about how and in what ways they may be showing preferential treatment toward well-dressed, well-spoken, traditionally feminine, and lighter-skinned students. But changing individual teacher behavior is not enough. Institutional practices and policies that acknowledge and validate certain types of students at the expense of others create the conditions which impede the success of disadvantaged children and teach *all* children not to comprehend social inequality.

Programs for academically "gifted and talented" students in grades as early as kindergarten provide a case in point. I am opposed to these programs when they separate and idealize already privileged students at the expense of others. That white, middle-class students are overrepresented in the ranks of the gifted and talented goes without saying. I have three quarrels with these programs. First I am concerned that those students who are not selected are set up to view school as a no-win situation in which they experience themselves as unwilling, unable, or disqualified contenders for success. At risk of feeling either personally betrayed by the teachers or torn between being untrue to themselves or others, *most* students (because by definition only the *few* are recognized as gifted and talented) will come to accept their personal and social limits as inevitable. These students, like the women I interviewed, may learn to doubt whether they are schoolsmart and whether they can expect themselves to succeed. Second, I am concerned that those who are chosen will learn to view their success only as an individual achievement and not also related to their social privileges. Especially troubling is that by participating in these programs students may learn to objectify and deny recognition to those whom school has defined as being "less than" gifted or talented. Meanwhile, the few poor and working-class children who are placed in these programs and who experience loyalty conflicts as a result of their selection may suffer.[11]

Part of the privilege of having a privilege is not knowing it is a privilege, and American schools are training grounds for this way of thinking. To redesign education means first acknowledging this unseen dimension; we need to break the silences and denials surrounding the *unearned advantages* of white, middle-class children in our efforts to reform and democratize American education.

RETHINKING AUTHORITY RELATIONS

The women's stories also suggest the need to reconsider the conditions under which teachers exercise their authority. There are material and psychological conditions that may lead teachers, who themselves feel inadequate and vulnerable, who may "have internalized the negative value accorded their occupation" (Biklen 1995:138), to deny students' capacities for knowing and feeling. Teachers' interests in controlling students may be driven, in part, by their own unresolved conflicts about the gap between their classroom authority and their own feelings of inadequacy or frustration about a job that is too big for any one person to handle. There are many ways to defend against or cover these feelings and anxieties, not the least of which is exercising teacherly authority in dominating or abusive ways. The women's stories remind us that teachers who exercised their authority through love, care, protection, and acceptance rather than fear, dominance, or punishment had positive impact.

How teachers exercise their authority affects student identities and stances towards school.[12] Authority is not in and of itself "bad" or "corrupt," although some of the most entrenched forms of authority appear to us in this way. Sociologists define "authority" as legitimized power. When people exercise power over others in ways that are considered "legitimate," we willingly assent.[13] Ironically, institutional authority can obscure other kinds of power that teachers have, which, when exercised, can actually disrupt the existing state of affairs. For example, teachers can exercise personal authority—I know this because of my relationship with you, because I respect and value you. Students can invest their teachers with authority based on personal, positive, affiliative relationships. Exercising this kind of teacherly authority can change students' lives.

The women's stories highlight the perception of women teachers as naturally nurturing figures who have the power to "make students feel good." This belief is supported by institutional, cultural, and psychodynamic processes in school.[14] Insofar as societal images of protection, acceptance, affiliation, and empathy evoke what the culture defines as "maternal," then as a feminist educator, I advocate that teachers (re)claim and transform maternal authority.[15] This means exercising authority in ways that promote and sustain mutual, egalitarian, and respectful relationships among teachers, parents, and students and among students themselves.

The women's stories also indicate that school mission influences how teachers exercise authority and how it is understood by students. To the extent that the urban-bureaucratic school mission corresponds to the needs of industry and reflects an authoritarian model of employer-employee relations, it is important that feminist teachers find ways to subvert these expectations and images. Without falling into a false nostalgia for the (segregated) rural-community school, we should acknowledge that the North Carolina women's fond memories point up the benefits of community-based over institutional-based school contexts. The one-room schoolhouse—with the autonomy it afforded the teachers and its premium placed on nurturance, love, and regard—enabled students to be more trusting of, engaged in, and joyful about school learning. Perhaps a version of this model is worth restoring. The nation's uncritical acceptance of the industrial/institutional training model of education limits our imagination about school reform.

RETHINKING SCHOOL MISSION

Students, teachers, and parents are personally and psychologically invested in what goes on in schools, and this is a *necessary condition*, not a side benefit, of learning and development. School success depends upon students, teachers, and parents viewing each other as partners, not adversaries. For this reason, I add mutual recognition to legitimacy, trust and assent as key factors to children's school success. When all parties can gain a sense of fit rather than contest between each others' feelings and concerns, then all can learn to recognize the others as sovereign, legitimate, and valued knowers. Meaningful and successful school relationships depend upon the abilities of students, teachers, and parents to sustain the tension between who each party imagines the others to be and who each are in their own right.

But certain conditions must be fulfilled for such mutually recognizing relationships to occur—conditions that are woefully unmet in American public schools and in children's material lives. The extent to which poor children are marginalized from education cannot be overstated. Children who live on the edge—who are homeless, neglected, hungry— go to school daily without any of the taken-for-granted necessities upon which success in school depends. We see these children and expect that their mothers (who themselves live on the edge) will somehow pull things together enough so that their children can learn and perform well in school. This expectation strikes me as wildly unreasonable, a fantasy or magical thinking on the part of school officials and the nation at large.[16]

To change this thinking means first acknowledging and valuing the caregiving side of teaching and learning. Reforms that support teachers' emotional labor should be put at the top of the agenda. This means "providing *resources* (especially time), teacher *autonomy* (because human relationships cannot be planned and human needs are unpredictable), *advice* (especially from networks of other teachers) and *recognition* (that this is an important part of teaching)" (Connell 1993: 64). It also means allowing teachers to be decision makers about curriculum and school governance so that the caregiving side of teachers' work can be made central to school life rather than being viewed as an "extra" demand on top of a load that is already too heavy to carry. It means reducing teachers' bureaucratic paperwork so that they can focus their best energies on students' academic, emotional, and social needs. Most important, school size should be small and student-teacher ratios low.

While we may pay lip service to the values and ethics of caregiving, we have yet to incorporate them into our educational mission, practices, and policies. The women's stories highlight the shortcomings of splitting schoolwise and motherwise skills and knowledge, rigidly separating family life from school life. While being careful not to reify these distinct spheres and knowledges, it is worth noting that these divisions have particularly damaging effects on poor and working-class girls who must invest considerable time and effort into personal survival and the care of others. Reallocating federal and state social service and school funds in ways that integrate rather than separate community, family, and school life (e.g., by providing on-site services and incentives such as child care, preventative health care, and nourishing meals in school settings) would be an important step toward achieving gender, race, and class equity in schools. That such a proposal sounds unrealistic or is perceived as having little benefit for middle-class children whose daily survival needs are already being met in ways that ensure their success in school is, in my view, a major obstacle to overcome on the road to equitable school reform. Broadening the mission of school will benefit *all* children by preparing them to become citizens who are treated with, instructed about, and have practice acting upon a combined ethic of social justice and care.

RETHINKING ADULT EDUCATION

My hope is that adult literacy educators will seize upon students' political and personal struggles to "become somebody" as the crux of adult literacy education. I would encourage literacy educators to be more attuned to how adult learners seek to establish at least the image of a valued and legitimate self as part of classroom exchanges or tutoring sessions. Adult education is about establishing a credible, worthy self and public identity as much as it is about gaining a diploma. Moreover, I would caution adult literacy educators against family literacy programs and curricula that may unwittingly deny or suppress women's wishes for intellectual mastery independent of the needs of children, for whom they are primarily responsible.[17] Women's lives and concerns should be put at the center of adult literacy education, which means focusing on issues such as violence against women, women's economic, physical, and mental health needs; recognizing the importance of child care and transportation; and organizing instruction in ways that do not further isolate women from each other.[18]

My research suggests that, at the very least, collecting and analyzing childhood memories of school, aspirations, and concepts of knowledge are worthwhile learning opportunities for both teachers and students.[19] Perhaps by tapping into adult literacy learners' urge to "tell it like it is," adult educators can serve as a community of supportive listeners for new and revised stories, and this, in turn, can lead to political action.

But in the final sense, for poor and working-class women to be visible and valuable, "to learn to speak in a unique and authentic voice, women [must] 'jump outside' the frames and systems authorities provide and create their own frame" (Belenky et al., 1986: 134). Jumping outside the frames is risky business; it requires courage and spirited conviction for students to learn and for instructors to teach against the view that some people and knowledge are worth more than others. This means refusing to accept or promote schooling as a badge of honor, a way to command respect or authority. School credentials are not answers to social inequalities, as the women's testimonies so powerfully attest. But acting on the desire to "be somebody"—to be seen, heard, and taken seriously as a citizen—is a necessary step toward change.

[Notes]

PREFACE

1. I am indebted to Hardy Frye for this wisdom.
2. These terms are borrowed from feminist psychologist and school ethnographer Michelle Fine (1992).
3. See Patti Lather (1991: 224–25) for her discussion of different storytelling conventions ("realist, critical, deconstructive, and reflexive"), all of which I have drawn upon to write this book.
4. Personal communication with Katherine Borman, September 1996.
5. I have published several articles based on aspects of this material. See Luttrell (1989, 1993, 1994, 1996a). Each article represents a piece of the story, but the whole is greater than the sum of these parts.
6. See Smith (1987) for her warning about creating feminist versions of reality that supersede those whose experiences are being investigated. I have tried to be sensitive to this warning by making it clear when I am presenting the women's words and interpretations and when I am presenting my own.

CHAPTER ONE

1. All names are pseudonyms and, when requested, the details of a woman's biography or background have been changed to assure anonymity.
2. Critics warn us that labels such as these can fix our understanding of how gender, race, and class shape our selfhood and identities. (Such critical works include but are not limited to Alcoff 1988; Barkley-Brown 1989; Butler 1990; Flax 1987b; Ginsburg and Tsing 1990; Hall 1991; Higginbotham 1992; hooks 1990; Mascia-Lees et.al. 1989; Scott 1992; Spelman 1988; Steedman 1986; Williams 1991.) With this in mind, I have chosen to refer to the groups by locality, as the Philadelphia women and the North Carolina women, and to focus on the similarities and differences in how they made sense of and negotiated gender, race, and class relations. Worth noting, however is that there was no single way that women in each group referred to themselves and their family backgrounds. For example, while the North Carolina women consistently referred to themselves and their family members as "black," the Philadelphia women never once referred to themselves as "white." The North Carolina women most often referred to their families as having been "poor" and/or having "country ways." Most of the Philadelphia women described their family backgrounds in religious (Catholic), ethnic (Irish or Polish), and/or class (such as "working-class," "blue collar," or "union") terms, yet some simply referred to themselves as being "working" or "neighborhood" women.

3. I will explain how I selected the women to interview in chapter 2. I have been influenced by and am indebted to the critical literature written by feminists on women's life histories, autobiographies, and oral histories, a literature that is quite large and growing constantly. See Catherine Bateson (1990); Ruth Behar (1993); Joanne Braxton (1989); Bella Brodzki and Celeste Schenck (1988); Susan Chase (1995); Susan G. Geiger (1986); Sherna Berger Gluck and Daphne Patai (1991); Carolyn Heilbrun (1988); Personal Narratives Group (1989) for examples.

4. Faye Ginsburg makes this same distinction in her study of abortion activists. She uses the term "life stories" in contrast to "life histories" to stress "the narrative devices used by activists to frame their lives, not actual experience or behavior (if one can ever know that, especially regarding the past)" (1989: 60). For examples of classic life histories see Vincent Crapanzano (1980), Sidney Mintz (1974) and Marjorie Shostak (1981). Also see Daniel Bertaux and Martin Kohli (1984) for further discussion of the distinction between life stories and life histories.

5. There is much debate about the use and meaning of life stories collected by anthropologists, particularly when anthropologists bring certain expectations about what should constitute the life story of any particular person. See Rosaldo (1989) for his inability to elicit from his subject, Tukbaw, what he considered to be an appropriate narrative of the "self," about inner life as we understand it. Similarly, Ruth Behar (1993) writes about how Esperanza refused to talk about certain matters, such as sexuality, which is a key subject that we have come to expect in treatments of women's lives. As Behar puts it, "Her life story, as she told it to me, was not a revelation of the 'real truth' of her inner life but an account of those emotional states (which were also often bodily and religious states) that she construed as worth talking about—physical suffering, martyrdom, rage, salvation" (1993: 273).

6. Susan Chase (1991, 1995) makes a similar point concerning her interviews with women about their career histories. "The request for a career history is essentially this: in a world in which so few women have highly paid, prestigious, leadership positions, there must be a story about how you acquired one of those jobs. The nature of the interaction surrounding the request and the telling—the smoothness of both the asking and the response, the ease with which the career history is formulated and told—show that women shared this assumption with us" (1991: 17).

7. For discussions about accounts and accounting strategies, see Burke (1954, 1969); Foote (1951); Hewitt and Stokes (1978); Mills (1940); Scott and Lyman (1968); Weinstein (1980). Arlene McLaren (1981, 1982, 1985) applies this concept to adult women's educational ambitions and pursuits.

8. See Kenneth Plummer (1995) for his review of the sociology of stories and storytelling, particularly how the stories people tell are part of the political process.

9. George Rosenwald and Richard Ochberg's (1992) book sets out a critical theory of personal narrative that borrows heavily on psychoanalytic thought and practice. George Rosenwald advocates a psychoanalytic viewpoint because "no other discipline has articulated the social formation and malformation of the individual more finely or more deeply, and none has taken the life-historical view of this formation so seriously. This is why the elaboration of the psychoanalytic life story can serve as a model for a broader concern with the social-developmental aspects of personal narratives"(267). I agree with Rosenwald, except to say that not all versions of psychoanalysis are useful. I advocate a feminist object relations version of psychoanalysis combined with symbolic interactionism and narrative analysis to be used as a model for theorizing personal narratives.

10. In most cases, memories unfolded through emotional displays (crying, halted speech, and frequent requests for me to turn off the tape recorder). Several of these incidences will be described in upcoming chapters. I am drawn to the term "memory work" for several reasons: Frigga Haug and others (1987) use it to

describe their feminist social scientific method; it corresponds to Arlie Hochschild's (1983) notion of "emotion work," which women are more prone to perform in our society than men; and as Jane Flax (1987a) asserts, memory (and the psychic force of repression) is different for women than for men in our culture. All these dimensions of "memory work" merit further discussion but are beyond the scope of this book.

11. Several black feminist scholars have cautioned, for example, that school may not be the best place to explore African American women's self-definitions or understandings. Instead, black churches or black community organizations may serve as more informative contexts. See Collins (1990); Giddings (1984); Gilkes (1985, 1988); Grant (1982). I suspect this is also the case for other groups of people whose identities are a mismatch for school and who struggle over the meanings and assertions of their identities in many different arenas of life. Moreover, identities vary as people move from one institutional setting to another—for instance from school to work—and as their stakes in those settings change. I draw attention to schools because they have far-reaching impact on the range of resources (cultural, symbolic, material, and psychological) that all people can use to establish and assert their social identities. I agree with Levinson and Holland (1996), who write that schools have been underexamined in recent years; "We urge anthropologists to avoid an exclusive attention to media which leaves schools largely unstudied and obscure" (1996: 19). Understanding why schools might be understudied, the authors aptly write: "We recognize that for individuals facing all the usual problems of carrying out field research, it may be easier to watch television in our informants' homes, or gather round the boom-box with dancing teenagers, than to enter the complexity of school relations. . . . Schools are difficult places to study" (19).

12. At the outset of my research I was greatly inspired by the ethnographic work of Paul Willis and those who followed in his footsteps as part of the Center for Contemporary Cultural Studies in Birmingham, England (e.g. Fuller 1980; McRobbie 1984, 1991). Willis's ethnography illuminated the cultural processes through which British high school lads resisted the "middle-class" ideology of school and teachers' authority in ways that sealed their destiny as manual laborers. His analysis informs my thinking regarding the women's stories about their resistance to school. Nonetheless, I agree with the many critics who found troubling blind spots regarding race and gender in Willis's discussion of cultural (re)production (For discussion of this work see Hall 1992; R. Johnson 1986/87; Lave et al. 1992; Levinson and Holland 1996; and Elizabeth Long 1986). But what I find most troubling is his lack of any attribution of inner struggle or emotional or psychological selfhood to the lads and their cultural forms of resistance. These psycho-cultural conflicts will occupy a central place in this book.

13. See Bernstein (1975); Bourdieu (1974, 1984); Bourdieu and Passeron (1977); Bourdieu and Saint Martin (1974). The main point of the cultural capital argument is that schools make it appear as if certain competencies and traits are objective and universal rather than signs or, in Lisa Delpit's (1995) words, "codes of power."

14. There are many compelling arguments about how schools reproduce the status quo, ranging from those that stress the importance of tracking mechanisms (Bowles and Gintis 1976); to those that focus on curriculum, i.e., how curricular silences and distortions about certain groups of Americans serve to keep students in their proper places (McCarthy and Crichlow 1993); to those that feature the effect of teachers' lowered expectations of students from less advantaged backgrounds. See Connell et al. (1982); Holland and Eisenhart 1990; Levinson, Foley and Holland (1996); MacLeod (1987); Weiler (1988); and Whitty (1985); for good reviews of the arguments about how schools reproduce inequality. I have found Bourdieu's analysis of cultural capital most relevant to the specific experiences

and views of the women I interviewed. I am aware of and agree with the critiques others have made of this notion, i.e., that class is overemphasized as the most determining factor and that the notion explains why middle-class students succeed better than it explains why working-class and poor students fail; see Connell (1983) and MacLeod (1987) for critiques. Nonetheless, I find the cultural capital notion useful for exploring the sorts of currency awarded certain groups of *black* students over others and certain groups of *female* students over others, currency which the women identified as greatly important in their school lives (see chapter 5).

15. This phrase comes from Susan Krieger (1991: 44), who writes about the importance of a view of the self that acknowledges inner experiences, a view that she says has all too often been overlooked by social scientists.

16. Some theories feature gender, race, and class as separate but related variables that determine social status and/or social mobility. Others take a more integrated view and feature race, gender, and class as interlocking systems of domination and oppression (Collins 1990). Still others highlight class, gender, and race as ideologies, discourses, and grand narratives that set "uncertain terms" for how people arrive at identities which perpetuate social inequalities (Ginsburg and Tsing 1990).

17. Ginsburg and Tsing (1990) make this point in their introduction and argue that when people become aware of the complexities of their position it can be politically empowering. See also Bookman and Morgen (eds.) (1988); R. W. Connell (1987); Angela Davis (1981); M. di Leonardo ed. (1991); Bonnie Thornton Dill (1983); J. Hall et al. (1989); Sherry Ortner (1984); Amy Smerdlow and Hanna Lessinger (eds.) 1983; and Young and Dickerson eds. (1994) for useful discussions about theorizing gender, race, and class relations.

18. Even the order in which one lists these three makes an implicit statement about the priority or salience of these oppressions or inequalities.

19. See Karen Sacks (1989) for an excellent review of how Marxists, white socialist-feminists, and feminists of color (Black, Latina and Asian women) have theorized the relationship between gender, race, and class oppression.

20. Alongside and supporting this view is the tendency to equate gender with women, race with people of color, and class with poor or disadvantaged people; and to focus on these groups as needing to be "fixed." Patricia Hill Collins (1990) has addressed this problematic "either/or" categorical thinking and advocates for a "both/and conceptual stance, one in which all groups possess varying amounts of penalty and privilege in one historically created system" (225).

21. I am using the term "social reproduction" broadly and inclusively to refer to processes of social and cultural production and reproduction—that is, to paraphrase Marx, that people make history, create and recreate their identities, take social action under conditions that are not of their own choosing. See Holland and Eisenhart (1990), Levinson and Holland (1996), Ortner (1984), and Willis (1981) for their reviews of how sociological, anthropological, and critical education theorists since the 1960's have examined human agency and creativity in the face of powerful structural constraints—how social differences, inequalities, modes of domination, and resistance get played out in ways that both challenge and maintain the status quo.

22. I draw upon symbolic interactionists (Cooley 1983; Goffman 1959, 1963; Mead 1962); object relation theorists (Fairbairn 1952; Greenberg and Mitchell 1983; Hughes 1989; Jacobson 1965; Klein 1975; Kohut 1978; Mahler et al. 1975; Stern 1985; Winnicott 1965, 1971, 1975) and most especially feminist object relation theorists (Benjamin 1988; Chodorow 1978, 1989; Dimen 1991; Flax 1990; Steedman 1986) to talk about both the conscious and unconscious dimensions of the women's relationships and interactions.

23. See Chodorow (1989) for her discussion of how object relations theorists view

self-formation as distinguished from Freudian or classical drive-theory. In her 1995 article, she discusses how images of and identifications with early caretakers are part of our self-definitions, even as these images and identifications change and become more or less salient over time. I am aware of (and sensitive to) the many critiques of Chodorow's account of self and identity formation, particularly those who point out the limitations of her empirical focus on European American middle-class families. See Gloria Joseph (1981: 76), Judith Lorber et al. (1981: 483), and Elizabeth Spelman (1988: 85). However, I agree with Segura and Pierce (1993: 64) that "the usefulness of Chodorow's theoretical framework, however, should not be obscured by the limitations of her empirical account." Rather, we should take advantage of the socially and historically specific context in which parenting takes place to help explain how racial, class, and ethnic differences shape self and identity formation.

24. A full review and critique of these concepts is beyond the scope of my project. See Jane Flax (1990) and J. Henriques et. al. (1984) for discussions of postmodern notions of self/subjectivity. Hawkesworth's (1989) discussion of the relationship between notions of self, identity and knowledge and Holland et al.'s (forthcoming) discussion of the cultural formation of selves and identities are particularly relevant to my research. See Taylor (1989) for an historical overview of notions of self and identity.

25. This notion also makes clear my union of psychological, cultural and institutional analyses. It helps me avoid featuring either the structure/culture or the individual/agent as the privileged vantage point as I relay and interpret the women's stories.

26. Carolyn Steedman critiques the field of "cultural criticism"—specifically the "positioning of mental life within Marxism," the work of Richard Hoggart, Jeremy Seabrook, E. P. Thompson, as well as traditional psychoanalytic accounts that depict fathers as patriarchs and daughters as the heroines of fairy tales. She says that a "delineation of emotional and psychological selfhood has been made by and through the testimony of people in a central relationship to the dominant culture, that is to say by and through people who are not working-class" (1986: 11). Steedman writes about her own working-class childhood and how she came to terms with her mother's politically conservative views, identifying in her mother what Steedman calls a "proper envy" for all that she was denied. Her point is "not to say that all working-class childhoods are the same, nor that experience of them produces unique psychic structures" (16). Rather, she calls for a theoretical stance that opens up the space for working-class people to "use the autobiographical 'I,' and tell the stories of their life" (16).

27. See Jessica Benjamin for her discussion of splitting as a psychoanalytic concept that, like repression, "has a narrow, technical use as well as broader metapsychological and metaphoric meaning. Just as repression became a paradigm for a larger cultural process, so might splitting be suggestive not only for individual psychic processes but also for supraindividual ones" (1988: 63).

Splitting may also help to explain why we are more willing to accept characteristic forms of western rational thought, what Patricia Hill Collins (1990) calls "either/or" forms of thinking that pit emotion against reason, mind against body, masculine against feminine. I discuss these splits further in chapter 3.

28. See anthropologist Katherine Ewing (1990) for her discussion of the "illusion of wholeness." She says that in all cultures people can be observed to project multiple and shifting self-representations, but they are often unaware of these shifts and inconsistencies. Despite these shifts, however, people experience their selves as whole and continuous. Melanie Klein (1975) writes that the experience of wholeness is aided by the process of splitting and the counteracting psychological process she calls "reparation." This reparative quest for coherence, whether an illusion or not, is a crucial feature of the women's stories. Linde (1993) writes

about this quest for coherence from a sociolinguistic vantage point and claims that the idea that people have a coherent "life story" to tell is a cultural form of self-representation that is common to American speakers.

CHAPTER TWO

1. John Lofland (1971), author of my early fieldwork bible, says that the fieldworker inevitably experiences emotional reactions and that these reactions can compromise the research. As an antidote to this, the author suggests that fieldworkers record and take account of their private feelings. As I recorded my feelings during the fieldwork process, I viewed my activity as a way to minimize, counterbalance, or neutralize the variable of my "self." In writing about the fieldwork, I found Susan Krieger's views most helpful. She says that social scientists "write to protect as much as we write to express the self and to describe the world. Although we speak of protecting others—usually the people our studies are about—the main object of our protective strategies is always our selves" (1991: 32). Hindsight lets me see that this self-protection kept me from representing all that I know about my subject. Many others have written about gaining insight into fieldwork observations vis-à-vis one's own emotional reactions as well as memories and dreams evoked during the research process. See Behar (1993); Briggs (1986); Collins (1990); Ewing (1990); Hunt (1989); Krieger (1991); Paget (1990); Thorne (1993); Williams (1988) for how the self can be a source rather than a contaminant of knowledge for the researcher. An especially helpful guide about emotions and fieldwork is written by Sherryl Kleinman and Martha Copp (1993).

2. Prior to the emergence of what Barbara Tedlock (1991: 69) calls "narrative ethnography," the ethnographer was faced with the choice of writing either an ethnographic memoir "centering on the Self" or a more traditional account "centering on the Other." I have attempted to avoid this either/or choice, and instead, to present both sides as "coparticipants" (not the same as equal participants) in the ethnographic encounter. See also Deborah Gordon (1988) and Margery Wolf (1992) for discussions of this dilemma in ethnographic writing.

3. I have been influenced by the work of several feminist scholars writing about the problems and possibilities of feminist research methods, including Anderson and Jacks (1991); Behar and Gordon (1995); Devault (1990); Griffin and Smith (1987); McRobbie (1982); Oakley (1981); Reinharz (1992); Smith (1987); Stacey (1988); Stanley (1990); Stanley and Wise (1983); Strathern (1987).

4. See Peter Binzen (1970) for a portrait of the same neighborhood. His account was not well liked among the women with whom I spoke.

5. These women also represented the basic demographic profile of white women in the community, including marital status, occupation, income, education level, religion, and race. I also selected women who represented the basic profile of Women's Program participants in terms of age, family situation, past attendance and type of school, academic achievement, and level of community or civic participation.

6. The Philadelphia women's school careers varied. Five of the women had attended local Catholic grammar schools for some part (not all) of their elementary years. At the time, the cost of attending these grammar schools was minimal, and in some cases, was free depending on whether one's family was a member of the local parish. Two of these women attended a Catholic all-girls high school; they both left (for different reasons) after the first year. Of the remaining women who attended public schools, two had attended the public girls' high school before it had become co-ed. I mention these variations because school context becomes an important factor in the women's identities and stance towards school. I hope my account will spur more research about the contrasts between Catholic and pub-

lic school contexts and between single-sex and coeducational contexts in shaping student identities in school.

7. This graduation rate reflected the neighborhood educational attainment figures reported in the 1980 census data.

8. I discovered, however, that wrapped up in these views about the dignity of manual work were implicit values about male privilege that I will discuss in chapter 3.

9. At the time I scribbled my reactions on the margins of my fieldnotes. They read, "I wonder about the gender dynamics at play; could this interaction be said to illustrate socialization patterns and developmental differences between boys and girls? Will Mikaela's verbal abilities and her social skills always be viewed so positively? Will they ever be turned against her? Will these social skills always earn her respect and will she come to see her communication skills as evidence of her intelligence?" All of these questions and conflicts will be addressed in chapter 3, in which I look at the women's definitions and values regarding intelligence.

10. My relatives on my mother's side are white, proper, Midwestern, Protestant, church-going, business-oriented, middle-class, people. My grandmother grew up on a farm. On my father's side are Scottish-Irish, hard-living, urban, blue-collar people. My grandfather left a Kentucky mining town for industrial work in Chicago. As a young girl I often felt torn between the two sides, especially when it came to my educational aspirations. The Philadelphia women often reminded me of my paternal cousin who seemed to have little invested in others' approval. I had always envied this in my cousin and I imagined that she did not feel pressured to perform or achieve in the same ways I did. Still I felt guilty about the discrepancy in our resources and opportunities, as if I had been unfairly bestowed with benefits that should rightfully be hers as well.

11. Stacey acknowledges that while her interviewee's statement is "true enough," as the author she does control the terms and textual forms of representing the women in her study. Stacey calls for a "greater respect for ambivalence as a worthy moral and theoretical stance" (1990: 544) as a result of this exchange. I see my work as a pitch for sustaining the tensions and ambivalences between self and other in dialogic relationships as a worthy moral and theoretical stance.

12. See Chodorow (1989: 154–162) for her discussion of the progression in psychoanalytic theory from a view of the self as a "pure, differentiated individuality based on rigid notions of autonomous separateness toward a relational individualism" (162).

13. Let me briefly explain my coding procedures. The material gathered in Philadelphia was coded according to recurrent themes that arose in the interview materials and observational notes. I examined what the women said, specifically what they identified as difficult or problematic in their schooling and family lives and how they sought to resolve these problems. I coded each woman's interview text separately (to discern the patterns that emerged in her own life narrative) and then looked across all fifteen texts to determine the patterns. In collecting the interview material in North Carolina, I started with a comparative frame of reference, i.e., the Philadelphia women's material. I noted the different themes raised by the North Carolina women, but began to discover a common pattern among women in both groups in how they narrated their stories. Thus, I developed a second coding strategy, whereby I examined the interview materials as school stories that followed certain storytelling patterns. Specifically, these patterns included *who* the women identified as primary actors and the events that characterized the problems they encountered in school; how they *ordered* their stories; and what *themes* tied the various stories together.

14. There were some significant differences between the two groups of women I interviewed. While equal numbers of them had become pregnant as teenagers, a higher proportion of the Philadelphia women had gotten married as a result. Whereas two-thirds of the Philadelphia women were or had been married, two-

thirds of the North Carolina women had been single heads of households for most of their lives. Because of life-cycle differences, several of the North Carolina women but none of the Philadelphia women were grandmothers raising school-aged children. Meanwhile, whereas none of the North Carolina women had spent any time out of the labor force since becoming mothers, roughly half of the Philadelphia women had been out of the paid labor force when raising children under school age. The North Carolina women on average earned less than the Philadelphia women, but all the women's family incomes had fluctuated considerably over the previous fifteen years.

15. The directness with which I handled this event is akin to the descriptions of young girls' development that Lyn Mikel Brown and Carol Gilligan (1992) describe. As a fourth grade girl, I was "allowed" this outrage (both internally and by the store manager) because the forces of good girl socialization had not yet set in. Indeed, as I grew older I learned to drive underground certain feelings and thoughts that did not seem appropriate. This story of course (re)presents my view only—in fact, my mother doesn't even remember this event, which I view as being so central to my childhood.

16. It is worth noting here that the reading skills of the Philadelphia and North Carolina women were similar and ranged from roughly third to ninth grade. Yet for reasons that will become clearer later, the North Carolina women held a lower opinion of themselves as competent learners.

17. See Jennifer Hunt (1989) about issues of transference and counter-transference in the interviewing process.

CHAPTER THREE

1. There is an ongoing dialogue about how gender shapes what and how women know. This debate has spanned the disciplines, including philosophy, psychology, sociology, and education (Belenky et al. 1986; Bordo and Jaggar 1989; Chodorow 1978; Collins 1990; Gilligan 1982, 1988, 1990; Harding and Hintikka 1983; Levesque-Lopman 1988; Lloyd 1984; Martin 1985; McMillan 1982; Ruddick 1989; Smith 1987).

2. See Cixous (1976, 1981); Daly (1973, 1978); Griffin (1980); Irigaray (1985); Trask (1986).

3. Collins (1990); Hartsock (1985); Jaggar (1983); O'Brien (1981); Rose (1983); and Smith (1987) and represent the range of feminist "standpoint" theorists.

4. See Bordo (1986); Gilligan (1982); Harding (1986); Keller (1984); and Tronto (1989).

5. *Women's Ways of Knowing* (Belenky et al. 1986) is a noteworthy example of research that considers the different contexts within which women claim and/or deny knowledge (as children in abusive relationships, as female students in school, as new mothers raising children, etc.). The conclusions they draw, however, have more to do with developmental stages of knowing than with the historical, political, or ideological conditions that shape women's knowing, which is my focus.

6. See also J. Grant (1987); Harding and Hintikka (1983); and Heckman (1987).

7. See also Alfred Schutz's (1967) concept of common sense as "the natural attitude."

8. See Arlene Fingeret (1983a) where she discusses what she calls a cultural clash between common sense and book learning among a group of non-literate adults she interviewed.

9. See Karla Holloway for her discussion of common sense and motherwit that opens her book *Codes of Conduct: Race, Ethics and the Color of Our Character*. She writes, and I agree (with some amendments), that common sense "contains the paradox of a self-destructive understanding imposed by race [I would add

gender and class here] as well as the creative tradition embraced by ethnic [and I would add gender and class] identity" (1995: 4).

10. Here I am adapting E. P. Thompson's (1963) views of class, culture, and consciousness as ways of living within certain relationships of power. These relationships are formed and change when people articulate and identify their class (and we can add gender or race) interests, capabilities, or concerns as being common to others like themselves and against those whose interests are different from (and usually opposed to) theirs. Cognitive processes are usually understood as being individual or at least psychological, not as part of class, racial, or gender culture and consciousness. I hope to expand the parameters of how "ways of knowing" are understood by way of this analysis.

11. See Richard Johnson (1979) for his historical description of working-class demands for schools to teach "really useful knowledge."

12. A full discussion of the controversial concept of intelligence, its historical emergence, and varied uses to justify inequality is beyond the scope of this book. Gilbert Gonzales (1979) argues that the concept of intelligence is historically linked to the development of monopoly capitalism. He puts forth that "mental abilities are social conditions reflected within the individual" and critiques the concept as an antidemocratic ideological construction. For a historical description of the mistaken claim that worth can be assigned to individuals or groups by quantitatively measuring a single intelligence score, see Stephen Jay Gould (1981). Meanwhile, Howard Gardner's theory of multiple intelligences posits that while those we generally view as smart possess a certain logical-mathematical intelligence, there are at least six other forms of intelligence that can be added to this: linguistic, spatial, musical, bodily, interpersonal, and intrapersonal. See Gardner (1993) for a synopsis of multiple-intelligence theory, its criticisms, and his own responses to those critiques. He also discusses the Key School in Indianapolis, where multiple-intelligence theory has been applied schoolwide. For a discussion of myths about black women's intelligence, see Reid 1975.

13. Carolyn Heilbrun (1988) suggests that women's life plots (marriage, child rearing, caring for others) are considered less interesting or noteworthy than are men's and as such shape the way women's lives are narrated and understood. The same might be said about how the Philadelphia women narrated and understood women's knowledge as it related to their life plots.

14. See Paul Willis (1977) for his discussion of British "lads" and their rejection of schoolwise values and knowledge as a way to express their masculinity and to identify with manual ways of knowing and shop-floor culture.

15. See Fee (1983); Rose (1983); Smith (1987).

16. Jane Roland Martin (1985, 1994) notes that this bias structures school mission, which I discuss further in chapter 5.

17. See Sandra Bartky (1990) for her discussion of the sexual division of labor, including the argument that housewifery is a task made impossible by its contradictions. Intended as an act of love, it also serves (and masks) domination. The same could be said about motherwise knowledge.

18. John Brown Childs (1984: 69–90) discusses the tradition of "motherwit" in African and Afro-American culture. Childs quotes Arthur Schomburg (1913), who wrote extensively on the culture and history of black Americans. Schomburg warned that black scholars must not become distanced from or neglectful of Afro-American history, culture, or social problems. "The university graduate is wont to overestimate his ability, fresh from the machinery that endows him with a parchment and crowns him with knowledge, he steps out into the world to meet the practical men with years of experience and motherwit. It is a contrast, the professional man with the veneer of high art, and the acquaintance with the best authors, and up to date histories demanding recognition. All these books take their proper places when applied to the white people, but when applied or mea-

sured up to the black people, they lack the substantial and the inspiring" (1913: 5–6). This view of motherwit, particularly in terms of the (racial) conflict between the veneer of (white) schoolwise knowledge pit against the practicality and value of (black) motherwit, resonates with the North Carolinians' views and values about common sense/motherwit. See also *Motherwit: An Alabama Midwife's Story*, which is the oral history of Onnie Lee Logan (1989). In the chapter entitled "Motherwit," she describes her knowledge of midwifery and her experiences of dealing with white racism, both in terms of her motherwit.

19. For example, see Jones (1985), Ladner (1972), and Stack (1974) for their discussions of how black women swap resources and child care and adapt to adverse economic constraints through extended kin networking and mutual support.

20. See also Davis (1971), Giddings (1984), and Higginbotham (1992), for support of this argument.

21. Evelyn Brooks Higginbotham (1992) writes about how class divisions have historically impacted the expression of black women's sexuality; it would be important to investigate differences in how African American women from different class backgrounds speak about their common sense and "motherwit" to fill out the picture I have provided.

22. See Frantz Fanon (1967), P. H. Collins (1990), and Karla Holloway (1995) for discussions about cultural narratives and images of blackness and femaleness through which we learn the rules of racial classification and our own racial identities, often without conscious teaching or inculcation. Frantz Fanon refers to these rules as a *racial schema* and makes a useful distinction between a person's "corporeal" and "racial epidermal" schema. The image of one's body located somewhere in physical space, an implicit knowledge that we possess about the position of our bodies in relation to other physical objects, is part of our corporeal schema. Fanon says that our racial epidermal schema is an interpreted image, an image "woven out of a thousand details, anecdotes, [and] stories" (1967: 35, 116, 112). Fanon writes about blackness as an image imposed on black, colonized (male) bodies in ways that haunt a person like a shadow and have diminishing and self-destructive effects, whereby black people come to exercise harsh dominion over their own self-esteem.

23. We might consider this way of knowing, this white ignorance, as an exercise of white privilege, a way of not having to attend to the daily assaults of racism (see Frankenberg 1993).

24. See Holloway for her discussion of the "tragic loneliness," "fear of fracture and invisibility," and "psychic conflict" that characterize the fiction written by black women writers and that are ever present in black women's everyday experiences (1995: 38–41). See also Patricia Williams (1991).

CHAPTER FOUR

1. Writing in the 1940s, C. W. Mills (1940) called on sociologists to "analyze, index, and gauge" how people speak about their actions in accordance to specific institutional practices and demands. Most important, he noted that specific institutional practices and their vocabularies of motive exercise control or at least profoundly shape how we view our options, choices, or lack thereof within any given situation. I am interested in how the women spoke about their childhood ambitions in relation to school and work-place practices and demands.

2. Patterned events at school or in work places—coupled with familiar and prototypical actors, motives, and outcomes—emerged across these stories, patterns that Holland and Quinn (1987) would call a *cultural model of success*.

3. The phrases "in the voice" and "in the image" are borrowed from Dorothy Holland's work on American understandings of attractiveness (1988). She notes that cognitive presentations of who is and is not attractive are evaluated in reference

to particular social practices or activities (e.g., "dating") and particular groups (e.g., "jerks," "jocks," "bitches") that comprise what she calls the "figured world of romance." For Holland's interviewees, critical self-appraisals were narrated in the voices of their peers—one interviewee "seemed to (re)experience the comparison of herself to the ideal through the questions and criticism of her peers" (1988: 2).

4. See E. Glenn, G. Chang and L. Forcey, eds. (1994) for a collection of articles that examine the ideology and experience of mothering among women of color.

5. See Judith Rollins (1985) for her discussion of all the various ways domestic workers establish their own sense of worth and authority in these conflicted settings.

6. I deal at more length with these regrets and sorrow about their selves in relation to mothers in chapter 7.

7. See Michelle M. Tokarczyk and Elizabeth A. Fay (1993) for their edited volume *Working-Class Women in the Academy*. Many writers in this volume speak about the same conflicts about not "belonging" in academic settings.

8. See Bowles and Gintis (1976) for the classic text on how schools "track" different groups of students, preparing them to take on jobs for which they are destined; and Willis (1977) for how students creatively (and sometimes oppositionally) respond to and internalize these school values and expectations.

9. References to their need to feel "comfortable" with others (particularly in school) were found in every Philadelphia woman's account.

10. This dominant image of femininity or the "cult of true womanhood," a term coined by Welter (1978), emerged during the mid-nineteenth century as part of the consolidation of the American middle class. Polite and proper middle-class manners, styles, and values were associated with "feminized" traits and were important for class mobility. These traits of so-called perfect womanhood were paradoxical—serving to justify white, upper-middle-class women's status and privilege, all the while serving to confine their power to the domestic sphere.

CHAPTER FIVE

1. "Abstract" is Labov's term (1972: 363).

2. See Young and Willmott (1962) for more discussion of this class-based view.

3. Rubin (1976) notes that the working-class parents she interviewed expressed similar concerns that by attending college their children might be exposed to views that conflicted with their family and community values. These parents also worried that a college education might encourage their children to be dismissive of or devalue a working-class way of life that these parents have worked so hard to achieve.

4. Bourdieu and Passeron (1977:115) refer to this as "symbolic violence" which is imposed on students whose cultural capital (such as Cora's country ways) does not match up with school styles or values. See also Signithia Fordham (1993) for her discussion of symbolic violence and the self-silencing of African American women in schools.

5. I discuss such responses to classroom materials in Luttrell (1981).

6. I want to re-emphasize here that the women in both groups shared a similar range of academic skills measured by standardized test scores.

7. Wexler (1992) found the same recurring reference among students that I found among the women interviewed. "In their own words, students are trying to 'become somebody.' They want to be somebody, a real and presentable self, anchored in the verifying eyes of friends whom they come to school to meet" (155).

8. See Collins (1990); Fields (1983); Giddings (1984); and Stuckey (1988).

9. Many black writers have used the metaphor of (in)visibility, from Ralph Ellison (1952) to Patricia Williams (1988).

10. These same issues have been noted in the lives and literature of black women such as Alice Walker, Toni Morrison, Mary Helen Washington, and Paule Marshall. The issue of women's physical self scrutiny is also well documented in feminist writings. See Bartky (1990).

11. I discuss in more depth the North Carolina women's invocation of such "good" teachers as well as their mothers' relationships to school in chapters 6 and 7.

12. This same observation is made by Lois Weis (1983: 235–61) in her study of black and white community college students in a large northeastern U.S. city, which she compares to two other accounts (London 1978; Willis 1977). These authors identified distinctly negative attitudes toward authority and school knowledge among white, working-class students, which they argue is based on a working-class rejection of mental labor. In contrast, I argue that the women's attitude toward authority stems from what they perceive is the school's dismissal of working-class women's labor. Paralleling my findings, Weis observed that black students did not reject the authority of teachers or question the legitimacy of their knowledge. Instead, they resented teachers for what they perceived were racist motives in ignoring or dismissing black students (1983: 244).

13. There were in fact two contexts (public and parochial) in which the Philadelphia women were schooled. The women viewed the nuns' authority slightly differently from public school teachers' authority in school. However, in terms of framing their school "problems," there were no differences between those Philadelphia women who attended public and those who attended parochial school. This may be due to the small number of women who attended Catholic school in the sample. Future research might yield important contrasts. See Lesko (1988) for a discussion of Catholic high school experiences.

14. This issue about familial responses to school is discussed at greater length in chapter 7.

15. I also found that, in response to the question about why they were returning to school, two-thirds of the Philadelphia women surveyed gave examples that drew on their desire to be able to "speak up" and "voice" their opinions and be heard by family members, social service agents, and school or city officials. See also Belenky et al. (1986) for their observations about women's silence and voice in the educational process.

16. This kind of interpretation follows from the Frankfurt school, specifically Adorno et al.'s 1950 study of the authoritarian personality. See Waller (1932) and Sennett (1980) for discussion of the fear and illusion of authority.

17. This is how Paul Willis (1977) interpreted the "lads'" resistance to teachers and school values as a "cultural penetration" (an admittedly male image; I prefer "insight") into work-place organization and their abilities to sabotage it.

18. I discuss the social control effects of this "good girl" school value in chapter 6.

19. In symbolic interactionist terms, the Philadelphia women's accounting strategies might be called "credentialing," i.e., they sought to establish their qualifications as vocational girls who didn't need to learn what the teachers wanted them to learn so that I would not view their behavior negatively. As we can see in this case, Debra was reconsidering the wisdom of the credentials that "the girls she hung with" shared.

20. This is especially interesting in light of current national rhetoric about teenage pregnancy being girls' major problem in school. Despite the fact that over 60 percent of girls who drop out of school give reasons other than pregnancy for their decision, this single focus continues to dominate and distort discussions about women's education (see Fine and Zane 1989; Weis, Farrar, and Petrie 1989). My current research addresses the historical shift in perspective on this issue.

21. McRobbie (1978) argues that fashion, beauty, and female sexuality all contribute to working-class, feminine antischool culture, which paradoxically pushes girls into compliance with stereotypical female roles. McRobbie observed that work-

ing-class girls asserted their sexualities within the classroom as part of their counterschool culture. The girls' corollary fascination with marriage (partly because it was the only legitimate means through which their sexualities could be expressed) was also part of their counterschool culture that ultimately worked to insure their complicity in dominant gender and class relations.

22. This notion of regimes of discipline and authority is borrowed from Foucault (1977, 1979).

23. It is interesting to note that while several North Carolina women mentioned that they had aspired to be teachers, none of the Philadelphia women expressed this same childhood ambition.

24. For example, see Fields (1983: 88–90) for her reference to this influence in her teacher training.

25. The "intimidation of color" is Mary Helen Washington's (1975) term, which I discuss more in chapter 7.

26. See Davis et al. (1931), which is instructive about class differences within black rural communities and resonates with the North Carolina women's descriptions of their rural childhoods.

27. Claude M. Steel and Joshua Aronson (1995) have shown that African Americans' achievements on a verbal test varied depending on whether they thought their performance was diagnostic of intellectual ability. "Blacks underperformed in relation to Whites in the ability-diagnostic condition but not in the nondiagnostic condition" (1995: 797). I believe their research findings support my observation that the North Carolina women were especially concerned about their abilities as learners.

28. I say purportedly because, as many educational critics have argued, schools teach specific versions of justice and freedom, versions that don't necessarily apply to all people equally. See Giroux (1992); Giroux and McLaren (1994); McCarthy and Crichlow (1993).

29. See the American Association of University Women's report, *How Schools Short-change Girls* (1992) for an excellent discussion of the "formal, hidden and evaded" curriculum and its negative effects on the education of girls.

30. See Gilligan (1990) and Fine (1991) for how schools distort, mute, or submerge girls' knowledge. The reference to girls' knowledge being driven "underground" is Brown and Gilligan's (1992). They write about adolescence being a time in girls' development when they "struggle over speaking and not speaking, knowing and not knowing, feeling and not feeling, and we see the makings of an inner division as girls come to a place where they feel they cannot say or feel or know what they have experienced—what they have felt and known" (1992: 4). My point is that schools further reinforce this inner division by idealizing some forms of knowledge adn devaluing others.

CHAPTER SIX

1. More empirical research would shed light on how the teacher-student bond gets negotiated differently by different groups of students.

2. There are some notable exceptions. See Sari Biklen (1995) for an excellent discussion and historical review of how gender relations and constructions of mothering define women's work as teachers.

3. See Gilligan (1982); Nodding (1984); Ruddick (1982); Wood (1994).

4. Meanwhile, teachers also see these knowledges as split and at odds and are likely to view their work according to myths about maternal love and power. For example, in their efforts to resist schools' attempts to rationalize or control their work with children, teachers borrow from the same gendered distinctions and divisions of labor, the association of women as naturally nurturing and well-suited for caregiving. Both M. W. Apple (1986, 1987) and R. W. Connell (1985) document

this conflict among the teachers they interviewed who were uncomfortable with (and at times actively undermined) their role as "managers," refusing to police children or to conform to rigid curricular programs.

5. My point here is that there is a relationship between outer loss and inner loss. See Winnicott (1971, 1975) and Klein (1975) for their discussions of the use of transitional objects (in this case, the teacher's books) in helping young children adapt to a loss of another as it impacts on a sense of inner loss.

6. I discuss these cultural myths about maternal power, love, and care and their limiting effects on women in chapter 7.

7. The phrase "reflexively self-denying split of self" comes from Chodorow and Contratto's (1982) discussion of women's relationships to mothers, which I am applying to teachers as well.

8. For example, see AAUW (1992); Best (1983); Brophy and Goode (1974); Dweck et al. (1978); Jones (1989); Martin (1972); Sadker and Sadker (1986); Serbin et al. (1973); Stacey, Bereaud and Daniels (1974); Stockard (1985).

9. Notable exceptions are the works of Linda Grant (1985, 1992, 1994) and Barrie Thorne (1993).

10. See Michelle Fine (1991) for her discussion of how the low-income girls of color she studied interpreted student-teacher interactions.

11. It would be important, of course, to know how the "Dorothys" felt about their approval from the teacher in order to fill out the picture of black students' experiences and interpretations of power relations in the classroom.

12. It could also be argued that the North Carolina women's schooling was regulated through confinement (because of their forced labor on tenant farms) and through protection (because of the need for [male] protection against potential racial violence).

13. See Sadker and Sadker (1986) for their review of the evidence that teachers pay more attention to boys, allow them to interrupt more, give more praise to their work, and so on.

14. I am indebted to John Wilson for starting me thinking about these particular ideological dimensions of the pet's power.

15. More often than not, academics have experienced being the teacher's pet, and as one woman said, "It is really hard to hear about what other girls might have been thinking about me." Some people who as graduate students experienced strong and affectionate/sexual bonds with their teachers/professors have yet another set of reactions. Some married these same professors. The variations abound.

CHAPTER SEVEN

1. This silence is interesting to consider in light of the fact that fathers were featured in other parts of their life stories, for example, when the women talked about their common sense or real intelligence, when they described their early romances with boys and before-marriage pregnancies, when they talked about being physically or sexually abused, but never when telling their "school story."

2. See Annette Lareau (1989) for her description and analysis of the differences between mothers' and fathers' roles in children's schooling, in which she shows that traditional gender roles shape the ways in which class privileges and inequalities are produced and reproduced in family-school relations. She describes the nature of maternal and paternal involvement in two school settings—a working-class and an upper-middle-class elementary school—and concludes that in both settings mothers shoulder the heaviest burden of supervising children's day-to-day school activities. Her descriptions of working-class mothers' activities, including their doubts and anxieties about confronting teachers and their self-perceived lack of appropriate knowledge (cultural capital) to help their children succeed in school, echo those of the women I studied.

I agree with Lareau that research about the mechanisms through which class inequalities are reproduced in school has overlooked the role of gender. My point is that these mechanisms are structural and psychological. In one sense, parents act upon their gender roles and their cultural capital as they negotiate with teachers and school officials about their children's school experiences in ways that impact on children's school success. In another sense, through the cultural and psychological idealizing and blaming of mothers' key role in children's schooling, class inequalities are both masked and internalized, as these women's accounts attest.

3. Griffith and Smith (1987) use the term "discourse" broadly to refer not only to so-called expert knowledge and texts, but also to ongoing and everyday conversation about education, teaching, learning, and child development that people have; and to the ways in which people organize their activities, make critical self-appraisals, and judge others in relationship to these several conversations (1987: 96).

4. Griffith and Smith (1987) write about how their own sense of guilt as inadequate mothers experienced in the interview setting informed their analytic work. My experience echoes theirs. The research process provided me with knowledge about mothering and provoked feelings in me about my own mother and my own mothering that would not otherwise have been available to me. But this is a subject for a different writing project than the one I endeavor here.

5. My thinking about these matters has been influenced by Chodorow and Contratto (1982); David (1980); Griffith and Smith (1987); and Lareau (1989).

6. See Michelle Fine (1991: 161–76) for her discussion about school-family collaborations and the different ways that the women she observed and interviewed thought about being involved in school. See also Sari Biklen (1995: 131) for a discussion of teachers' views of mothers as good and bad.

7. See Lillian Rubin (1976) for her observation that the working-class men and women she interviewed did not blame their parents for their difficult childhoods, in contrast to the middle-class respondents in her study who did blame their parents.

8. Perhaps these mothers felt able to take up their daughter's side because there were other options to fall back on, for example, enrolling their child in the public school.

9. See also Madeline Grumet (1988) for her discussion of how the social construction of gender puts women, as teachers and as mothers, at odds with one another. Lightfoot also notes this when she writes: "Mothers and teachers are caught in a struggle that reflects the devaluation of both roles in this society" (1977: 404). My point is that we also need to understand better how daughters get caught up in this conflicted relationship.

10. Of the thirty women I interviewed in depth, only one woman expressed anger more than gratitude toward her mother. There are several reasons for this anger; most notable was what she perceived as her mother's lack of protection against a violent and sexually abusive father.

11. The difference between these two experiences, particularly as they relate to the women's construction of gender identity, merits attention and further study.

12. Chodorow notes this form of guilt in some non-Euro-American women who have grown up in classically patriarchal families (1995: 534.) She cites Alarcon (1985), Espin (1984), and Moraga (1986) for their descriptions of weeping for mothers among Latina women. Ruth Behar writes about "mother-daughter mirroring" in the life story of Esperanza, which she describes as being "darkened by an awareness of the class limitations that make mothering for rural working women a bittersweet wager at best, entered into with reluctance and ambivalence" (1993: 279). See Patricia Hill Collins (1990) for her chapter on "Black Women and Motherhood" in which she examines controlling images, within society at large and in African American communities, which may cause black women to weep for their

mothers. She observes that a fully articulated Afrocentric feminist standpoint on motherhood is missing. In her 1994 article, "Shifting the Center: Race, Class and Feminist Theorizing About Motherhood," she calls for an examination of motherhood and mothers-as-subjects from multiple perspectives, which she speculates will uncover rich textures of ethnic, racial, and class difference.

13. Not surprisingly, the taped version took some new turns, but the main abstract of the story and her regrets about not having been more understanding of her (now-dead) mother remained the same.

14. My thinking about the women's stories as transitional objects has been influenced by Larry Hirschhorn's (1988) discussion of work—the services and products we provide and connections we establish through exchange—that can function as transitional objects in postindustrial society. "Just as the transitional object enables the child to take a round trip from mother to the world and back, in the process changing the relationships to each, so can the products of our work, the goods or services we produce, help us take a round trip from our internal fantasies to the client or customer and back. In the process we change our relationship to each" (213). From this perspective, by telling her story, Kate moves from her internal fantasies to the external world and back, and in the process changes her relationship to herself and others.

15. Kate's story reminds me of Caffeline Allen who grew up in Tumbling Creek, Tennessee, and wrote the following:

> Thinking back on those times and conflicts, I find my emotions toward my mother and my teachers still bound up in the same love-hate web most of us reserve for our families only. In a way my teachers were my family. They were the first to encourage my love for learning, to find scholarships for me, to bring me books to read during the long, lonely summer months, to encourage my writing, to express their belief that I could even make a living as a writer. But at the same time, they taught me to hate my culture, to despise people who had a different linguistic approach to life, even if one of those people was my mother. After many long years, I have managed finally to reconcile to some extent my world with my mother's. Regaining a sense of pride in my Appalachian heritage and an appreciation for who my mother was as a person was one of the hardest and most valuable tasks of my adult life. (1994: 27)

16. I think it is interesting that school decisions were described as being made by mothers, even in families where fathers were cast as the ultimate authority figure. This was as true for the Philadelphia as for the North Carolina women.

17. See Luttrell (1988) for a discussion of this organizing effort in Philadelphia. Two of the women I interviewed were participants in the Edison School struggle.

18. This interview was difficult for me and I left feeling badly. To deny my feelings of vulnerability and dependency in this research process, I focused excessively on what happened at the end of the interview, taking pride in the "data" I had collected for its richness and depth. Yet, for weeks I felt bad and unconfident (in retrospect depressed and anxious) about my upcoming interview with Tina, worried that she was still upset with me. I believe that part of my discomfort in relating to Tina was that I identified with her feelings—that she became a symbol of many past relationships in which I felt abandoned or unprotected. In taking the risk of reaching out again to Tina, despite my fears of rejection, I began a reparative process of my own. Research often functions in this way for researchers, and the more conscious we are of the emotional and relational dimensions of this work, the better we are able to use the insights we glean in our analysis. See Gluck and Patai (1991), Hunt (1989), Kleinman and Copp (1995), Thorne (1993), and selections from Personal Narratives Group (1989) for discussions about emotions and counter-transference in fieldwork and interviewing.

19. According to critic Elizabeth Abel, the point of Steedman's account is that "femi-

ninity (re)produced through this working-class female genealogy has more to do with self-sufficiency than with relationality. . . . The withholding, not the offer, of empathic merger here structures female subjectivity" (1990: 195).

20. See Bruno Bettelheim (1987: 69), where he writes, "The fantasy of the wicked stepmother not only preserves the good mother intact, it also prevents having to feel guilty about one's angry thoughts or wishes about her."

21. See Jessica Benjamin (1988) for her discussion of the "first bond" of love, in which she reviews recent research on infants' responses to mothers and argues that many theories of the self have missed the need for mutual recognition—the "necessity of recognizing as well as being recognized by others" (23).

22. See also Alice Miller (1981) for her discussion about how, for some parents, the child is viewed as an extension of parents' own needs to care for themselves.

23. That poverty, hunger, and violence are conditions of early experiences of mothering that get internalized into the development of selfhood and self-understandings, with consequent profound effects on a person's sense of agency and happiness, has yet to be fully explicated. Carolyn Steedman's (1986) book certainly stands out as an example of how gendered subjectivity is historically specific and socially variable according to specific class-based caretaking/mothering arrangements. I believe there is great promise in feminist object relations theory in exploring these specificities. As Jane Flax writes, "The caretaker brings to the relationship . . . the whole range of social experience—work, friends, interaction with political and economic institutions, and so on. The seemingly abstract and suprapersonal relations of class, race, and male dominance enter into the construction of 'individual' human development" (1990: 122). Nancy Chodorow (1989) also takes this position, as do Denise Segura and Jennifer Pierce (1993) in their review and critique of Chodorow's work.

24. Jessica Benjamin also makes this point (1988).

25. There are also myths about people of color's "natural" talents for taking care of whites (Wong 1994). See Valerie Polakow for her discussion of motherhood and the ideology of care (1993: 22–41) and its negative effects on women's lives.

26. Chodorow and Contratto (1982) suggest that unresolved childhood images and fantasies of an all-powerful mother (upon whom children are dependent and yet seek autonomy from) fuel these maternal myths and images. Black feminist scholar Patricia Hill Collins, however, has faulted such feminist theorizing on motherhood, particularly, "the emphasis placed on all-powerful mothers as conduits for gender oppression." For according to Collins, "Instead of emphasizing maternal power in dealing with father as patriarch (Chodorow 1978; Rich 1986), or with male dominance in general (Ferguson 1989), women of color are concerned with their power and powerlessness within an array of social institutions that frame their lives" (1994: 53).

27. This is not to say that as mothers we have no power to act. As Collins states: "The existence of Afrocentric feminist thought suggests that there is always choice, and power to act, no matter how bleak the situation may be" (1990: 237).

CHAPTER EIGHT

1. Approximately 94,000,000 people are affected by low literacy skills in America, based on the National Adult Literacy Survey (Kirsch et al. 1993; Quigley 1997). Less than half of these (44.1 million) are the target population for adult literacy education and this figure constitutes 26.8 percent of the adult population. Only about 8 percent of these are served by federal adult literacy education programs per year (Beder 1994). Meanwhile, the dropout rate for adults in adult literacy programs is "18 percent before 12 hours of instruction, 20 percent at 16 weeks of instruction, and 50 percent at over 16 weeks" (Beder 1994: 16). See Quigley (1997) for a discussion of the scope of the problem and his recommendations for change.

2. Her resulting self-doubt parallels the North Carolina women's doubts about their academic abilities related to their educational marginalization.

3. But, according to Margaret, this was based on his need for her to increase her status within his family. Margaret characterized her husband's family as "looking down on her" and considering her less than what their son deserved. She wanted to be able to "wave the diploma in their faces."

4. Chodorow writes that "the integration of a 'true self' that feels alive and whole involves a particular set of internalized feelings about others in relation to the self. These include developing a sense that one is able to affect others and one's environment (a sense that one has not been inhibited by over-anticipation of all one's needs), a sense that one has been accorded one's own feelings and a spontaneity about these feelings (a sense that one's feelings or needs have not been projected onto one), and a sense that there is a fit between one's feelings and those of the mother or caretaker. These feelings all give the self a sense of agency and authenticity" (1989: 106).

5. Jane Flax offers a model of women's conflicted selfhood and gender identity, which resonates with the way the women narrated their lives. She describes the conflicts between "a mostly false (but predominant) 'social self,' an autonomous (and highly underdeveloped) self, and a 'sexual' self (also underdeveloped, but not as forbidden or constricted as the autonomous self)" (1987a: 98). Flax offers this model as an alternative to one proposed by other feminist scholars, who cast western women's selves as "relational" in contrast to men's selves, which are said to be "autonomous." Gilligan (1982) and Ruddick (1989) are examples of the models that Flax rejects. Also see Sandra Bartky, who writes about different modes of psychological oppression and "fragmentation, the splitting of the whole person into parts of a person which, in stereotyping, may take the form of a war between a 'true' and 'false' self" (1990: 23).

6. The second most cited reason was to get a better job but, as I have already explained, most of the North Carolina women did not believe that education was a sure ticket for job mobility. Indeed, structural features of university job categories and wage and salary levels meant that employees who received their GEDs and thus were eligible to transfer into "better" units than housekeeping, lost financial ground in the transfer because they could not take their wage rate with them. Starting at the bottom of the pay scale in the new unit was not an option for most employees I knew.

7. There are several layers of beliefs linking schooling and mothering discourses that deserve attention. First, the women did not count as "educational" those daily caregiving and socialization tasks they performed raising children. See Kathleen Rockhill (1987: 315–33) for her discussion of why the group of Hispanic literacy learners she studied do not count as "literacy" those things they do to rear their children, and how threatening women's pursuits of literacy can be to others. Second, the women believed that children could not be expected to want to go to school; indeed, it was their responsibility as individual mothers (not the responsibility of school or society) to get their children to see the importance and value of the educational enterprise. Third, it could be argued that the women's own motivations for returning to school reflected the institutional imperatives of an educational system built upon the psychological edifice of the omnipotent mother, in which women are at once idealized and blamed for their role in children's development. See Luttrell (1996b).

CHAPTER NINE

1. See Gavin Mackenzie (1973:2) for his summary of nineteenth-century discussions of "American exceptionalism" and David Halle (1984) for his review of debates about why Americans lack institutionalized forms of working-class consciousness

and solidarity. Claudia Strauss (1988) refers to the phenomenon I am describing as the "American individualistic success model," a cultural model that combines individualism with "economic utilitarianism, blended with the rational capitalist ethos" and with "American culture's optimism, materialism and work ethic" (37). I am concerned about how this cultural model gets acquired in and passed on through American schooling.

2. See Signithia Fordham (1993) for her explanation of how African American girls learn to censor themselves in response to the symbolic violence of school. My study demonstrates the role of specific school context and mission in shaping African American girls' adaptations to school.

3. Here I am referring to the process of "interpellation" set out by Althusser (1971)—that is, how state apparatuses such as education and the media, socially control people by making them subjects of, and subjects to, certain ideologies about who they are, what they can expect for themselves and so forth. My point is that the women in each group were differently interpellated by each school setting.

4. Nancy Chodorow (1995) advocates for a more complex picture of how gender is constructed at the personal level, how individuals appropriate larger discourses about gender in ways that are both unconscious and emotionally-charged. As a clinician and social theorist, she believes that this process is best investigated "under the clinical illumination in the transference process" (541). I believe that more empirical research about the personal construction of gender in school, under the light of a psychoanalytically-informed ethnography would be useful for understanding, and therefore improving, the ways in which girls construct their gendered identities in relation to school.

5. Karen Sacks (1989) notes that while social class has traditionally been viewed as a relationship of *individual* workers in relation to their employers, it may be better to view class as a relationship of *communities* in relation to capitalist political economies. I think the same can be said about gender and race.

6. I find the implanting notion troubling because it over-emphasizes the force of an external "other" to impose a view or an idea onto another. Still, it is a compelling image that evokes the depth and tenacious hold of certain forms of domination.

7. This phrase comes from Jessica Benjamin (1988:45–46), who writes about the contrast between intersubjective and internalization theories which she describes as "radically different" but not "mutually exclusive" ways of looking at development. She also describes how these different views of development get played out in critical social theories. She advocates the intersubjective approach because it holds more promise for self and social transformation.

8. As a fieldworker and interviewer, I would replace the notion of truth with the notion of value. I would not want to imply that what the women said or did are free-floating fictions.

9. Kenneth Plummer (1995) uses the example of rape stories as a case in point, how it is only in the past two decades that women could speak publicly about being raped or of childhood sexual abuse and still be viewed as credible or legitimate speakers. His point is that stories must be "seen as socially produced in social contexts" and that power relations are always involved (16).

10. Dorothy Allison, speech given at Carolina Theater, Durham, North Carolina, October 25, 1996.

11. See Richard Rodriguez's (1982) account of his schooling, particularly his description of being a "scholarship boy" and its damaging effects on his identity as a learner.

12. I should note here that teachers' identities are as complex as students' identities and are formed in relation to each other, in relation to institutional imperatives, cultural meanings about womanliness and manliness, and personal understandings about gender, authority, care, and nurturance. See Biklen (1995) for a good

discussion of gendered discourses about teaching (for example, about professionalism, autonomy, and motherhood) that make "the teacher's identity a complex site" (143).

13. Teachers have many choices about how they exercise authority in the classroom; these choices send important messages to students about the meaning of power, nurturance, and learning. Teachers can draw on moral or religious authority—I know this or can do this because I represent a higher source. Or they can exercise patriarchal or racist authority—I know this or can do this because I am a man or because I am white. By virtue of their position in schools, teachers exercise institutional authority—it's my job to know or to teach this, to be powerful in this way.

14. I am hardly the first to bring psychodynamic interpretations to bear on these matters, particularly as they concern student-teacher relationships (Waller 1932; Lightfoot 1977; Wexler 1992; Walkerdine 1990).

15. Sara Ruddick's (1982, 1989) work about "maternal thinking" is useful in thinking about maternal authority. She says that the social practice of mothering generates a way of thinking that is governed by interests to preserve life and relationships, to promote growth and self-acceptance. She calls for a transformation of maternal thought through feminist consciousness as the basis for women's authority and social activism.

16. When I consider how much effort it takes me—an educated, middle-class mother who is not intimidated by teachers or treated disrespectfully by them—to be involved and act as an advocate on behalf of my children in their school lives, I simply can't imagine the will and energy it must take for mothers who aren't tied to school and teachers in the same way I am to advocate for their children. See Lareau (1989) for more discussion about class and gender differences in parent involvement in schooling.

17. See Luttrell (1996b) for more discussion of this problem in adult literacy programs.

18. See Lloyd (1994) for a discussion of what she calls "woman-positive literacy education." Also see Horsman (1990); Luttrell (1981, 1982, 1996b); Robinson et al. (1973, 1978) and Thompson (1980) for more discussion of this point.

19. Others have written about the value of storytelling in education. See Robert Coles (1989) and Carol Witherell and Nel Noddings (1991).

[References]

Abel, Elizabeth. 1990. "Race, Class and Psychoanalysis? Opening Questions." In *Conflicts in Feminism*, ed. Marianne Hirsh and Evelyn Fox Keller, 184–204. London and New York: Routledge.

Adorno, Theodor, Else-Frenkel Brunswick, Daniel J. Levinson, and R. N. Sanford in collaboration with Betty Aron, Maria Hertz Levinson, and William Morrow. 1950. *The Authoritarian Personality.* New York: Harper & Brothers.

Alarcon, Norma. 1985. "What Kind of Lover Have You Made Me, Mother: Toward a Theory of Chicanas' Feminism and Cultural Identity Through Poetry." In *Perspectives on Feminism and Identity in Women of Color,* ed. Audrey T. McCluskey, 85–110. Bloomington: Indiana University Press.

Alcoff, Linda. 1988. "Cultural Feminism versus Post-Structuralism: The Identity Crisis in Feminist Theory." *Signs: Journal of Women in Culture and Society* 13 (3): 405–36.

Allen, Caffelene. 1994. "First They Changed My Name . . . Deep in Appalachia, Education Came with a Price." *Ms.,* January/Februrary, 25–27.

Allison, Dorothy. 1996. *Two or Three Things I Know for Sure.* New York: Penguin.

Althusser, Louis. 1971. "Ideology and Ideological State Apparatuses." In *Lenin and Philosophy and Other Essays.* New York: Monthly Review Press.

American Association of University Women Report (AAUW), 1992. *How Schools Shortchange Girls: A Study of Major Findings on Girls and Education,* researched by the Wellesley College Center for Research on Women, Wellesley, Mass.

Anderson, Kathryn, and Dana Jacks. 1991. "Learning to Listen: Interview Techniques and Analyses." In *Women's Words: The Feminist Practice of Oral History,* ed. S. Gluck and D. Patai, 11–27. New York: Routledge.

Apple, M. W. 1986. *Teachers and Texts: A Political Economy of Class and Gender Relations in Education.* New York and London: Routledge and Kegan Paul.

———. 1987. "Gendered Teaching, Gendered Labor." In *Critical Studies in Teacher Education,* ed. Thomas S. Popkewitz. Hampshire, England: Falmer.

Barkley-Brown, Elsa. 1989. "African American Women's Quilting: A Framework for Conceptualizing and Teaching African American Women's History." *Signs: Journal of Women in Culture and Society* 14 (4): 921–29.

Bartky, Sandra Lee. 1990. *Feminity and Domination: Studies of the Phenomenology of Oppression.* New York and London: Routledge.

Bateson, Catherine. 1990. *Composing a Life.* New York: Penguin.

Beder, Hal. 1994. "The Current Status of Adult Literacy Education in the United States." *PAACE Journal of Lifelong Learning* 3: 14–25.

Behar, Ruth. 1993. *Translated Woman: Crossing the Border With Esperanza's Story.* Boston: Beacon.

Behar, Ruth, and Deborah Gordon. 1995. *Women Writing Culture*. Berkeley: University of California Press.

Belenky, Mary Field, Blythe McVicker Clinchy, Nancy Rule Goldberger, and Jill Mattuck Tarule. 1986. *Women's Ways of Knowing: The Development of Self, Voice, and Mind*. New York: Basic.

Benjamin, Jessica. 1988. *The Bonds of Love: Psychoanalysis, Feminism, and the Problem of Domination*. New York: Pantheon.

———. 1994. "The Omnipotent Mother: A Psychoanalytic Study of Fantasy and Reality." In *Representations of Motherhood*, ed. Donna Bassin, Margaret Honey, and Meryle Mahrer Kaplan, 129–46. New Haven: Yale University Press.

Bernstein, Basil. 1975. *Class, Codes and Control*, vol. 3. London: Routledge and Kegan Paul.

Bertaux, Daniel, and Martin Kohli. 1984. "The Life Story Approach: A Continental View." *Annual Review of Sociology* 10: 215–37.

Best, Raphaela. 1983. *We've All Got Scars: What Boys and Girls Learn in Elementary School*. Bloomington: Indiana University Press.

Bettelheim, Bruno. 1987. *The Uses of Enchantment: The Meaning and Importance of Fairy Tales*. New York: Vintage.

Biklen, Sari. 1995. *School Work: Gender and the Cultural Construction of Teaching*. New York: Teachers College Press.

Binzen, Peter. 1970. *Whitetown, USA*. New York: Random House.

Bookman, Ann, and Sandra Morgen, eds. 1988. *Women and the Politics of Empowerment*. Philadelphia: Temple University Press.

Bordo, Susan. 1986. "The Cartesian Masculinization of Thought." *Signs: Journal of Women in Culture and Society* 11 (3): 439–56.

Bordo, Susan, and Alison Jaggar, eds. 1989. *Gender, Body, Knowledge: Feminist Reconstructions of Being and Knowing*. New Brunswick, NJ: Rutgers University Press.

Bourdieu, Pierre. 1974. "The School as a Conservative Force: Scholastic and Cultural Inequalities." In *Contemporary Research in the Sociology of Education*, ed. John Eggleston, 32–46. London: Methuen.

———. 1977. *Outline of a Theory of Practice*. Cambridge: Cambridge University Press.

———. 1984. *Distinction: A Social Critique of the Judgment of Taste*. Cambridge, MA: Harvard University Press.

Bourdieu, Pierre, and Jean-Claude Passeron. 1977. *Reproduction in Education, Society and Culture*. Beverly Hills: Sage.

Bourdieu, Pierre, and Monique Saint Martin. 1974. "Scholastic Excellence and the Values of the Educational System." In *Contemporary Research in the Sociology of Education*, ed. John Eggleston, 338–71. London: Methuen.

Bowles, Samuel, and Herbert Gintis. 1976. *Schooling in Capitalist America*. New York: Basic Books.

Braxton, Joanne. 1989. *Black Women Writing Autobiography: A Tradition Within a Tradition*. Philadelphia: Temple University Press.

Briggs, Jean. 1986. "Kapluna Daughter." In *Women in the Field: Anthropological Experiences*, ed. Peggy Golde, 19–44. Berkeley: University of California Press.

Brodzki, Bella, and Celeste Schenck, eds. 1988. *Life/Lines: Theorizing Women's Autobiography*. Ithaca, NY: Cornell University Press.

Brophy, Jere, and Thomas Goode. 1974. *Teacher-Student Relationships: Causes and Consequences*. New York: Holt, Rinehart & Winston.

Brown, Lyn Mikel, and Carol Gilligan. 1992. *Meeting at the Crossroads: Women's Psychology and Girls' Development*. Cambridge and London: Harvard University Press.

Burke, Kenneth. 1954. *Permanence and Change: An Anatomy of Purpose*. Los Altos, CA: Hermes Publications.

———. 1969. *A Grammar of Motives*. Berkeley: University of California Press.

Butler, Judith. 1990. *Gender Trouble: Feminism and the Subversion of Identity*. New York and London: Routledge.
———. 1991. "Imitation and Gender Insubordination." *Inside/Out: Lesbian Theories, Gay Theories*, ed. D. Fuss. New York and London: Routledge.
Chase, Susan. 1991. "Interpreting Women's Narratives: Toward an Alternative Methodology." Paper presented at the Southern Sociological Society Meetings, Atlanta, Georgia, April 6.
———. 1995. *Ambiguous Empowerment: The Work Narratives of Women School Superintendents*. Amherst: University of Massachusetts Press.
Childs, John Brown. 1984. "Afro-American Intellectuals and the People's Culture." *Theory and Society* 13: 69–90.
Chodorow, Nancy. 1978. *The Reproduction of Mothering: Psychoanalysis and the Sociology of Gender*. Berkeley: University of California Press.
———. 1989. *Feminism and Psychoanalytic Theory*. New Haven and London: Yale University Press.
———. 1995. "Gender as a Personal and Cultural Construction." *Signs: Journal of Women in Culture and Society* 20 (3): 516–44.
Chodorow, Nancy, and Contratto, S. 1982. "The Fantasy of the Perfect Mother." In *Rethinking the Family: Some Feminist Questions*, ed. Barrie Thorne and Marilyn Yalom, 54–75. New York: Longman.
Cixous, Helene. 1976. "The Laugh of the Medusa." *Signs: Journal of Women in Culture and Society* 1 (4): 875–93.
———. 1981. "Castration or Decapitation?" *Signs: Journal of Women in Culture and Society* 7 (1): 41–55.
Clark, Lorenne. 1976. "The Rights of Women: The Theory and Practice of Ideology of Male Supremacy." In *Contemporary Issues in Political Philosophy*, ed. William R. Shea and John King-Farlow, 49–65. New York: Science History Publications.
Coles, Robert. 1989. *The Call of Stories: Teaching and the Moral Imagination*. Boston: Houghton Mifflin.
Collins, Patricia Hill. 1990. *Black Feminist Thought: Knowledge, Consciousness, and the Politics of Empowerment*. London: Harper Collins Academic.
———. 1994. "Shifting the Center: Race, Class and Feminist Theorizing About Motherhood." In *Mothering: Ideology, Experience, and Agency*, ed. Evelyn Nakano Glenn, Grace Chang, and Linda Rennie Forcey. New York and London: Routledge.
Connell, R. W. 1983. *Which Way Is Up? Essays on Class, Sex, and Culture*. London: George Allen and Unwin.
———. 1985. *Teachers' Work*. London: George Allen and Unwin.
———. 1987. *Gender and Power*. Stanford, CA: Stanford University Press.
———. 1993. *Schools and Social Justice*. Philadelphia: Temple University Press.
Connell, R. W., D. J. Ashenden, S. Kessler, and G. W. Dowsett. 1982. *Making The Difference: Schools, Families and Social Division*. Sydney: George Allen and Unwin.
Cooley, Charles H. 1983. *Human Nature and the Social Order*. New Brunswick, NJ: Transaction.
Crapanzano, Vincent. 1980. *Tuhami: Portrait of a Moroccan*. Chicago: University of Chicago Press.
Daly, Mary. 1973. *Beyond God the Father*. Boston: Beacon.
———. 1978. *Gyn/Ecology: The Metaethics of Radical Feminism*. Boston: Beacon.
David, M. E. 1980. *The State, the Family and Education*. London: Routledge and Kegan Paul.
Davis, Allison, B. Burleigh Gardner, and Mary Gardner, directed by Lloyd Warner. 1931. *Deep South: A Social Anthropological Study of Caste and Class*. Chicago: University of Chicago Press.
Davis, Angela. 1971. "The Black Woman's Role in the Community of Slaves." *The Black Scholar* 3: 2–153.
———. 1981. *Women, Race and Class*. New York: Random House.

Delpit, Lisa. 1995. *Other People's Children: Cultural Conflict in the Classroom.* New York: New Press.

Devault, Marjorie. 1990. "Talking and Listening from Women's Standpoint: Feminist Strategies for Interviewing and Analysis." *Social Problems* 37 (1): 96–116.

di Leonardo, Micaela, ed. 1991. *Gender at the Crossroads of Knowledge: Feminist Anthropology in the Postmodern Era.* Berkeley: University of California Press.

Dill, Bonnie Thornton. 1983. "On the Hem of Life: Race, Class and Prospects for Sisterhood." In *Class, Race and Sex: The Dynamics of Control,* ed. A. Swerdlow and H. Lessinger, 173–188. Boston: G. K. Hall.

Dimen, Muriel. 1989. "Power, Sexuality and Intimacy." In *Gender/Body/Knowledge: Feminist Reconstructions of Being and Knowing,* ed. Alison Jaggar and Susan Bordo, 34–53. New Brunswick and London: Rutgers University Press.

———. 1991. "Deconstructing Difference: Gender, Splitting and 'Transitional Space.'" *Psychoanalytic Dialogues* 1: 335–52.

Dinnerstein, Dorothy. 1976. *The Mermaid and the Minotaur: Sexual Arrangements and Human Malaise.* New York: Harper Colophon Books.

Dweck, Carol S., William Davidson, Sharon Nelson, and Bradley Enna. 1978. "Sex Differences in Learned Helplessness: II. The Contingencies of Evaluation Feedback in the Classroom. III. An Experimental Analysis." *Developmental Psychology* 14: 268–76.

Ellison, Ralph. 1952. *Invisible Man.* New York: Random House.

Erickson, Frederick. 1987. "Transformation and School Success: The Politics and Culture of Educational Achievement." *Anthropology and Education Quarterly* 18 (4): 335–56.

Espin, Olivia. 1984. "Cultural and Historical Influences on Sexuality in Hispanic Women: Implications for Psychotherapy." In *Pleasure and Danger: Exploring Female Sexuality,* ed. Carole Vance, 149–64. New York: Monthly Review Press.

Ewing, Katherine. 1990. "The Illusion of Wholeness: Culture, Self and the Experience of Inconsistency." *Ethos* 18 (3): 251–78.

Fairbairn, W. R. D. 1952. *An Object Relations Theory of the Personality.* New York: Basic Books.

Fanon, Frantz. 1967. *Black Skins, White Masks.* New York: Grove Press.

Fee, E. 1983. "Women's Nature and Scientific Objectivity." In *Women's Nature: Rationalizations of Inequality,* ed. M. Lowe and R. Hubbard. New York: Pergamon.

Ferguson, Ann. 1989. *Blood at the Root: Motherhood, Sexuality, and Male Dominance.* London and Winchester, MA: Pandora.

Fields, Mamie Garvin, with Karen Fields. 1983. *Lemon Swamp and Other Places.* New York: Free Press.

Fine, Michelle. 1991. *Framing Dropouts: Notes on the Politics of an Urban Public High School.* Albany: State University of New York Press.

———. 1992. *Disruptive Voices: The Possibilities of Feminist Research.* Ann Arbor: University of Michigan Press.

Fine, Michelle, and Nancie Zane. 1989. "On Bein' Wrapped Too Tight: When Low Income Females Drop Out of School." In *Dropouts in Schools: Issues, Dilemmas, and Solutions,* ed. Lois Weis, 23–54. Albany: State University of New York Press.

Fingeret, Arlene. 1983a. "Common Sense and Book Learning: Cultural Clash?" *Lifelong Learning: the Adult Years* 6 (8): 22–24.

———. 1983b. "Social Network: A New Perspective on Independence and Illiterate Adults." *Adult Education Quarterly* 33 (3): 133–46.

Flax, Jane. 1987a. "Re-membering the Selves: Is the Repressed Gendered?" *Michigan Quarterly* 26 (1): 92–110.

———. 1987b. "Postmodernism and Gender Relations in Feminist Theory." *Signs: Journal of Women in Culture and Society* 12 (4): 621–43.

———. 1990. *Thinking Fragments: Psychoanalysis, Feminism, and Postmodernism in the Contemporary West.* Berkeley and Los Angeles: University of California Press.

Foote, Nelson. 1951. "Identification as the Basis for a Theory of Motivation." *American Sociological Review* 16: 14–21.

Fordham, Signithia. 1993. "'Those Loud Black girls': (Black) Women, Silence, and Gender 'Passing' in the Academy." *Anthropology and Education Quarterly* 24 (1): 3–32.

Frankenberg, Ruth. 1993. *White Women, Race Matters: The Social Construction of Whiteness.* Minneapolis: University of Minnesota Press.

Freud, Sigmund. 1963. *Sexuality and the Psychology of Love.* New York: Collier.

Foucault, Michel. 1977. *Discipline and Punish: The Birth of the Prison.* New York: Pantheon.

———. 1979. *The History of Sexuality, vol. 1: An Introduction,* trans. Robert Hurley. London: Allen Lane.

Fox, Greer Litton. 1977. "Nice Girls: Social Control of Women Through a Value Construct." *Signs: Journal of Women in Culture and Society* 2 (4): 805–17.

Fuller, M. 1980. "Black Girls in a London Comprehensive School." In *Schooling for Women's Work,* ed. R. Deem, 52–65. London: Routledge and Kegan Paul.

Gardner, Howard. 1993. *Multiple Intelligences: The Theory in Practice.* New York: Basic Books.

Gaskell, J. 1985. "Course Enrollment in the High School: The Perspective of Working-Class Females." *Sociology of Education* 58: 48–57.

Geertz, Clifford. 1983. *Local Knowledge: Further Essays in Interpretive Anthropology.* New York: Basic Books.

Geiger, Susan G. 1986. "Women's Life Histories: Method and Content." *Signs: Journal of Women in Culture and Society* 11: 334–51.

Giddings, Paula. 1984. *When and Where I Enter: The Impact of Black Women on Race and Sex in America.* New York: Bantam.

Gilkes, Cheryl Townsend. 1985. "'Together and in Harness': Women's Traditions in the Sanctified Church." *Signs: Journal of Women in Culture and Society* 10 (4): 678–99.

———. 1988. "Building in Many Places: Multiple Commitments and Ideologies in Black Women's Community Work." In *Women and the Politics of Empowerment,* ed. Ann Bookman and Sandra Morgen, 53–76. Philadelphia: Temple University Press.

Gilligan, Carol. 1982. *In a Different Voice: Psychological Theory and Women's Development.* Cambridge, MA: Harvard University Press.

———. 1988. *Mapping the Moral Domain: A Contribution of Women's Thinking to Psychological Theory and Education.* Cambridge, MA: Harvard University Press.

———. 1990. *Making Connections: The Relational Worlds of Adolescent Girls at Emma Willard School.* Cambridge, MA.: Harvard University Press.

Ginsburg, Faye. 1989. "Dissonance and Harmony: The Symbolic Function of Abortion in Activists' Life Stories." In *Interpreting Women's Lives: Feminist Theory and Personal Narratives,* ed. Personal Narratives Group, 59–84. Bloomington: Indiana University Press.

Ginsburg, Faye, and Anna Tsing. 1990. *Uncertain Terms: Negotiating Gender in American Culture.* Boston: Beacon.

Giroux, Henry. 1992. *Border Crossings: Cultural Workers and the Politics of Education.* New York: Routledge.

Giroux, Henry, and Peter McLaren, eds. 1994. *Between Borders: Pedagogy and the Politics of Cultural Studies.* New York and London: Routledge.

Glenn, Evelyn Nakano, Grace Chang, and Linda R. Forcey, eds. 1994. *Mothering: Ideology, Experience, and Agency.* New York and London: Routledge.

Gluck, Sherna Berger, and Daphne Patai. 1991. *Women's Words: The Feminist Practice of Oral History.* New York: Routledge.

Goffman, Erving. 1959. *The Presentation of Self in Everyday Life.* New York: Doubleday, Anchor.

———. 1963. *Stigma: Notes on the Management of Spoiled Identity.* Englewood Cliffs, NJ: Prentice-Hall.

Gonzales, Gilbert. 1979. "The Historical Development of the Concept of Intelligence." *Review of Radical Political Economics* 11 (2): 44–54.

Gordon, Deborah. 1988. "Writing Culture, Writing Feminism: The Poetics and Politics of Experimental Ethnography." *Inscriptions* 3/4: 7–24.

Gordon, Linda. 1988. *Heroes of Their Own Lives*. New York: Penguin.

Gould, Stephen Jay. 1981. *The Mismeasure of Man*. New York: Norton.

Grant, Jacquelyn. 1982. "Black Women and the Church." In *All the Women Are White and All the Blacks Are Men, But Some of Us Are Brave*, ed. Gloria T. Hull, Patricia Bell Scott, and Barbara Smith, 141–52. Old Westbury, NY: Feminist Press.

Grant, Judith. 1987. "I Feel Therefore I Am: A Critique of Female Experience as a Basis for Feminist Epistemology." *Women and Politics* 7 (3): 99–114.

Grant, Linda. 1985. "Race-gender Status, Classroom Interaction, and Children's Socialization in Classrooms." In *Gender Influences in Classroom Interaction*, ed. L. C. Wilkinson, and C. B. Marrett, 57–77. New York: Academic.

———. 1992. "Race and the Schooling of Young Girls." In *Education and Gender Equality*, ed. Julia Wrigley, 91–114. London and Washington, DC: Falmer.

———. 1994. "Helpers, Enforcers and Go-Betweens: Black Girls in Elementary Schools." In *Women of Color in America*, ed. Maxine Baca Zinn and Bonnie Thornton Dill, 43–63. Philadelphia: Temple University Press.

Greenberg, Jay, and Stephen Mitchell. 1983. *Object Relations in Psychoanalytic Theory*. Cambridge, MA: Harvard University Press.

Griffin, Susan. 1980. *Woman and Nature: The Roaring Inside Her*. New York: Harper Colophon.

Griffith, Alison, and Dorothy Smith. 1987. "Constructing Cultural Knowledge: Mothering as Discourse." In *Women and Education: A Canadian Perspective*, ed. Jane Gaskell and Arlene McLaren, 87–103. Calgary, Alberta: Detselig Enterprises.

Grumet, Madeline. 1988. *Bitter Milk: Women and Teaching*. Amherst: University of Massachusetts Press.

Hall, Stuart. 1991. "Old and New Identities, Old and New Ethnicities," In *Culture Globalization and the World System*, ed. A. D. King, 41–68. London: Macmillan.

———. 1992. "Cultural Studies and Its Theoretical Legacies." In *Cultural Studies*, ed. Lawrence Grossberg, Cary Nelson, and Paula Treichler, 277–94. New York: Routledge.

Hall, Jacqueline, J. Deloudis, R. Korstad, M. Murphy, L. Jones, and C. Daly. 1987. *Like a Family: The Making of a Southern Mill World*. Chapel Hill: University of North Carolina Press.

Halle, David. 1984. *America's Working Man: Work, Home, and Politics among Blue-Collar Property Owners*. Chicago: University of Chicago Press.

Hansot, Elisabeth, and David Tyack. 1988. "Gender in American Public Schools: Thinking Institutionally." *Signs: Journal of Women in Culture and Society* 13 (4): 741–60.

Harding, Sandra. 1986. *The Science Question in Feminism*. Ithaca: Cornell University Press.

Harding, Sandra, and Merrill Hintikka, eds. 1983. *Discovering Reality: Feminist Perspectives on Epistemology, Metaphysics, and Philosophy of Science*. Dordrecht: Reidel.

Hartsock, Nancy. 1985. *Money, Sex and Power: Toward a Feminist Historical Materialism*. Boston: Northeastern University Press.

Haug, Frigga, et al. 1987. *Female Sexualization: A Collective Work of Memory*, trans. from German by Erica Carter. London: Verso.

Hawkesworth, Mary E. 1989. "Knowers, Knowing, Known: Feminist Theory and Claims of Truth." *Signs: Journal of Women in Culture and Society* 14 (3): 533–57.

Heath, Shirley Brice. 1983. *Ways with Words: Language, Life and Work in Communities and Classrooms*. Cambridge: Cambridge University Press.

Heckman, Susan. 1987. "The Feminization of Epistemology: Gender and the Social Sciences." *Women and Politics* 7 (3): 65–83.

Heilbrun, Carolyn. 1988. *Writing a Woman's Life*. New York: Norton.

Henriques, Julian, Wendy Holloway, Cathy Urwin, Couze Venn, and Valerie Walkerdine. 1984. *Changing the Subject: Psychology, Social Regulation and Subjectivity*. London and New York: Methuen.

Hewitt, J. P., and R. Stokes. 1978. "Disclaimers." In *Symbolic Interaction: A Reader in Social Psychology*, ed. J. Manis, and B. Meltzer, 308–18. Boston: Allyn and Bacon.

Higginbotham, Evelyn Brooks. 1992. "African-American Women's History and the Metalanguage of Race." *Signs: Journal of Women in Culture and Society* 17 (2): 251–74.

Hine, Darlene Clark. 1989. "Rape and the Inner Lives of Black Women in the Middle West: Preliminary Thoughts on the Culture of Dissemblance." *Signs: Journal of Women in Culture and Society* 14 (4): 912–20.

Hirschhorn, Larry. 1988. *The Workplace Within: Psychodynamics of Organizational Life*. Cambridge, MA: MIT Press.

Hochschild, Arlie. 1983. *The Managed Heart: Commercialization of Human Feeling*. Berkeley: University of California Press.

Holland, Dorothy. 1988. "In the Voice of, in the Image of: Socially Situated Presentations of Attractiveness." *Papers in Pragmatics* 2 (1/2): 106–135.

Holland, Dorothy, Carole Cain, William Lashicotte, Deborah Skinner, and Renee Prillamann. Forthcoming. *Emerging Selves: Identities Forming in and Against Cultural Worlds*. Cambridge, MA: Harvard University Press.

Holland, Dorothy, and Margaret Eisenhart. 1990. *Educated in Romance: Women, Achievement and College Culture*. Chicago: University of Chicago Press.

Holland, Dorothy, and Naomi Quinn. 1987. *Cultural Models in Language and Thought*. Cambridge: Cambridge University Press.

Holloway, Karla. 1995. *Codes of Conduct: Race, Ethics and the Color of Our Character*. New Brunswick, NJ: Rutgers University Press.

hooks, bell. 1990. *Yearning: Race, Gender, and Cultural Politics*. Boston: South End Press.

Horsman, Jennifer. 1990. *Something in My Mind Besides the Everyday: Women and Literacy*. Ontario, Canada: Women's Press.

Hughes, Judith. 1989. *Reshaping the Psychoanalytic Domain: The Work of Melanie Klein, W.R.D. Fairbairn and D. W. Winnicott*. Berkeley: University of California Press.

Hunt, Jennifer. 1989. *Psychoanalytic Aspects of Fieldwork*. Newbury Park, CA: Sage.

Irigaray, Luce. 1985. *Speculum of the Other Woman*, trans. Gillian Gill. Ithaca: Cornell University Press.

Jacobson, Edith. 1965. *The Self and the Object World*. London: Hogarth.

Jaggar, Alison. 1983. *Feminist Politics and Human Nature*. Totowa, NJ: Rowman and Littlefield.

Johnson, Miriam. 1988. *Strong Mothers, Weak Wives*. Berkeley: University of California Press.

Johnson, Richard. 1979. "'Really Useful Knowledge': Radical Education and Working-Class Culture, 1790–1848." In *Working Class Culture: Studies in History and Theory*, ed. J. Clarke, C. Critcher, and R. Johnson, 75–102. New York: St. Martin's.

———. 1986/87. "What Is Cultural Studies Anyway?" *Social Text: Theory, Culture, Ideology* 16: 38–40.

Jones, Jacqueline. 1985. *Labor of Love, Labor of Sorrow: Black Women, Work and the Family from Slavery to the Present*. New York: Basic Books.

Jones, M. Gail. 1989. "Gender Bias in Classroom Interactions." *Contemporary Education* 60 (4): 218–22.

Joseph, Gloria. 1981. "Black Mothers and Daughters." In *Common Differences: Con-*

flicts in Black and White Feminist Perspectives, ed. Gloria Joseph and Jill Lewis, 75–126. New York: Anchor.

Kaplan, Temma. 1982. "Female Consciousness and Collective Action: The Case of Barcelona, 1910–1918." Signs: Journal of Women in Culture and Society 7 (3): 545–66.

Keller, Evelyn Fox. 1978. "Gender and Science." Psychoanalysis and Contemporary Thought 1: 409–33.

———. 1987. "Feminism and Science." In Sex and Scientific Inquiry, ed. S. Harding and J. O'Barr, 233–46. Chicago: University of Chicago Press.

———. 1984. Reflections on Gender and Science. New Haven: Yale University Press.

Kincaid, Jamaica. 1985. Annie John. New York: Farrar, Straus and Giroux.

Kirsch, I., A. Jungeblute, L. Jenkins and A. Kolstad. 1993. Adult Literacy in America: A First Look at the Results of the National Adult Literacy Survey. Washington, DC: U.S. Department of Education.

Klein, Melanie. 1975. Love, Guilt and Reparation and Other Works, 1921–1945. London: Hogarth.

Klein, Melanie, and Joan Riviere. 1974. Love, Hate and Reparation. New York: Norton.

Kleinman, Sherryl, and Martha Copp. 1993. Emotions and Fieldwork. Newbury Park, CA: Sage.

Kohut, Heinz. 1978. The Search for the Self: Selected Writings of Heinz Kohut, 1950–1978. New York: International Universities Press.

Krieger, Susan. 1991. Social Science and the Self: Personal Essays on an Art Form. New Brunswick, NJ: Rutgers University Press.

Labov, William. 1972. Language in the Inner City: Studies in the Black English Vernacular. Philadelphia: University of Pennsylvania Press.

Ladner, Joyce. 1972. Tomorrow's Tomorrow: The Black Woman. Garden City, NY: Doubleday Anchor Press.

Lamphere, Louise 1987. From Working Daughters to Working Mothers in a New England Industrial Community. Ithaca: Cornell University Press

Lareau, Annette. 1989. Home Advantage: Social Class and Parental Intervention in Elementary Education. London and New York: Falmer.

Lather, Patti. 1991. Getting Smart: Feminist Research and Pedagogy With/In the Postmodern. New York and London: Routledge.

Lave, Jean, Paul Duguid, Nadine Fernandez, and Erik Axel. 1992. "Coming of Age in Birmingham: Cultural Studies and Conceptions of Subjectivity." Annual Reviews of Anthropology 21: 257–82.

Lesko, Nancy. 1988. Symbolizing Society: Stories, Rites and Structure in a Catholic High School. New York: Falmer.

Levesque-Lopman, Louise. 1988. Claiming Reality: Phenomenology and Women's Experience. Totowa, NJ: Rowman and Littlefield.

Levinson, Bradley, Douglas Foley, and Dorothy Holland. 1996. The Cultural Production of the Educated Person: Critical Ethnographies of Schooling and Local Practice. Albany: State University of New York Press.

Levinson, Bradley, and Dorothy Holland. 1996. "The Cultural Production of the Educated Person: An Introduction." In The Cultural Production of the Educated Person, ed. Bradley Levinson, Douglas Foley and Dorothy Holland, 1–54. Albany: State University of New York Press.

Lightfoot, Sarah Lawrence. 1977. "Family-School Interactions: The Cultural Image of Mothers and Teachers." Signs: Journal of Women in Culture and Society (3): 395–408.

Linde, Charlotte. 1993. Life Stories: The Creation of Coherence. New York: Oxford University Press.

Lloyd, B., with F. Ennis and T. Atkinson. 1994. Women in Literacy Speak: The Power of Woman-Positive Literacy Work. Halifax, Canada: Fernwood.

Lloyd, Genevieve. 1984. *The Man of Reason: Male and Female in Western Philosophy.* London: Methuen.

Lofland, John. 1971. *Analyzing Social Settings: A Guide to Qualitative Observation and Analysis.* Belmont, CA: Wadsworth.

Logan, Onnie Lee. 1989. *Motherwit: An Alabama Midwife's Story.* New York: Penguin.

London, Howard B. 1978. *The Culture of a Community College.* New York: Praeger.

Long, Elizabeth. 1986. "Women, Reading, and Cultural Authority: Some Implications of the Audience Perspective in Cultural Studies." *American Quarterly* 38 (4): 591–612.

Lorber, Judith, et al. 1981. "On *The Reproduction of Mothering*: A Methodological Debate." *Signs: Journal of Women in Culture and Society* 6 (3): 482–513.

Lorde, Audrey. 1984. *Sister Outsider.* Trumansberg, NY: The Crossing Press.

Luttrell, Wendy. 1981. *Women in the Community: A Curriculum Guide for Students and Teachers.* Lutheran Settlement House. Philadelphia: Pennsylvania State Department of Education.

———. 1982. *Curriculum-Issues in Feminist Community-based Education*, published by the Fund for the Improvement of Post-secondary Education, U.S. Department of Education.

———. 1984. "The Getting of Knowledge: A Study of Working-Class Women and Education." Unpublished Ph.D. dissertation, University of California at Santa Cruz.

———. 1985. *Making Sense: A Resource Guide for a Collaborative Learning to Read Process.* North Carolina Department of Community Colleges, Raleigh, North Carolina.

———. 1988. "The Edison School Story: Reshaping Working-Class Education and Women's Consciousness." In *Women and the Politics of Empowerment*, ed. Ann Bookman and Sandra Morgen, 136–56. Philadelphia: Temple University Press.

———. 1989. "Working-Class Women's Ways of Knowing: Effects of Gender, Race, and Class." *Sociology of Education* 62 (1): 33–46.

———. 1993. "'The Teachers They All Had Their Pets': Concepts of Gender, Knowledge and Power." *Signs: Journal of Women in Culture and Society* 18 (3): 505–46.

———. 1994. "'Becoming Somebody': Aspirations, Opportunities, and Womanhood." In *Color, Class and Country: Experiences of Gender*, ed. Gay Young and Bette Dickerson, 17–35. London and New Jersey: Zed Books.

———. 1996a. "'Becoming Somebody' in and Against School: Towards a Psychocultural Theory of Gender and Self Making." In *The Cultural Production of the Educated Person: Critical Ethnographies of Schooling and Local Practice*, ed. Bradley Levinson, Douglas Foley, and Dorothy Holland, 93–118. Albany: State University of New York Press

———. 1996b. "Taking Care of Literacy: One Feminist's Critique." *Educational Policy* 10 (3): 342–65.

Mackenzie, Gavin. 1973. *The Aristocracy of Labor: The Position of Skilled Craftsmen in the American Class Structure.* Cambridge: Cambridge University Press.

MacLeod, Jay. 1987. *Ain't No Makin' It: Leveled Aspirations in a Low-Income Neighborhood.* Boulder, CO: Westview.

McCarthy, Cameron, and Warren Crichlow, eds. 1993. *Race and Representation in Education.* New York and London: Routledge.

McLaren, Arlene T. 1981. "Women in Adult Education: The Neglected Majority." *International Journal of Women's Studies* 4 (2): 245–58.

———. 1982. "Ambition and Accounts: A Study of Working-Class Women in Adult Education." *Psychiatry* 45: 235–46.

———. 1985. *Ambitions and Realizations: Women in Adult Education.* London: Peter Owen.

McMillan, Carol. 1982. *Women, Reason and Nature.* Princeton, NJ: Princeton University Press.

McRobbie, Angela. 1978. "Working Class Girls and the Culture of Femininity." In *Women Take Issue: Aspects of Women's Subordination*, ed. Women's Studies Group CCCS, 96–108. London: Hutchinson.

———. 1982. "The Politics of Feminist Research: Between Talk, Text and Action." *Feminist Review* 12: 46–57.

———. 1984. *Gender and Generation*. London: Macmillan.

———. 1991. *Feminism and Youth Culture: From "Jackie" to "Just Seventeen."* Boston: Unwin Hyman.

Mahler, Margaret, Fred Pine, and Anni Bergman. 1975. *The Psychological Birth of the Human Infant: Symbiosis and Individuation*. New York: Basic Books.

Martin, Jane Roland. 1985. *Reclaiming a Conversation*. New Haven: Yale University Press.

———. 1994. *Changing the Educational Landscape*. New York and London: Routledge.

Martin, Roy. 1972. "Student Sex and Behavior as Determinants of the Type and Frequency of Teacher-Student Contact." *Journal of School Psychology* 10 (4): 339–44.

Mascia-Lees, Frances, Patricia Sharpe, and Colleen Ballerino Cohen. 1989. "The Postmodern Turn in Anthropology: Cautions from a Feminist Perspective." *Signs: Journal of Women in Culture and Society* 15 (1): 7–33.

Matthews, Jill Julius. 1984. *Good and Mad Women: The Historical Construction of Femininity in Twentieth Century Australia*. Sydney: George Allen and Unwin.

Mead, George H. 1962. *Mind, Self, and Society*. Chicago: University of Chicago Press.

Miller, Alice. 1981. *Drama of the Gifted Child*, trans. Ruth Ward. New York: Basic Books.

Mills, C. W. 1940. "Situated Actions and Vocabularies of Motive." *American Sociological Review* 5: 905–13.

Mintz, Sidney. 1974. *Worker in the Cane*. New York: Norton.

Mishler, Elliot. 1986. *Research Interviewing: Context and Narrative*. Cambridge, MA: Harvard University Press.

Moody, Anne. 1968. *Coming of Age in Mississippi*. New York: Dial Press.

Moraga, Cherrie. 1986. "From a Long Line of Vendidas: Chicanas and Feminism." In *Feminist Studies/Critical Studies*, ed. Teresa De Lauretis, 173–90. Madison: University of Wisconsin Press.

Noddings, Nel. 1984. *Caring: A Feminine Approach to Ethics and Moral Education*. Berkeley: University of California Press.

Oakley, Ann. 1981. "Interviewing Women: A Contradiction in Terms." In *Doing Feminist Research*, ed. H. Roberts, 30–61. London: Routledge and Kegan Paul.

O'Brien, Mary. 1981. *The Politics of Reproduction*. London: Routledge and Kegan Paul.

———. 1988. "Class Stratification, Racial Stratification, and Schooling." In *Class, Race and Gender in American Education*, ed. Lois Weis, 163–82. Albany: State University of New York Press.

Ogbu, John. 1988. "Class Stratification, Racial Stratification, and Schooling." In *Class, Race and Gender in American Education*, ed. Lois Weis, 163–182. Albany: State University of New York Press.

Omi, Michael, and Howard Winant. 1986. *Racial Formation in the United States: From the 1960's to the 1980's*. New York and London: Routledge.

Ortner, Sherry B. 1984. "Theory in Anthropology Since the Sixties." *Comparative Studies in Society and History* 26: 126–65.

Paget, Marianne. 1990. "Life Mirrors Work Mirrors Text Mirrors Life." *Social Problems* 37 (2): 137–48.

Palmer, Phyllis M. 1983. "White Women/Black Women: The Dualism of Female Identity and Experience in the United States." *Feminist Studies* 9 (1): 153–70.

Personal Narratives Group. 1989. *Interpreting Women's Lives: Feminist Theory and Personal Narratives*. Bloomington: Indiana University Press.

Plummer, Kenneth. 1995. *Telling Sexual Stories: Power, Change and Social Worlds*. London and New York: Routledge.

Polakow, Valerie. 1993. *Lives on the Edge: Single Mothers and Their Children in the Other America.* Chicago: University of Chicago Press.

Quigley, Allan. 1997. *Rethinking Literacy Education: The Critical Need for Practice-Based Change.* San Francisco: Jossey-Bass.

Reid, Inez. 1975. "Science, Politics, and Race." *Signs: Journal of Women in Culture and Society* 1 (2): 397–422.

Reinharz, Shulamit. 1992. *Feminist Methods in Social Research.* New York and Oxford: Oxford University Press.

Rich, Adrienne. 1986 (1976). *Of Woman Born: Motherhood as Experience and Institution.* New York: W.W. Norton.

Robinson, J., S. Paul, and G. Smith. 1973. *Project Second Start: A Study of the Experience of a Group of Low-income Women in Adult Programs at Brooklyn College.* New York: John Hay Whitney Foundation.

———. 1978. *Second Start Revisited.* New York: John Hay Whitney Foundation.

Rockhill, Kathleen. 1987. "Literacy as Threat/Desire: Longing to be Somebody." In *Women and Education: A Canadian Perspective,* ed. Jane Gaskel and Arlene McLaren, 315–33. Calgary, Alberta: Detselig Enterprises.

Rodriguez, Richard. 1982. *The Hunger of Memory: The Education of Richard Rodriguez.* New York: Bantam.

Rollins, Judith. 1985. *Between Women: Domestics and Their Employers.* Philadelphia: Temple University Press.

Rosaldo, Renato. 1989. *Culture and Truth.* Boston: Beacon.

Rose, H. 1983. "Hand, Brain, and Heart: A Feminist Epistemology for the Natural Sciences." *Signs: Journal of Women in Culture and Society* 9 (1): 73–90.

Rosenwald, George. 1992. "Conclusion: Reflections on Narrative Self-Understanding." In *Storied Lives: The Cultural Politics of Self-Understanding.* ed. G. Rosenwald and R. Ochberg, 265–89. New Haven: Yale University Press.

Rosenwald, George, and Richard Ochberg, eds. 1992. *Storied Lives: The Cultural Politics of Self-Understanding.* New Haven: Yale University Press.

Rubin, Lillian. 1976. *Worlds of Pain: Life in the Working-Class Family.* New York: Basic Books.

Ruddick, S. 1982. "Maternal Thinking." In *Rethinking The Family: Some Feminist Questions,* ed. B. Thorne and M. Yalom, 76–93. New York: Longman.

———. 1989. *Maternal Thinking: Toward a Politics of Peace.* Boston: Beacon.

Sacks, Karen. 1989. "Toward a Unified Theory of Class, Race and Gender." *American Ethnologist* 16: 534–50.

Sadker, Myra, and David Sadker. 1986. "Sexism in the Classroom: From Grade School to Graduate School." *Phi Delta Kappan* 68: 512.

Schomburg, Arthur. 1913. "Racial Integrity: A Plea for the Establishment of a Chair of Negro History in Our Schools and Colleges, etc." *Negro Society for Historical Research Occasional Paper,* No. 3 (July).

Schutz, Alfred. 1967. *The Phenomenology of the Social World,* trans. George Walsh and Frederick Lehnert. Evanston, IL: Northwestern University Press.

Scott, Joan. 1992. "Experience." In *Feminists Theorize the Political,* ed. Judith Butler and Joan Scott, 22–40. New York and London: Routledge.

Scott, Marvin B., and Stanford M. Lyman. 1968. "Accounts." *American Sociological Review* 33: 46–62.

Scott, N. A. 1980. *Returning Women Students: A Review of Research and Descriptive Studies.* Washington, DC: National Association for Women Deans, Administrators, and Counselors.

Segura, Denise, and Jennifer Pierce. 1993. "Chicana/o Family Structure and Gender Personality: Chodorow, Familism, and Psychoanalytic Sociology Revisited." *Signs: Journal of Women in Culture and Society* 19 (1): 62–83.

Sennett, Richard. 1980. *Authority.* New York: Vintage.

Sennett, Richard, and Jonathan Cobb. 1972. *The Hidden Injuries of Class.* New York: W. W. Norton and Co..

Serbin, Lisa K., Daniel O'Leary, Ronald Kent, and Illene Tonick. 1973. "A Comparison of Teacher Response to the Preacademic and Problem Behavior of Boys and Girls." *Child Development* 44 (4): 796–804.

Shostak, Marjorie. 1981. *Nisa: The Life and Words of a !Kung Woman.* New York: Vintage.

Smerdlow, Amy, and H. Lessinger, eds. 1983. *Class, Race and Sex: The Dynamics of Control.* Boston: G. K. Hall.

Smith, Dorothy. 1987. *The Everyday World as Problematic: A Feminist Sociology.* Boston: Northeastern University Press.

Spelman, Elizabeth. 1988. *Inessential Woman: The Problem of Exclusion in Feminist Thought.* Boston: Beacon.

Stacey, Judith. 1988. "Can There Be a Feminist Ethnography?" *Women's Studies International Forum* 11 (1): 21–27.

———. 1990. "On Resistance, Ambivalence and Feminist Theory: A Response to Carol Gilligan." *Michigan Quarterly Review* 29 (4): 537–46.

Stacey, Judith, Susan Bereaud, and Joan Daniels, eds. 1974. *And Jill Came Tumbling After: Sexism in American Education.* New York: Dell.

Stack, Carol. 1974. *All Our Kin: Strategies for Survival in the Black Community.* New York: Random House.

Stanley, Liz, ed. 1990. *Feminist Praxis: Theory and Epistemology in Feminist Sociology.* New York and London: Routledge.

Stanley, Liz, and Sue Wise. 1983. *Breaking Out: Feminist Consciousness and Feminist Research.* London: Routledge and Kegan Paul.

Steedman, Carolyn. 1986. *Landscape for a Good Woman.* New Brunswick, NJ: Rutgers University Press.

Steel, Claude, and Joshua Aronson. 1995. "Stereotype Threat and the Intellectual Test Performance of African Americans." *Journal of Personality and Social Psychology* 69 (5): 797–811.

Stern, Daniel. 1985. *The Interpersonal World of the Infant: A View from Psychoanalysis and Development Psychology.* New York: Basic Books.

Stockard, Jean. 1985. "Education and Gender Equality: A Critical View." In *Research in Sociology of Education and Socialization*, ed. Alan C. Kerckhoff, 5: 293–321. Greenwich, CT: JAI.

Strathern, Marilyn. 1987. "An Awkward Relationship: The Case of Feminism and Anthropology." *Signs: Journal of Women in Culture and Society* 12 (2): 276–92.

Strauss, Claudia. 1988. *Culture, Discourse, and Cognition: Forms of Belief in Some Rhode Island Working Men's Talk About Success.* Ph.D. diss., Harvard University.

Stuckey, Elspeth. 1988. "Invisible Women: The Black Female Educator in the Segregated South." Paper presented at the Southeastern Women's Studies Association Annual Meeting, University of North Carolina, Chapel Hill.

Suleiman, Susan Rubin. 1988. "On Maternal Splitting: A Propos of Mary Gordon's Men and Angels." *Signs: Journal of Women in Culture and Society* 14 (1): 25–41.

Taylor, Charles. 1989. *Sources of the Self: The Making of Modern Identity.* Cambridge, MA: Harvard University Press.

Tedlock, Barbara. 1991. "From Participant Observation to the Observation of Participation: The Emergence of Narrative Ethnography." *Journal of Anthropological Research* 47 (1): 69–94.

Thompson, E. P. 1963. *The Making of the English Working-Class.* New York: Vintage.

Thorne, Barrie. 1993. *Gender Play: Girls and Boys in School.* New Brunswick, NJ: Rutgers University Press.

Tokarczyk, Michelle, and Elizabeth Fay, eds. 1993. *Working-Class Women in the Academy.* Amherst: University of Massachusetts Press.

Trask, Haunani-Kay. 1986. *Eros and Power: The Promise of Feminist Theory*. Philadelphia: University of Pennsylvania Press.

Tronto, Joan. 1989. "Women and Caring: What Can Feminists Learn about Morality from Caring?" In *Gender, Body, Knowledge*, ed. S. Bordo and A. Jaggar, 172–88. New Brunswick, NJ: Rutgers University Press.

Walkerdine, Valerie. 1990. *Schoolgirl Fictions*. New York: Verso.

Waller, Willard. 1932. *Sociology of Teaching*. New York: Wiley.

Washington, Mary Helen. 1982. "Teaching Black-Eyed Susans: An Approach to the Study of Black Women Writers." In *All the Women Are White and All the Blacks Are Men, But Some of Us Are Brave*, ed. G. Hull, P. B. Scott, and B. Smith, 208–17. Old Westbury, NY: Feminist Press.

———, ed. 1975. *Black-Eyed Susans*. New York: Doubleday Anchor Press.

Weiler, K. 1988. *Women Teaching for Change: Gender, Class, and Power*. South Hadley, MA: Bergin and Garvey.

Weinstein, R. M. 1980. "Vocabularies of Motive for Illicit Drug Use: An Application of the Accounts Framework." *Sociological Quarterly* 21: 577–93.

Weis, Lois. 1983. "Schooling and Cultural Production: A Comparison of Black and White Lived Culture." In *Ideology and Practice in Schooling*, ed. Michael Apple and Lois Weis, 235–255. Philadelphia: Temple University Press.

Weis, Lois, Farrar, Eleanor, and Petrie, Hugh G., eds. 1989. *Dropouts from School: Issues, Dilemmas, and Solutions*. Albany: State University of New York Press.

Wellesley College Center for Research on Women. 1992. *How Schools Shortchange Girls: A Study of Major Findings on Girls and Education*. Washington, DC: American Association of University Women.

Welter, Barbara. 1978. "The Cult of True Womanhood: 1820–1860." In *The American Family in Social-Historical Perspective*, ed. Michael Gordon, 313–33. New York: St. Martin's.

Wexler, Philip. 1992. *Becoming Somebody: Toward a Social Psychology of School*. London: Falmer.

Whitty, Geoff. 1985. *Sociology and School Knowledge: Curriculum Theory, Research and Politics*. London: Methuen.

Williams, Patricia. 1988. "On the Object of Property." *Signs: Journal of Women in Culture and Society* 14 (1): 5–24.

———. 1991. *The Alchemy of Race and Rights: Diary of a Law Professor*. Cambridge, MA: Harvard University Press.

Williams, Raymond. 1976. *Keywords: A Vocabulary of Culture and Society*. New York: Oxford University Press.

Willis, Paul. 1977. *Learning to Labour: How Working-Class Kids Get Working-Class Jobs*. Westmead, England: Saxon House, Teakfield.

———. 1981. "Cultural Production is Different from Cultural Reproduction is Different from Social Reproduction is Different from Reproduction." *Interchange* 12 (2/3): 48–67.

Winnicott, D. W. 1965. *The Maturational Processes and the Facilitating Environment*. New York: International Universities Press.

———. 1971. *Playing and Reality*. New York: Basic Books.

———. 1975. *Through Paediatrics to Psycho-analysis*. New York: Basic Books.

Witherell, Carol, and Nel Noddings, eds. 1991. *Stories Lives Tell: Narrative and Dialogue in Education*. New York: Teachers College Press.

Wolf, Margery. 1992. *A Thrice Told Tale: Feminism, Postmodernism and Ethnographic Responsibility*. Stanford, CA: Stanford University Press.

Wong, Sau-ling C. 1994. "Diverted Mothering: Representations of Caregivers of Color in the Age of 'Multiculturalism.'" In *Mothering: Ideology, Experience and Agency*, ed. Evelyn Nakano Glenn, Grace Chang, and Linda Rennie Forcey, 67–91. London and New York: Routledge.

Wood, Julia T. 1994. *Who Cares? Women, Care and Culture.* Carbondale, IL: Southern Illinois University Press.

Young, Gay, and Bette Dickerson, eds. 1994. *Color, Class and Country: Experiences of Gender.* London and New Jersey: Zed Books.

Young, Michael, and Peter Willmott. 1962. *Family and Kinship in East London.* Baltimore: Penguin.

[Index]

INDEX OF WOMEN
IN THE STUDY

DATE DUE

JUL 19 '98		
SEP 0 4 1998		
SEP 30 '98		
OCT 26 1999		
APR 1 7 2001		
AP 12 '04		
4 15 07		